MARGERY SPRING RICE

Margery Spring Rice

Pioneer of Women's Health
in the Early Twentieth Century

Lucy Pollard

OpenBook
Publishers

ISBN Paperback: 978-1-78374-881-5
ISBN Hardback: 978-1-78374-882-2
ISBN Digital (PDF): 978-1-78374-883-9
ISBN Digital ebook (epub): 978-1-78374-884-6
ISBN Digital ebook (mobi): 978-1-78374-885-3
ISBN Digital (XML): 978-1-78374-886-0
DOI: 10.11647/OBP.0215

Cover image: Margery pushing a young friend along the Crag Path in Aldeburgh, New Year, 1968. Drawing by Christopher Ellis (1968). Photograph: the author (2020).
Cover design by Anna Gatti.

Contents

For Caitlin and Malcolm

'I thought it possible that your habitual opinion that valour is the better part of discretion might seize upon you...'

Eileen Power, letter to Margery Spring Rice, 18 August 1910

Preface and Acknowledgements

This book could not have been written without the collections of family letters and papers preserved by Anna Mercer, Sam Garrett-Jones, Camilla Garrett-Jones, Robert Robertson, Sebastian Garrett and Stephen Robertson. I am immensely grateful to them for keeping so much, for all the family knowledge they have so generously shared, for the suggestions they have made and the mistakes they have corrected. Many of the photographs have been provided by Sam Garrett-Jones and Robert Robertson. I am also particularly grateful to Margaret Young for sharing her huge knowledge of the Garrett family.

Many other people have helped me with this project: I want to thank Jane Abraham, Brian Boulton, John Charlton, Jane Darke, Marlene Baldwin Davis, Sylvia Dunkley, Emma Ellis, Rachel Forbes, Constantine Gras, Jeremy Greenwood, Heather Holden-Brown, Barney Hopkinson, Matt Jolly, Ben Johnston, Pamela King, Nina Lambert, Sonia Lambert, Stephen Mael, Marcos Magariños, Julian Minns, Dominick Robertson, Matthew Robertson, Stephen Robertson, Thomas Robertson, Catherine Sandbrook, Sally Schweitzer, Sarah Slinn, Charlie Spring Rice, Tom Stevens, Hew Stevenson, Alison Stuart-Klein, Karen Taylor, the late Michael Wheeler-Booth, Joane Whitmore and Richard Wilson. The librarians and archivists of the British Library, Cambridge University Library, Girton College Cambridge, the Women's Library at the London School of Economics, the Suffolk Record Office, the Britten-Pears Library, the Wellcome Collection, the Church of England Children's Society, Leeds University Brotherton Library, the Law Society Library, Pembroke College Cambridge, King's College Cambridge, the Imperial War Museum and the Royal Voluntary Service have been unfailingly helpful.

I am also enormously indebted to my editors at Open Book Publishers for their friendly professionalism.

I am extremely grateful to the Old Girtonians Fund for their financial support for the publication of this book

I would also like to thank my husband; my sons and their partners; and other members of my family for their support and encouragement, and for reading and commenting on sections of the book at various stages.

The family trees (which are simplified) were made by Stephen Robertson. The battle area map was made by Brian Boulton.

I have to confess a personal interest: I am one of Spring Rice's grandchildren. Writing this book has taken me on a sometimes-uncomfortable journey from child's-eye view to biographer's view. It is a journey that began, I think, over sixty years ago — long before I ever thought of writing about it. When I was eleven, my grandmother wanted to take me to a big society wedding at St Martin's-in-the-Fields Church in London, followed by a reception in the House of Commons. She also suggested a shopping trip on the morning of the wedding. My mother tried, without being at all specific, to persuade me to forego the shopping, but I was adamant that I wanted to spend the whole day with my grandmother. It was only the experience of my grandmother complaining about every item she looked at, to my great embarrassment, that made me realise what my mother's unspoken message had been: how difficult my grandmother could sometimes be. On the other hand, I cannot imagine a more wonderful grandmother. Despite all her failings, in her public life she was, as one of her North Kensington clinic colleagues said, 'far in advance of the rest of us & far in advance of [her own] time'.[1] As her biographer, I have tried both to be dispassionate and to do justice to her great strengths; but in the end, leaving aside my faults and hers, what I am left with is still my childhood love and admiration for her — love and admiration that are, in Seamus Heaney's words, 'something else the tide won't wash away'.[2]

Any mistakes are my own.

Lucy Pollard
Suffolk, 2020

---

1   Phyllis Bowen, letter to Margery Spring Rice, 15 June 1958.
2   Seamus Heaney, 'The Strand', in *The Spirit Level* (London: Faber & Faber, 1996), p. 62.

Note on Sources

The principal sources for Margery Spring Rice's personal life are the letters and papers preserved by members of her family. These include hundreds of letters, unevenly distributed in terms of date, but nevertheless extending over the whole course of her life. The Garrett and Jones families are both well-represented in these letters, but there is almost nothing from the Spring Rice side. Most of the letters are to her, from family and friends, rather than from her. Spring Rice kept two brief diaries, one in childhood and one when she was a young woman, which have survived, and her brother Douglas kept a diary over a twenty-five-year period. Towards the end of her life, one of Spring Rice's grandsons recorded, transcribed and annotated her recollections of various incidents in her life. The visitors' books that she kept from 1936 until 1970, far more than just a record of names and dates, also survive. One other extant document is a copy of the fifty-page statement that Spring Rice made to the court in 1929, when she was thinking of applying for custody of her two youngest children. I very much hope that some, at least, of these papers will end up in a public archive.

Where I have quoted from diaries and letters, I have not made any editorial alterations, but have kept the quotations exactly as in the originals. In footnotes to letters, I thought it clearer to refer to Spring Rice throughout as 'Margery Spring Rice', even when the letters date to periods when her name was 'Garrett' or 'Garrett Jones'. On the same principle, I have referred to Spring Rice by that name throughout the book. I have treated other women's names in the same way, using the most appropriate surname for each.

There is a mass of material, particularly for Spring Rice's public life, available in public archives: the records of the North Kensington Women's Welfare Centre and the Family Planning Association are in the Wellcome Archive; Eileen Power's letters to Spring Rice are in the archives at Girton College, Cambridge; Spring Rice's correspondence with Benjamin Britten is in the archives at the Red House in Aldeburgh (now part of Britten Pears Arts); and Stella Benson's diary is in Cambridge University Library. Unfortunately, none of these has been digitised. There are also copies of Edward Jones's World War I letters in the Imperial War Museum.

A biographer will always have to contend with gaps in the record, some of which may not even be recognised. In this case, there is one large gap that I am aware of: the great majority of the surviving letters are addressed to Margery Spring Rice, not written by her, so the contents of her letters often have to be deduced from the replies. The exceptions to this are the correspondence with Britten (of which both sides are extant) and, to a lesser extent, the records of the North Kensington clinic, which contain a number of her letters, though of course these are not primarily personal. It is particularly frustrating not to have Spring Rice's letters to Dick Mitchison — they may possibly survive in private hands but are not accessible at the present time.

Many people have parts in Spring Rice's story. To make it easier for the reader, in the index, I have given family members' relationships to Spring Rice under their names.

Family Trees

Garrett family tree

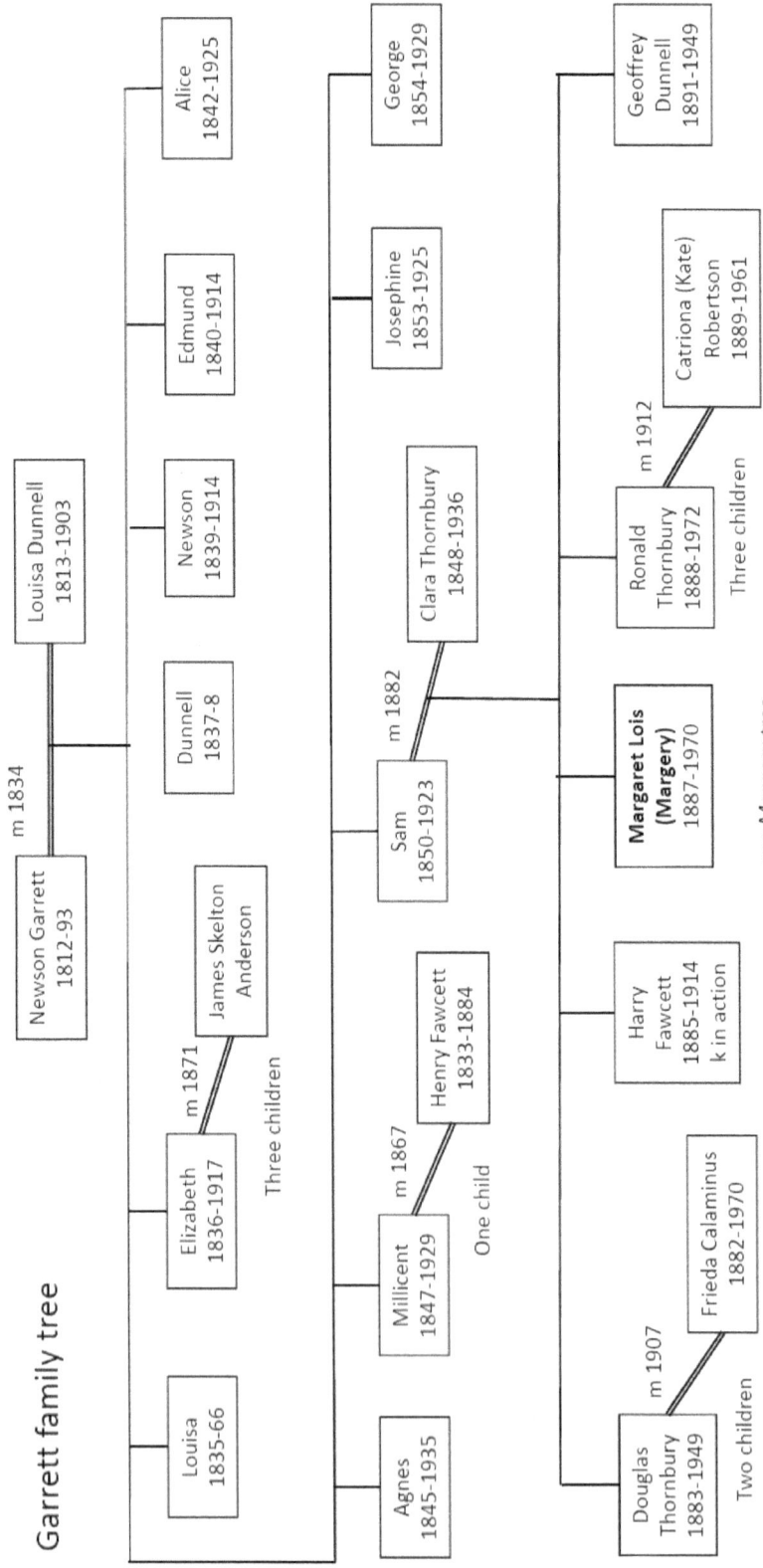

Newson Garrett 1812-93 — m 1834 — **Louisa Dunnell** 1813-1903

Children:
- Louisa 1835-66
- Elizabeth 1836-1917 — m 1871 — James Skelton Anderson — Three children
- Dunnell 1837-8
- Newson 1839-1914
- Edmund 1840-1914
- Alice 1842-1925
- Agnes 1845-1935
- Millicent 1847-1929 — m 1867 — Henry Fawcett 1833-1884 — One child
- Sam 1850-1923 — m 1882 — Clara Thornbury 1848-1936
- Josephine 1853-1925
- George 1854-1929

Children of Sam and Clara:
- Douglas Thornbury 1883-1949 — m 1907 — Frieda Calaminus 1882-1970 — Two children
- Harry Fawcett 1885-1914 k in action
- Margaret Lois (**Margery**) 1887-1970
- Ronald Thornbury 1888-1972 — m 1912 — Catriona (Kate) Robertson 1889-1961 — Three children
- Geoffrey Dunnell 1891-1949

see Margery tree

Jones family tree

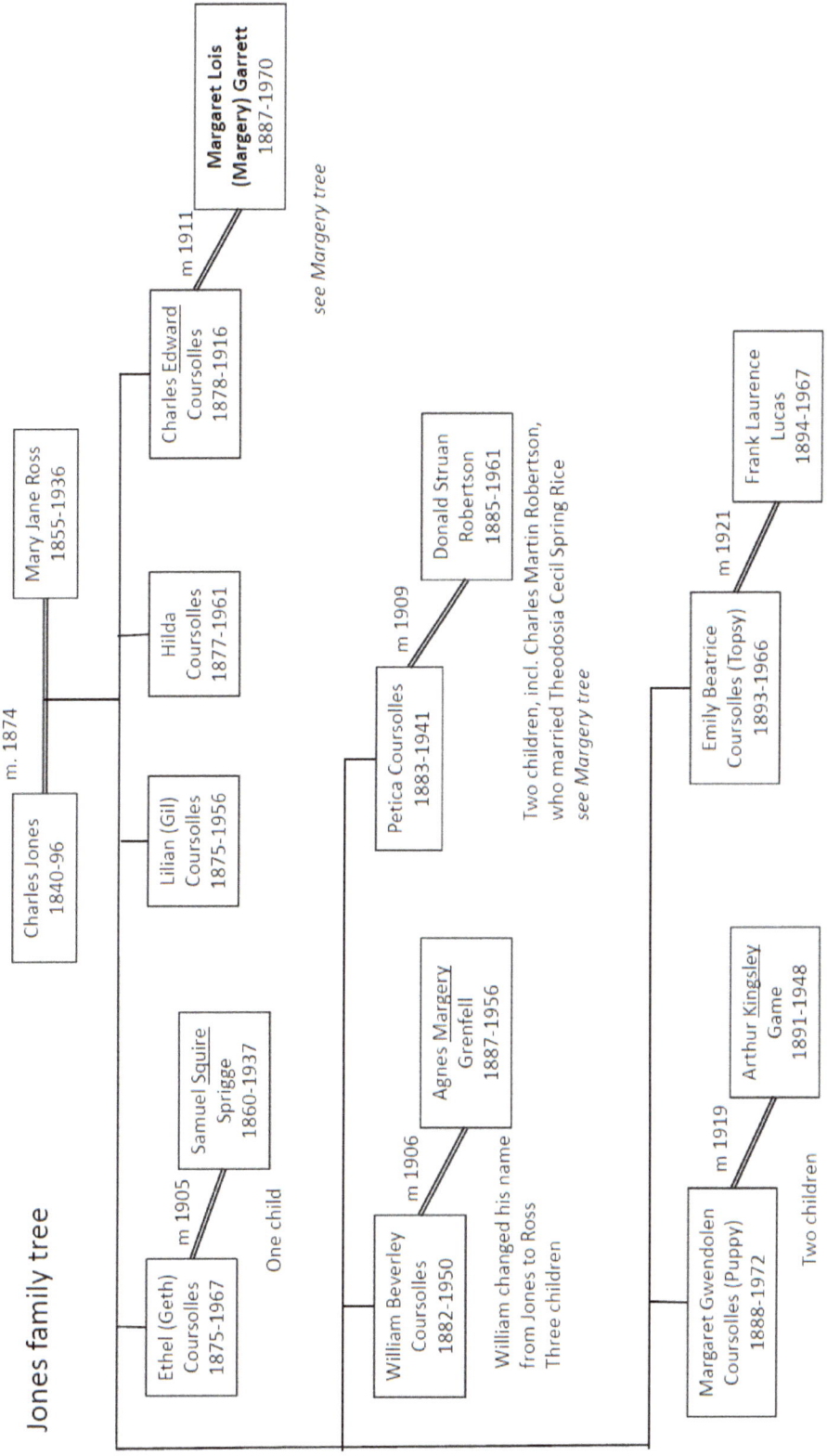

Charles Jones
1840-96

m. 1874

Mary Jane Ross
1855-1936

Lilian (Gil)
Coursolles
1875-1956

Hilda
Coursolles
1877-1961

Charles Edward Coursolles
1878-1916

m 1911

Margaret Lois (Margery) Garrett
1887-1970

see Margery tree

Ethel (Geth) Coursolles
1875-1967

m 1905

Samuel Squire Sprigge
1860-1937

One child

William Beverley Coursolles
1882-1950

m 1906

Agnes Margery Grenfell
1887-1956

William changed his name
from Jones to Ross
Three children

Petica Coursolles
1883-1941

m 1909

Donald Struan Robertson
1885-1961

Two children, incl. Charles Martin Robertson,
who married Theodosia Cecil Spring Rice
see Margery tree

Margaret Gwendolen Coursolles (Puppy)
1888-1972

m 1919

Arthur Kingsley Game
1891-1948

Two children

Emily Beatrice Coursolles (Topsy)
1893-1966

m 1921

Frank Laurence Lucas
1894-1967

Spring Rice family tree

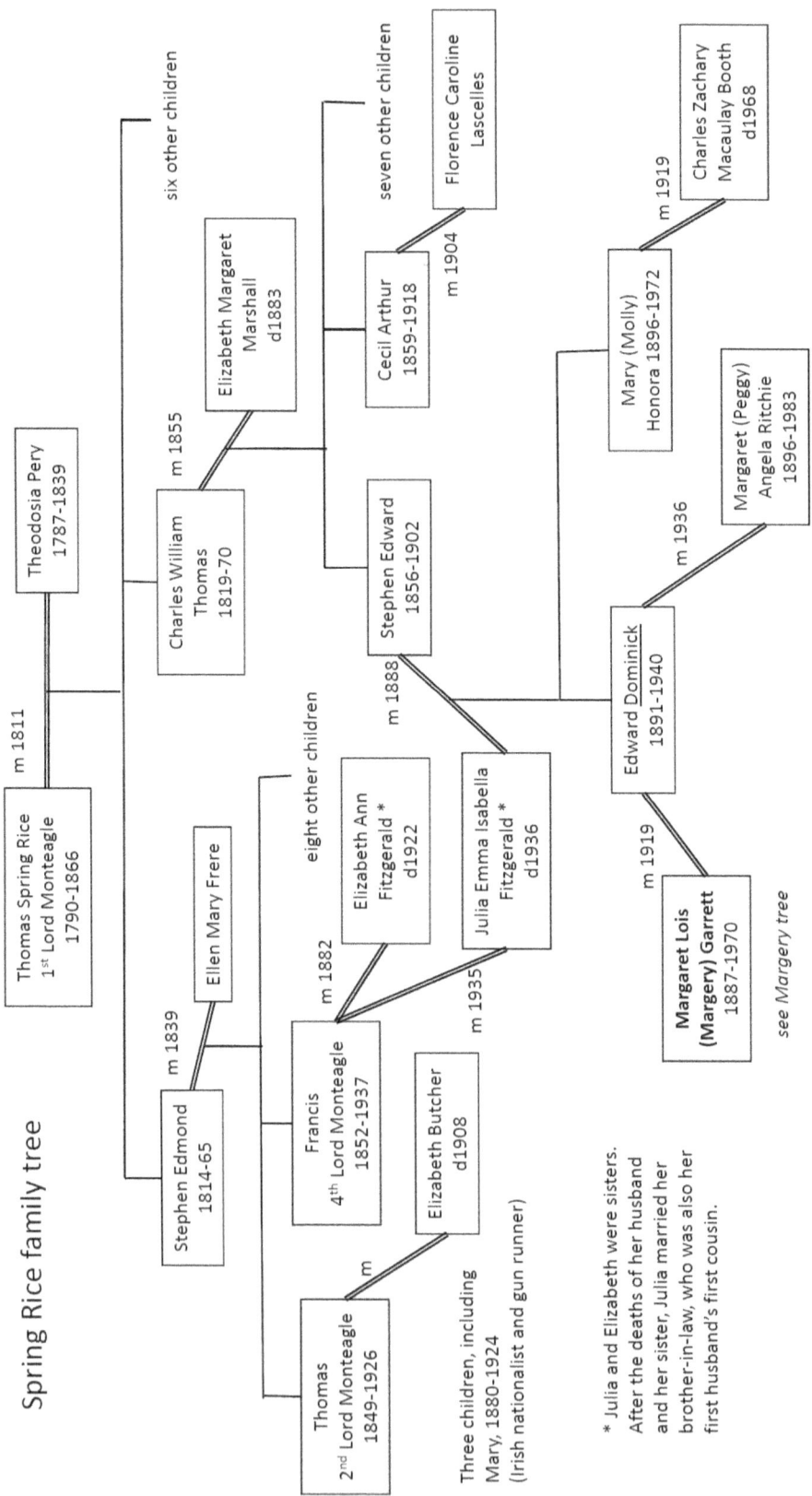

Thomas Spring Rice
1st Lord Monteagle
1790-1866

m 1811

Theodosia Pery
1787-1839

six other children

Stephen Edmond
1814-65

m 1839

Ellen Mary Frere

Charles William
Thomas
1819-70

m 1855

Elizabeth Margaret
Marshall
d1883

seven other children

Florence Caroline
Lascelles

m 1904

Cecil Arthur
1859-1918

Stephen Edward
1856-1902

Mary (Molly)
Honora 1896-1972

m 1919

Charles Zachary
Macaulay Booth
d1968

Margaret (Peggy)
Angela Ritchie
1896-1983

Francis
4th Lord Monteagle
1852-1937

m 1882

Elizabeth Ann
Fitzgerald *
d1922

eight other children

Julia Emma Isabella
Fitzgerald *
d1936

m 1888

m 1936

Edward Dominick
1891-1940

m 1919

m 1935

Thomas
2nd Lord Monteagle
1849-1926

m

Elizabeth Butcher
d1908

Three children, including
Mary, 1880-1924
(Irish nationalist and gun runner)

Margaret Lois
(Margery) Garrett
1887-1970

see Margery tree

* Julia and Elizabeth were sisters.
After the deaths of her husband
and her sister, Julia married her
brother-in-law, who was also her
first husband's first cousin.

Margery family tree

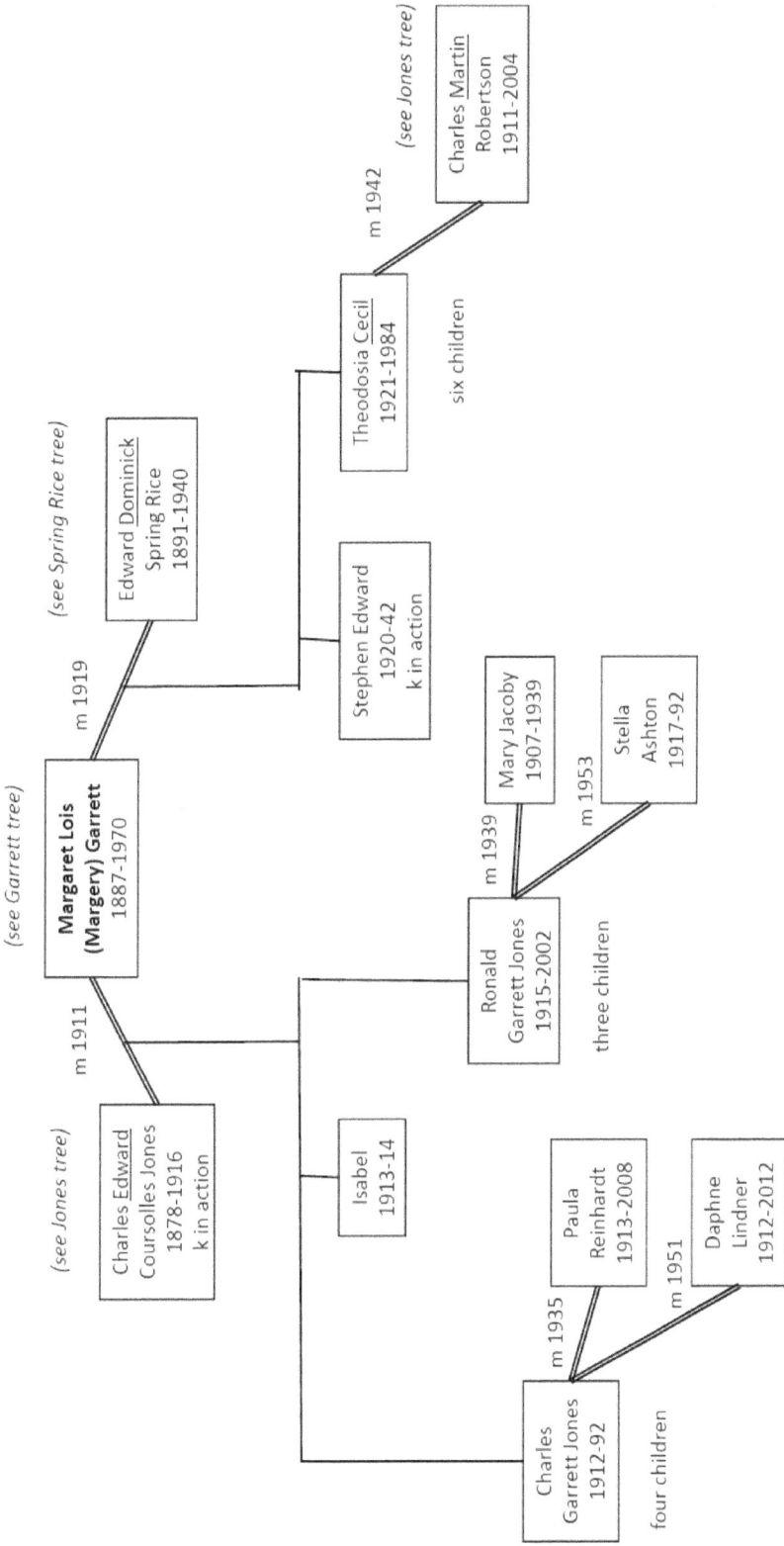

(see Garrett tree)

(see Jones tree)

(see Spring Rice tree)

(see Jones tree)

Margaret Lois (Margery) Garrett 1887-1970

Edward Dominick Spring Rice 1891-1940

m 1919

Charles Edward Coursolles Jones 1878-1916 k in action

m 1911

Theodosia Cecil 1921-1984

Charles Martin Robertson 1911-2004

m 1942

six children

Stephen Edward 1920-42 k in action

Isabel 1913-14

Ronald Garrett Jones 1915-2002

Mary Jacoby 1907-1939

m 1939

Stella Ashton 1917-92

m 1953

three children

Charles Garrett Jones 1912-92

Paula Reinhardt 1913-2008

m 1935

Daphne Lindner 1912-2012

m 1951

four children

1. Cherished daughter (1887–1907)

The writer Naomi Mitchison, in a short biography of the pioneer doctor Elizabeth Garrett Anderson, suggests a steam roller as a symbol for the Garrett family.[1] This is apt, not only because the Garretts had been making agricultural machinery for generations, but also because some individual Garretts — especially the women — possessed the capacity to drive doggedly over obstacles in pursuit of their goals. When the third child of Elizabeth's brother Sam was born in 1887, a welcome daughter after two sons, Elizabeth arrived to meet the new baby, promptly offered the parents five hundred pounds for her and was astonished to have her offer refused.[2] The baby was Margery, the subject of this book, and although Elizabeth did not succeed in adopting her, she did become Margery's godmother. One might imagine the story as a fairy tale in which this steamroller quality is the gift bestowed by the godmother: Margery's life certainly demonstrated that she too possessed it, and it was a gift that would make her both fierce enemies and loyal friends.

***

I only have to add, that she was very happy as a child, but as I only write this when she was the age of 14, I cannot say what her future may be, but she has all prospects of an extremely happy life, in the company of an exceptionally good Father, & an exceptionally good Mother, & exceptionally good brothers, & an exceptionally good home.[3]

---

1   Naomi Mitchison, 'Elizabeth Garrett Anderson', in *Revaluations: Studies in Biography*, Lascelles Abercrombie, Lord David Cecil, G. K. Chesterton, et al. (London: Oxford University Press, 1931), pp. 155–95 (p. 161).
2   Ibid., p. 190. This story was also related to the author by Margery herself. At the time of Margery's birth, Elizabeth was fifty-one, and her own children were ten and thirteen. The children of her sister Louisa (always known as Louie), whom she had cared for after Louie's premature death from appendicitis in 1867, were adults.
3   The majority of archival material throughout this book is drawn from the private collections of the Garrett Family Papers and the Jones Family Papers, unless otherwise specified.

     https://doi.org/10.11647/OBP.0215.01

These are the final words of the introduction to the diary kept by Margery Garrett over the period 1901–1905, which she had received as a fourteenth birthday present in June, 1901. The diary largely covers her journeys to Italy and Scotland, while her introduction gives us an indication of how she saw her life in 1901, and how she was already beginning to visualise herself as a person with standing in a wider world.

***

Margery was born into a comfortably well-off, but by no means conventional, middle class household. Her father Sam, who had studied classics at Peterhouse College, Cambridge, was a solicitor in London (a first-generation professional whose father Newson Garrett came from very humble origins) while her mother Clara had been a teacher before marriage.[4] We do not know how Sam and Clara had met, but it is likely to have been through their siblings' links with the women's suffrage movement, in which three of Sam's sisters and Clara's sister, Kate, were deeply involved. It is also possible that Kate, a decorative artist, had an artistic connection with Sam's sister Agnes and her cousin Rhoda Garrett, who ran an interior design business together. In 1882, Sam and Clara were married in the village of Sullington, Sussex, about twelve miles from Rustington, where Rhoda and Agnes used to take their holidays.

Although their daughter's name is stated as Margaret Lois on her birth certificate, in her childhood her family addressed their letters to 'Marjorie'. In fact, it seems that she never liked either of these versions of her name and, over the course of her life, used many other variants and nicknames, most frequently 'Margery'. She had two older brothers, Douglas (born 1883) and Harry (1885), and two younger ones, Ronald (1888) and Geoffrey (1891). In 1897, they were joined by Clara's orphaned nephew, Brian, who came between Ronald and Geoffrey in age. The house they lived in during Margery's childhood[5] — 13 Nottingham

---

4   In the 1881 census, before her marriage, Clara is described as a visitor in the family of Arthur and Emmeline Cohen in Kensington; her occupation is given as 'teacher', with 'school' added in another hand. There were small children in this family, and perhaps she was teaching them? The nickname by which she was known to her nieces and nephews, 'Da', is a shortened version of 'darling': Margery's explanation for this was that it was what Clara's pupils had called her, but it had been shortened to 'Da' as 'darling' was not thought appropriate.

5   The family had previously lived at 59a Abbey Road, Marylebone, where Douglas and Harry had been born.

Place, Marylebone — still stands, a five-storey Victorian end-of-terrace house that provided plenty of room for servants and family. The 1901 census states that they had a cook and five maids. At the time of the previous census, in 1891, Clara was staying in Aldeburgh, Suffolk, in Gower House[6] with a nurse and three maids, while Sam remained at home in London with two more servants. Sam and Clara spent a good deal of time in Suffolk, where Clara's passion for gardening had space to flourish[7] and Sam could indulge his penchant for chopping down and replanting trees. Clara's sister Grace Mallock, widowed in 1896, spent a lot of time with her sister and brother-in-law and was involved with the upbringing of her niece and nephews.

Fig. 1. 13 Nottingham Place, Marylebone, London. Photograph: the author (2015).

---

6   There is a mystery here. The census lists the house as '5 River View, Station Road': what is now Park Road (where Gower House is) was originally called Station Road, but I can find no other trace of anything called River View; Gower House is listed in *History, Gazeteer and Directory of Suffolk, 1891–92* (Sheffield: William White Ltd., 1891–1892), p. 101, as being the home of Samuel Garrett.

7   There is a story that she habitually wore a pith helmet for gardening — perhaps a relic from the days of her childhood in India, where she had been born — but in an extant portrait of her by Thomas Dugdale she is wearing an ordinary straw gardening hat.

Though they were very different in temperament, both Sam and Clara had wide cultural and social interests and there were lively discussions on politics, music, art and literature among parents and children. Sam was dearly loved in his wider family for his sweet nature: his sister Millicent Fawcett wrote of him in her memoirs:

> His was a remarkable character, for he possessed a wonderful combination of qualities: first-rate brain-power, an absolutely selfless nature, a keen appreciation of public duty, and added to all these a strong sense of humour, which made me save up every amusing incident I met with in order that I might tell him and hear his explosion of hearty laughter.[8]

When he died, his obituary in *The Law Society's Gazette* recorded that his colleagues found him the kindest of friends, one of whose 'most pleasant characteristics to those who knew him well was a certain gruffness of manner and speech which was almost ludicrously contradicted by a benevolent twinkle in his eyes'.[9] Clara too had a strong character unlike that of a submissive Victorian wife, and as Margery grew older, there were clashes of will and of opinion between mother and daughter, partly because they were too alike, and partly because Clara was more conservative than Margery. It is clear that from an early age, Margery was unafraid to differ from her parents and brothers in her views and to express herself forcefully. However, it was thanks to Clara that Margery developed her love of literature, music and, later in life, gardening too. Clara was also — as Margery was later — extremely hospitable and loved gathering friends and family around her. From both her parents, Margery inherited a strong social conscience which was to find outlets in varying ways throughout her life.

Both Sam and Clara, along with other members of the Garrett family, especially Sam's sisters Elizabeth and Millicent, were strong advocates of rights for women. Sam, who rose to be president of the Law Society, was probably among the first to admit women as articled clerks — a big leap towards opening the profession to women. Progress had been painfully slow: in 1859, a law stationers' business was set up in Lincoln's Inn, London, to train women in legal copying, but it was not until nearly twenty years later that Janet Wood became the first woman to complete a law degree, at Girton College, Cambridge. Wood did not actually

---

8   Millicent Fawcett, *What I Remember* (London: Fisher Unwin, 1924), p. 30.
9   'The Late Mr. Samuel Garrett', *The Law Society's Gazette* (May, 1923), 20, p. 108.

receive a degree because women could not do so at that date. In the same year of 1878, however, University College London began to admit women to law degree courses on the same basis as men. In the following year, Eliza Orme applied to take the Law Society's examinations to become a solicitor, but was refused. In 1913, four women, aspiring to become barristers, took legal action to try to get the Law Society to admit them to its examinations. Although they were also refused, times were beginning to change. At a meeting of the Law Society in August 1918, Sam, in his role as president, said:

> I ask every member of the profession to consider this matter seriously, and to ask whether, considering the spirit of the times towards the status of women in the industrial world, considering the work women have done in connection with the war, considering the political rights women have obtained,[10] it is possible any longer to maintain an opposition to their entrance into a profession in which they are already employed as clerks, and of their fitness to practise which no thoughtful person would venture now to express a doubt.[11]

In March the following year, at a special general meeting of the Society, Sam moved 'That in view of the present economic and political position of women, it is in the opinion of this meeting expedient that the existing obstacles to their entry into the legal profession should be removed; and the Council is requested to report this opinion to the Lord Chancellor'.[12] The motion was passed by fifty votes to thirty-three; at the end of that year, Parliament passed the Sex Disqualification (Removal) Act.

Margery had a happy childhood within her close and loving family. As was usual in families of that time and class, the boys were sent to boarding school quite early, first to Horton, a preparatory school near Biggleswade (where some of their cousins also went), and then to Rugby, which sent a large proportion of its students into the army and where (as in many public schools of the time) there was a heavy emphasis on religious and moral education.[13] Many letters from her brothers to

---

10   The Representation of the People Act, giving some women the vote, had been passed in February 1918.

11   The Law Society Gazette, 'Memory Lane', *Obiter* (6 August 2018), https://www.lawgazette.co.uk/obiter/memory-lane-6-august-2018/5067167.article

12   The Law Society Gazette, 'Memory Lane', *Obiter* (30 April 2009), https://www.lawgazette.co.uk/obiter/memory-lane/50540.article

13   Sam had also been educated at Rugby. His father, Newson, did not find the written word easy: a couple of letters from him to the headmaster of Rugby about Sam's

Margery, written from school, survive: they are mostly unremarkable, but convey their closeness to their sister, whom they tease, amuse and, in the case of Douglas and Harry, advise. Throughout his life, Douglas was to remain Margery's trusted advisor through the most difficult and stressful times, even if his views — always more conventional than hers — sometimes enraged her. Her brothers' letters are full of their accounts of school life: cycle rides, sporting events (in Harry's case), lines having to be written for offences that nobody had owned up to, horse-riding, carpentry, going to plays and concerts and agonising about what they were to buy each other for birthday presents. Harry, who was eventually to choose a career as an artist, also wrote a lot about his drawings and discussed with Margery her own aspirations in the artistic line.

Holidays were spent either at Gower House (built by Newson Garrett), in Aldeburgh, on the Suffolk coast, where the boys sailed, cycled and built a wigwam in the garden, or with their cousins the Gibb family in Scarborough in Yorkshire. Dorothea Gibb (always known as 'Aunt Theo') was Sam's niece. Though only eleven years younger than him, she was the daughter of his oldest sister Louisa. Theo and her husband had five children roughly similar in age to Sam's children. One of them was Roger, who remained a lifelong friend of Margery's. The two families were close, and Aunt Theo was one of Margery's godmothers (the other being her aunt, Elizabeth Garrett Anderson). Holidays together often involved writing and performing plays: for Christmas 1903, in Scarborough, Clara wrote a play in blank verse for the two families to act. Cycling, in London as well as in Aldeburgh, was enthusiastically enjoyed by parents as well as children. In 1897, Sam wrote to Margery, who was spending three months in Scarborough with the Gibbs, 'Mother is becoming quite a scorcher & goes quite easily 8 miles an hour now';[14] he went on to report that she had had a fall from her bicycle, but had suffered nothing more than a bruise. Gwen Raverat, a near contemporary of Margery's, has given a delightful description of her family's participation in the 'cycling craze' in Cambridge: her mother too suffered some quite

---

admission to the school are extant, but the letters that purported to come from Newson had actually been written by Sam's older sister Elizabeth. I am grateful to Margaret Young for drawing my attention to this.

14   Sam Garrett, letter to Margery Spring Rice, 6 June 1897.

severe tumbles from her bicycle.[15] It is worth remembering that in that
same year of 1897, male Cambridge undergraduates hung an effigy of
a woman on a bicycle, dressed in 'rational' clothing, out of a window
in order to ridicule the academic success of Margery's cousin Philippa
Fawcett.[16] So-called rational dress, worn by women when they rode
bicycles, was in itself the subject of ridicule for some: unfortunately, we
have no photograph of Clara on a bicycle and it is not known what she
wore. On another occasion, Sam wrote that he and Ronald had cycled
six times round the inner circle of Regent's Park. Sam and Clara were
not unusual for their time and class in believing in the importance
of the outdoors, holidays and exercise, but Clara had a particularly
passionate belief in the healthy properties of fresh air.

Every Christmas, the family carried out a ritual of taking presents
to the crew of the *Shipwash* light-ship in the North Sea off Harwich,
which Sam, as a keen amateur sailor, must have greatly enjoyed. The
year before her death, Margery recalled the event, and the ceremony
of it:

> I am sitting, on a grey October evening at dusk in my flat in Aldeburgh;
> looking out onto the Crag Path [the promenade along the sea front], and
> beyond, to the sea. As always, if one watches carefully the light from the
> Lightship keeps up its constant flash and my memory jumps back 75 years
> or so to the time when my father Samuel Garrett and my four brothers
> packed a large hamper full of Christmas foods and drinks (innocuous!)
> and more tangible presents for the crew of the 'Shipwash'[...] on their
> bank.
>
> It is pitch dark now over the sea already, and indeed over Aldeburgh
> itself. The welcome which we received when we reached the Shipwash
> is indescribable for those men stay at their posts in all weathers to keep
> the trained and untrained mariners guided and safe. It was an annual
> celebration which we [...] never failed to keep. The joy with which we
> climbed aboard the ship, and the ceremony of unpacking the gifts [...]
> was an adventure which came first in our Christmas celebrations.[17]

---

15 Gwen Raverat, *Period Piece: A Cambridge Childhood* (London: Faber & Faber, 1960),
    pp. 238–42.

16 Philippa, daughter of Sam's sister Millicent, was ranked above the Senior Wrangler
    (i.e. the student scoring the highest marks in the final mathematics degree exams at
    Cambridge), but could not be given the title of Senior Wrangler herself because she
    was a woman.

17 Margery Spring Rice, fragmentary memoirs, recorded by Sam Garrett-Jones,
    October/November 1969, transcribed 12 January 2006 by Sam Garrett-Jones.

Margery's roots in Aldeburgh and the surrounding area went deep; her Garrett inheritance was a matter of interest and pride to her all her life. There had been Garretts in that part of the world at least since the seventeenth century and possibly the sixteenth, but it was two brothers (Margery's grandfather Newson and his older brother Richard) in the early nineteenth who wrote their name indelibly on to the Suffolk map. Richard (born 1807, the sixth Richard Garrett in the family) took over the agricultural engineering firm in Leiston that his grandfather had inherited from his father-in-law, and hugely expanded it.[18] He and Newson (born 1812) married sisters, Elizabeth and Louisa Dunnell. The brothers often came into conflict, and though their wives did their utmost to keep the peace, there were long periods of estrangement between their families. One of the many triggers of conflict was the proposal of marriage by Richard's son Richard to Newson's daughter Louisa, which she turned down.[19] According to Margery,[20] it was only the losses on the two sides of the family in World War I, more than twenty years after Newson's death, that finally healed the breach. Newson's daughter Millicent wrote in her memoirs that her father's temperament was 'sanguine, generous, daring, impulsive, and impatient, and I am afraid I must add, quarrelsome'.[21] Apart from his brother, another person Newson regularly quarrelled with was the vicar of Aldeburgh, as a result of which, on some Sundays, his family was to be found worshipping at the dissenting chapel or at the nearby village of Snape instead of in Aldeburgh church. Sam was baptised in Snape church during one of these periods.

When Richard, as expected, took over the family engineering works in 1826, Newson left for London and began his career managing a pawnbroker's shop belonging to John Dunnell, his brother's and later his own father-in-law, in Whitechapel.[22] In the early 1840s, however, after the death of their father, Newson brought his family back to Aldeburgh

---

18   This business now has an afterlife as the Long Shop Museum.

19   In biological terms, this would have been a very unwise marriage as the prospective couple were first cousins twice over.

20   Margery Spring Rice, fragmentary memoirs, recorded 24 November 1968 by Sam Garrett-Jones, transcribed 12 January 2006 by Sam Garrett-Jones.

21   Fawcett, *What I Remember*, p. 30.

22   He also worked in the Beehive Inn in Crawford St, Marylebone, owned by John Dunnell; Newson and Louisa were married in St Marylebone parish church in 1834. The Dunnell family, like the Garretts, came from Suffolk.

Fig. 2. Newson Garrett, by John Pettie (1886). Courtesy of Hew Stevenson. Photograph: Hew Stevenson (c. 2015).

Fig. 3. Louisa Garrett, by James Elder Christie (1888). Courtesy of Snape Parish Council. Photograph: Matt Jolly (2019).

and set about building up a business as a merchant, ship-owner and maltster. Having bought a coal and corn warehouse at Snape Bridge from a Mr Fennell, he began to malt barley there for the brewery trade, hugely extending his business over the next few decades. He was responsible for the construction of the beautiful range of buildings that now constitute the Snape Maltings cultural centre and provide the Aldeburgh Festival with its home; he managed ships that sailed up and down the east coast; he founded his own brickworks; and was instrumental in persuading Great Eastern Railway to build a branch railway line from Campsea Ashe[23] to Snape. In Aldeburgh, he built a row of houses for his sons and daughters; converted the town's reading room into the Jubilee Hall at his own expense (it is still in use as a concert hall and theatre);[24] served as mayor of Aldeburgh four times; and, having converted from Conservatism, was active as a Liberal in local politics. Proud of the town on which he had such a strong influence physically, economically and socially, he was capable of acting with extremely imperiousness. In the 1860s, he decided that he was the only person with the right to take a horse and carriage along the Crag Path[25] and physically prevented at least one visitor from doing so. More benignly, when he was planning to build the Maltings, he marked out its line of frontage in the ground with his stick, but no-one dared to point out to him that there was a slight curve on it — a curve that in fact contributes to its beauty.

Newson and Louisa had eleven children, of whom ten survived to adulthood. His second child, Elizabeth (later Garrett Anderson), was the first woman in England to qualify openly as a doctor.[26] After his initial opposition to her ambitions, Newson became her fiercest advocate and defender; Louisa, having at first been horrified at the idea, later admitted that Newson was right and came to enjoy her daughter's fame and success. Their seventh child, Agnes, was another

---

23 A tiny village, later immortalised by a line in the libretto of Benjamin Britten's comic opera *Albert Herring*.

24 When the building was re-opened after renovations in July 1931, Clara Garrett (by then a widow) did the honours (Amanda Davies, '*A Room Worthy of the Town': A History of Aldeburgh Jubilee Hall* (Leiston: Leiston Press, 2016), p. 18).

25 Then, and until the 1950s, the Crag Path was surfaced with crag and was a distinctive and attractive orange colour. It was tarmacked in the fifties.

26 The first to do so, in the guise of a man, was Margaret Bulkley, alias James Barry. Another Englishwoman, Elizabeth Blackwell, qualified in the US in 1849 and subsequently practised on both sides of the Atlantic. A lecture by Blackwell, and a meeting of the two women, inspired Elizabeth Garrett's decision to become a doctor.

Fig. 4. Snape Maltings today. The frontage has barely been altered since Newson Garrett's day. Photograph: the author (2019).

innovator, who went on to set up an interior design business with her cousin Rhoda Garrett. Their eighth child, Millicent (later Fawcett), spent her life fighting the cause of women's suffrage. Their ninth child was Margery's father Sam. The world was changing for women and Margery's family were instrumental in effecting some of that change. The legal position of women improved in various ways in the late nineteenth century with the Married Women's Property Acts (1870 and 1882) and changes in child custody laws, even though, in terms of sexual relationships, women remained subservient to their husbands. New opportunities in education were slowly opening up and women were beginning to contribute to political life in local government. Elizabeth, amply endowed with the family characteristics of stamina and determination, was prising open the medical profession for women at a time when many other professions were far behind.

In 1887, the year of Margery's birth, the ownership of the land designated for the building of the Jubilee Hall was put into a trust overseen by a Board of Trustees, among whom were Newson and several other members of the Garrett family. It was stipulated that the Board should always include two women, and Elizabeth was one of the first two. It is likely that Newson and Elizabeth were both instrumental in ensuring that women would always be represented.[27]

---

27   Davies, *'A Room Worthy of the Town'*, p. 9.

Elizabeth, fourteen years older than Sam, seems to have acted as his third parent. It was she who wrote to the headmaster of Rugby, Dr Temple, about Sam's admission to the school; in fact, she unashamedly forged Newson's signature on the letter: 'I thought it did not matter forging the signature as mine is a hand which might be a man's'.[28] Although Newson has sometimes been described as being illiterate, he had been to school and could read and write, but his relationship with the written word was an uneasy one and he often used Louisa as his amanuensis. According to Elizabeth, he 'had always wished to have a scholarly son' and he thought it important that his daughters should get a decent education — another difference between him and his brother Richard. Elizabeth, demonstrating a remarkable attitude for the time, showed her concern for Sam's emotional well-being at school by making sure that he had a bedroom of his own: she thought this would allow him to 'escape the worst chances of harm in public school life'. She had also taken the trouble to consult a cousin, an old boy of Rugby, who told her that there was 'not much of what is generally called "bullying"' in the school.[29]

In 1870, when Sam was a twenty-year-old undergraduate, Elizabeth took him and their sister Josephine, who was still a teenager at the time, for a short 'holiday' to see the battlefields of the Franco-Prussian War — in the course of which they spent some hours distributing chocolate, tobacco, water and apples to wounded soldiers.[30] This is an extraordinary choice of destination and the adventure must surely have had an influence on Sam when he became a parent himself. It illustrates the level of political consciousness in the Garrett family as well as the character of their patriotism: in Millicent's memoirs, she recalls walking on Aldeburgh beach as a small child with her father while he tried (unsuccessfully) to persuade local fishermen to enlist to fight in Crimea. When Sebastopol fell in 1855, he strode into the room where his family were having breakfast to issue the command: '[h]eads up and shoulders down; Sebastopol is taken'.[31] Towards the end of the Boer War, Millicent,

---

28 Elizabeth Garrett Anderson, letter to Louisa and Newson Garrett, 5 January 1865.
29 Elizabeth Garrett Anderson, letter to Sam Garrett, 21 January 1865; Elizabeth Garrett Anderson, letter to Newson Garrett, 28 January 1865.
30 Louisa Garrett Anderson, *Elizabeth Garrett Anderson* (London: Faber & Faber, 1939), p. 140.
31 Fawcett, *What I Remember*, p. 10.

by that time a distinguished public figure although the achievement of women's suffrage was still years away, was to head a delegation to look into conditions in the concentration camps in South Africa.

Clara came from a military background, socially very different from Sam's though alike in terms of their broad outlook on the world. She was the daughter of Nathaniel Henry Thornbury (1806–1881), a colonel in the 4th Bombay Native Infantry and secretary to the Bombay Military Board (part of the East India Company's Bombay Presidency Army), and his third wife, Louisa Jane Kelly. Clara herself was born in India. They were very much a family of the Empire: Clara's brother, Edward Barton Thornbury, worked as a railway surveyor in South Africa in the 1870s and eventually in Australia.[32] Nathaniel and Louisa are recorded as having lived in Kent at the time of the 1871 census, as was Nathaniel in 1881 after Louisa's death in 1879. Another of Nathaniel's sons, Frank, also worked in South Africa — in the mines and, at various times, as a ship's mate. In 1881, Nathaniel sailed for Sydney with Edward Barton's family but died en route, so Margery never knew either of her maternal grandparents. Clara's sister Grace, a nurse, played a significant part in Sam's family; in her forties, she had married a much older man (a retired captain from the Madras Native Infantry) but was widowed in 1896 after only four years of marriage. Her sister Kate was active in both the suffrage and the arts and crafts movements, which linked her in multiple ways with Margery's Garrett aunts.[33] Clara's brother Bruce and his wife Helen both died in Aldeburgh in the 1890s, leaving their young son, Brian, to be cared for by Sam and Clara.

Margery did know her paternal grandparents. Although Newson died shortly before her sixth birthday,[34] he was nevertheless a towering figure in her life, both in terms of the influence of his personality on his family and also because of the fundamental role he played in making the Aldeburgh of her childhood the place that it was.

---

32 His diaries are in the State Library of New South Wales.

33 See Elizabeth Crawford, 'Suffrage Stories: House Decorating and Suffrage: Annie Atherton, Kate Thornbury, And The Society of Artists', *Woman and Her Sphere* (8 May 2017) https://womanandhersphere.com/2017/05/08/suffrage-stories-house-decorating-and-suffrage-annie-atherton-kate-thornbury-and-the-society-of-artists/. Crawford explores the links between Kate and the Garrett family. She also quotes a letter from Kate to the *Pall Mall Gazette* in 1887, which shows how forthrightly she could express herself.

34 Louisa died ten years later.

Aldeburgh was a town of a few thousand people (which had lost its
MP in 1832), sited on a low coastal strip on the eastern side of England
and on the hill behind. The river Alde flows down from its source in
the north of Suffolk, through Snape to Aldeburgh, and then makes a
right-angle turn south to run parallel to the sea for several miles more,
past Orford, to its mouth at Shingle Street — thus creating a long
shingle spit. The distance between the sea and the river at Slaughden,
the southern-end of the town of Aldeburgh, is only a matter of yards
and one of Newson's many projects — one that was never carried out,
though it has resurfaced from time to time since Newson's day — was
the cutting of a channel between river and sea to enhance the port of
Aldeburgh. The number of pilots vastly increased under his influence
and the coastguard and lifeboat services were expanded and improved.
Newson himself was a man of great bravery, who, for example, joined
the human chain bringing ashore crew members from a Swedish ship
after a terrible storm in November 1855 which left seventeen ships
wrecked off Aldeburgh.[35] He obtained a long lease on thirty-five acres
of land belonging to Aldeburgh Corporation and built a row of houses
on Park Road on the western side of the town, of which Gower House
(now called Garrett House) is one. He was also a moving force behind
the renovation of the disused Elizabethan Moot Hall. In addition to
his service as mayor of Aldeburgh, in 1889, he was the first Aldeburgh
representative on the County Council. It has been said that the changes
that took place in the town between 1840 and 1855 are 'intelligible
only in terms of Garrett's impulsive energy'.[36] This is not to say that
Aldeburgh was a place without culture: Millicent's memoirs record how
a shipbuilder from the Tyne, Percy Metcalf, who came to build ships for
Newson at Snape, brought his passion for music to the town (especially
Bach, Handel and, above all, Mozart), 'open[ing] a new world of music'
for Newson's family.[37]

Of course, Aldeburgh was a small-town society but it is possible that,
for this very reason, Margery may have met a wider social range there
than she did in London — the fishermen on the beach, for example.

---

35 The lifeboatman who relieved Newson in the chain that night, George Cable, was
    drowned there; Louisa regarded him as having saved Newson's life.

36 Norman Scarfe, 'Victorian Aldeburgh', in *Programme Book for the Fifteenth Aldeburgh
    Festival* (1962), pp. 16–20 (p. 17).

37 Fawcett, *What I Remember*, p. 27.

Besides, she had another wider perspective on the world through the activities and careers of her aunts: Elizabeth had been qualified as a doctor for more than twenty years when Margery was born, and Agnes and Rhoda Garrett had launched their decorating business in the mid-1870s. For Millicent, who was to devote her life single-mindedly to the cause of women's suffrage (strictly as a suffragist, never endorsing the violent methods of the suffragettes),[38] there were still three decades of fighting before any women were to get the vote. From her earliest years, Margery was conscious of what women could do, what needed to be done and what her extended family might expect of her.

Fig. 5. Garrett family group at Gower House, 1907. Left to right: Geoffrey, Sam, Grace Mallock, Clara, Godfrey Garrett Smith (a cousin), Margery. Photograph: family archives (1907).

For both Sam and Clara, the education as well as the schooling of their daughter was as important a matter as that of their sons. Clara, who had been a teacher before her marriage, was a well-educated and cultured woman, who passed on her love of literature and theatre in particular to her daughter. We know that Margery saw Shakespeare, but it would be interesting to know whether she also saw Shaw — many of whose

---

38   Several of Margery's grandchildren remember having the difference between suffragists and suffragettes impressed on them from an early age. However, Millicent, at the end of her career, recognised that the suffragette movement had played its part in achieving the aim.

plays were first performed in the first decade of the twentieth century. Nor do we know anything about what she read: Hardy perhaps? H. G. Wells? Arnold Bennett? Titles by all of these were certainly on her bookshelves later in her life. For her formal education, Margery was sent first to a nursery in Baker Street, following which she did her lessons in a small private class taught by two women — Constance Crommelin, who later married the poet John Masefield, and Isabel Fry, who came from one of the big Quaker families and was a sister of the artist and critic Roger Fry. Among Margery's papers is the manuscript of a sonnet (whether by herself or one of her fellow students is unclear) addressed to Miss Crommelin, beginning: 'O sleepy one! O thou great drowsy one!' and carrying on in the same vein, which hardly suggests an energetic teacher. Though it was clearly not serious, one would like to know whether Miss Crommelin was allowed to see it! Later in life, Margery referred to both Fry and Crommelin as remarkable women. Isabel Fry was an innovative and admired teacher who went on to found the progressive Farmhouse School at Mayortorne near Wendover, Buckinghamshire, in 1917. In around 1902, Margery was sent to a girls' school in Stratford run by a Mrs Stuart, which gave her the opportunity of regularly seeing plays performed there. Music, too, was a very important part of her education: she became a competent pianist and began to learn the violin at some stage, though she struggled with this and did not continue into adulthood. As a young woman, she also took singing lessons and even considered, at one point in time, a professional career as a singer.

At a period when the economic centre of British life was shifting from the northern industrial cities to London, from manufacturing towards financial services, the Garrett family in Nottingham Place took full advantage of the cultural hub that London was becoming. It was easier than ever to get around the city as well as to get out into the country — the construction of the underground had begun with the Metropolitan Line in the 1860s and, by 1890, all the rail termini had been built. Although horse-drawn buses continued in service up until World War I, there were cars and petrol-engine cabs and buses running from the turn of the century.[39]

---

39   Christopher Hibbert, *The English: A Social History* (London: Paladin, 1988), pp. 647, 653, 656–57, 659–60.

Fig. 6. Margery as a girl. Photograph: family archives (c. 1895).

As Margery entered her teenage years, the Victorian age was coming to an end: when Victoria died in 1901, the thirteen-year-old Margery watched the funeral procession;[40] she also had permission from Mrs Stuart to visit her family in London for the coronation of Edward VII. Sam had acquired tickets for himself and his son Ronald to watch the celebratory naval review at Portsmouth from a boat belonging to the ship-owner Donald Currie; however, there is no evidence as to whether they actually went since the coronation and accompanying celebrations were postponed, owing to the king's ill-health. It was at this time, on 9 June 1902, that Sam wrote to Margery:

> My dear little girl / Alas I shall not be able so to call you much longer. To think that you are 15 tomorrow & that in 2 or 3 years you will be in long frocks & considering yourself a young lady & expecting to be treated as such! [...] I hope my dear daughter that as you get older you will feel your life fuller & more full of interest & occupation & therefore happier, happy though your childhood I hope & believe, has been.

---

40 The author remembers as a child reading Margery's account of this, but it is not among the extant papers.

Part of the transition from girlhood to young womanhood involved travel — regarded by Sam and Clara as both enjoyable and educational. On Clara's part, this may have stemmed partly from the fact that she had been born in India; moreover, several members of the Garrett and Thornbury families lived and worked in Australia and South Africa. Margery used the diary given to her for her fourteenth birthday to record trips to Italy in the autumns of 1902 and 1903, and one to Scotland in 1905. The journeys were largely made by train, for which the tea basket, refilled wherever possible, was their most indispensable piece of luggage. While Margery was thrilled by the art and scenery of Italy, she also comments on more down-to earth aspects of their trips. In Venice (which they were lucky enough to see in the period when St Mark's square had no campanile),[41] a Miss Percy attached herself to them and they were torn between accepting that she was lonely and being irritated by her.[42] They watched glassblowing and mosaic-making, took a steamer across to the Lido and walked for a mile or so along the seashore; one evening, they heard a band in the Piazza playing Beethoven and Wagner. As well as sightseeing, they were reading John Ruskin's *Stones of Venice* and George Eliot's *Romola*, presumably aloud to one another. In Siena, the Belle Arti gallery was closed, 'but [they] got the man to let [them] in'. In Verona, Sam lost his wallet and went through the necessary bureaucratic procedures at the police station, to no avail. In November that year, back at school, Margery received a letter from her father thanking her for a pocket book she had sent him as a replacement for 'the one which is now reposing in the pocket of some thief at Milan [sic]'.[43]

In September 1903, Margery wrote in the diary: 'You didn't think that I should use you again this year [...] for the same purpose as last, did you?'. This time they visited different Italian cities, including Assisi and Rome. In Assisi, Clara and Sam were particularly intrigued by some of the plants growing in old walls and collected some seeds to take home. However, the splendours of Rome were too much for Margery's powers of description and, after a few entries, the account of this trip ends in mid-sentence: 'In the afternoon we'.

---

41   It fell down in 1902 and was not rebuilt until 1912.
42   Had they been a few years later, they might have thought of Miss Lavish in E. M. Forster's *A Room with a View* (first published 1908) and wondered whether she was putting them in a novel.
43   Sam Garrett, letter to Margery Spring Rice, 20 November 1902.

In 1905, she resumed: 'What a long time it seems since I have written in this dear old diary. But out it comes again, when Father, Mother & I go touring'. The year before, Clara and Sam had gone to Greece[44] but Margery had not shared that trip with them. This year, they went first to Glenbuchat in Aberdeenshire, as guests of their friends Mr and Mrs Barclay; Margery enjoyed herself with energetic activities — walking, horse-riding and dancing (sustained by whisky toddy and sandwiches). On one walk, Mr Barclay had to carry Margery across the Water of Buchat: 'Poor man, I shd think he regretted the undertaking'.[45] Leaving the Barclays' estate, they went on to Braemar. Sam and Margery set off for a walk along the Dee (she gives the impression that Clara was a less keen walker, though she was a fresh air enthusiast)[46] and typically ignored a 'strictly private' sign. When an old man warned them to turn back, Sam dismissed him, and they kept going even when the old man tried to physically stop them, fording a burn when he blocked their path across a bridge. Eventually they met someone else who explained that the road they were on led into the Duke of Fife's deer forests and they must retrace their steps. Perhaps this experience was the genesis of Margery's fierce fight to protect public footpaths in East Suffolk later in her life.

In the autumn of 1903, returning from Italy, her parents left Margery with a Madame Dussan in Paris for a few months. There were several English girls there so it was difficult to practise speaking French as Clara urged her to do: the latter thought it a disgrace to travel without trying to express oneself in the language of the country and went as far as to write parts of her own letters to Margery in French. Margery must have learnt some French, as she achieved the 'brevet supérieur'[47] of the Alliance française but, in any case, Madame wrote to Clara that her daughter was working hard. Margery also enjoyed musical opportunities, such as

---

44 Another echo of *A Room with a View*, where the Miss Alans daringly take off for Greece. The country was probably of particular interest to Sam, who had studied Classics.

45 Margery was very overweight in later life, but photographs of her as a young woman show a slimmer girl.

46 On 10 June 1903, when Clara had a bad cold, Sam wrote to Margery that her mother was 'a bad patient & insists on sitting & sleeping in the same draughts in wh. she delights when in health'. Margery inherited this attitude of Clara's.

47 The term 'brevet supérieure' (higher certificate') covers a multitude of sins, and it is impossible to be certain of the standard required in this case.

seeing Richard Wagner's *Tannhäuser* and visiting the sights of the city, particularly the Père Lachaise cemetery. 'This hankering after sarcophagi seems in your blood as well as fathers', wrote Clara, who hated both Père Lachaise and the Protestant cemetery in Rome, only prepared to like monuments that deserved to be regarded as works of art in their own right.[48] As Easter 1904 approached, Margery was still in Paris and Geoffrey had joined her there. Clara wrote that she might come out for a visit: 'I don't think that will be much of an interruption to your Frenchification'.[49] However, the visit did not happen as Clara caught the flu and was ill enough to cause her family serious anxiety. Aunt Grace went to Aldeburgh to look after her, and Sam (having consulted his sister Elizabeth) rushed from London to Aldeburgh to be with her. However, Clara had a strong constitution and recovered, even though it evidently took her some weeks before she was fully herself again.

In politics, the family was liberal and Margery became a committed and active Liberal Party member in her early adult life. But while she was still living at home, she seems to have enjoyed politically standing up to the rest of her family. In November 1907, her brother Ronald wrote to her: 'I am really very sorry to hear that you have turned socialist; my only consolation is that the chances are 10 to 1 that you don't know what you are talking about'.[50] His view was that the possibility of implementing socialism depended on the unlikely condition that humans learnt to solve disputes without fighting: although Margery's socialism did not last long, a commitment to solving disputes without violence was to play an important part in her life.

It is difficult to gauge Sam and Clara's attitude to religion. Sam's mother Louisa was deeply, evangelically religious and Newson went along with the outward observances of the Anglican church. However, according to Newson's daughter, Millicent, he was apt to deliberately turn over two pages at a time during family prayers so as to shorten the whole business. Their children and grandchildren varied in their enthusiasm. Millicent married a free-thinker, Henry Fawcett, but remained a devout Christian herself — as demonstrated by her accounts of her journeys to Palestine in the 1920s. Elizabeth's letters include many references

---

48   Clara Garrett, letter to Margery Spring Rice, 11 November 1903.
49   Clara Garrett, letter to Margery Spring Rice, 22 March 1904.
50   Ronald Garrett, letter to Margery Spring Rice, 5 November 1907.

to sermons she had heard, while the Scottish medical missionary Jane Waterston's description of her as 'hard and godless' may say as much about the writer as about Elizabeth.[51] Margery's other godmother, Theo, was also devout, though later in life she leaned away from Anglicanism towards Quakerism. Clara makes conventional references to religion in her letters (and her paternal grandfather and his father were both clergyman), but there is no sense that it was a particularly important part of family life. For example, no reference is made to family prayers in her letters or any other surviving family correspondence. On the other hand, Margery, as a teenager, clearly went through a phase of passionate conviction: a series of letters from a clergyman called Robert Laffan is extant, written to her between 1904 and 1907. He was, at this date, Rector of St Stephen's, Walbrook, in the City of London, having previously been head of King Edward VI School in Stratford-upon-Avon and of Cheltenham College.[52] Perhaps she had met him in Stratford in 1902; he almost certainly prepared her for her confirmation in 1905. He and his wife were supporters of women's suffrage, which may well have endeared him to Margery. Her side of the correspondence is lost, but his consists of long and encouraging answers to the theological questions she was posing him: he never loses patience with her although one has the impression that she was a demanding student. Margery lost her faith as an adult, perhaps at Cambridge, but she was married in St Stephen's in 1911, when Laffan was still rector there, which suggests that the friendship endured for several years.

Margery's brothers were, of course, growing up alongside her. In December 1901, Douglas, whose career plan was to join Sam as a solicitor in his office in the city, had won a scholarship to Emmanuel College, Cambridge, where he started in the autumn of 1902. His letters to Margery from Cambridge are full of anecdotes about university life. When Margery was in Paris, he wrote to her about the dinner party he was giving for the May Ball, suggesting that next year she might perhaps 'condescend to live in England, & [...] even if she be not yet "out", will just have to put her hair up & come all the same'.[53]

---

51 John Mackenzie, *The Scots in South Africa* (Manchester: Manchester University Press, 2007), p. 133.
52 He was also instrumental in the establishment of the modern Olympic games.
53 Douglas Garrett, letter to Margery Spring Rice, 15 May 1904.

Harry — bright, sporty and a talented artist, but perhaps more mercurial in character than Douglas — found it hard to settle on what to do, causing his parents a good deal of anxiety as well as expense. At one stage, he intended to be an architect, but agonised about whether to go to university first, noting that many of his father's friendships were formed in his university days. In the summer of 1903, when he was seventeen, he tried unsuccessfully to persuade Sam to let him leave Rugby. Another possibility was joining the civil service — likely his parents' choice rather than his own. In the autumn of 1904, he won a place at Pembroke College, Cambridge, but suffered some kind of breakdown when he came to sit, and subsequently fail, his final exams — perhaps because his heart was not really in academic work. Some years later, when Margery too was facing her final exams, Harry wrote to her: 'My own disappointment at the time of my unfortunate collapse was very great, on Father's behalf. But for myself it was nothing to the regret which I feel now. I want you to profit from this experience of mine. I thought that in a year or two I shouldn't care. I was wrong'.[54] After Cambridge, Harry travelled in Italy and then trained as an artist at the Slade School of Fine Art, London. He and Margery, who shared both his artistic interests and his tendency to regard locked gates as an invitation to enter, were close until his early death.

Between 1904 and 1907, Margery studied at Bedford College, London, which may have been chosen because Aunt Theo's daughter, Lesley, had been there and because Margery could live at home as the college was, at that time, situated in York Place, near Baker Street. On 20 September 1904, Aunt Theo wrote to her: 'You too like some others of us, begin a new stage this term — Go on as you are going my Beloved God-daughter — & the gentleness of all the gods go with thee'. At this point, there is a gap in the sequence of family letters and we know very little about her life at Bedford, except that she studied a matriculation course in mathematics in her first year and English in the two subsequent years. It is likely, also, that the college was seen as preparation for Cambridge, though we have no idea when that idea germinated: all we know is that Margery begged her parents to let her try for a place at Cambridge and that, in the autumn of 1907, she went up to Girton College to read Moral Sciences. This was another and more significant new stage for

---

54 Harry Garrett, letter to Margery Spring Rice, 13 February 1910.

her, an experience that deeply affected the course of her personal life and helped shape her into the adult she became. Harry was right that one of the most important aspects of university was the formation of friendships.

2. Independence (1907–1912)

Margery had been independently-minded since her teenage years. Though she had lived away from home during her education in Stratford, and subsequently in Paris, going to Cambridge allowed her much greater scope to develop autonomously. There were family links with both Newnham and Girton, the only two Cambridge options for women at the time: her aunt Millicent had been involved with the founding of Newnham and her aunt Elizabeth's close friend Emily Davies was the founder of Girton.[1] There is no evidence for why Girton was chosen by (or for) Margery.

The Cambridge in which she arrived in 1907, as one of a cohort of forty-four Girton students, was a place where the academic opportunities for women were highly restricted. Although the two colleges had been founded more than three decades earlier, there had been almost no progress in terms of women's circumstances as students: they were not members of the university and they could not gain degrees. They could attend lectures only by courtesy of individual lecturers and their access (and that of the women teaching them) to the University Library was restricted to the hours of 10am to 2pm. The successes of Girton's Agnata Ramsay (top student in Classics in 1887) and of Newnham's Philippa Fawcett, Margery's cousin, (who in 1890 was ranked above the Senior Wrangler) had brought no change to entrenched male attitudes. The dogged and painstaking work of advocates such as Emily Davies and Henry Sidgwick had been no more successful, and, by the early years of the twentieth century, some of the zeal had gone out of the campaign. Women were formally allowed to be examined, have their names listed in class lists, and receive certificates: this was the sum of their rights. The

---

1   Elizabeth served on the House Committee of Girton in its first incarnation as the Cambridge College for Women, in Hitchin. She helped to raise money for the college, as well as giving money herself.

    https://doi.org/10.11647/OBP.0215.02

inadequacy and illogicality of the arguments used by their opponents are laughable, but nothing would shift the university: by the end of the century, degrees were open to women at London, Durham and the Scottish universities, but at Cambridge the proposal had been turned down in 1888 and 1897. Shamefully, it was not until after World War II that women in Cambridge could graduate, nearly thirty years after Oxford, which itself was hardly in the vanguard.[2]

The restrictions were not only academic but also social. It was a new experience for most of the women at Girton to be living away from home, but their social lives were still governed by strict rules. Emily Davies, an unbending character who did not deal easily with views that opposed her own, had been determined that her students should be irreproachable in their conduct, so Girton students were chaperoned whenever they were, or might be, in the presence of men. The same policy was pursued by Davies's successors as Mistress of the college, including (in Margery's day) Constance Jones, who was also a lecturer in Moral Sciences. One student had got into trouble because she had been seen walking in the college gardens with a man who was revealed to be her brother. The result of this policy was that non-academic activities, such as music and drama, took place within the college — Margery was on the committee of the college debating society in the spring of 1909 — and intense, often lifelong friendships were formed. Constance Jones, in a little book of memoirs, described life in college as offering an opportunity 'to combine social intercourse and solitude in a way not often met with'. Every member of the college had a bedroom and a study while there were communal gardens, a dining hall and libraries. Students were encouraged to manage their time well: 'Girton aimed at being the abode of disciplined freedom — at giving the girl students the same kind of life and teaching that have helped to make Cambridge and Oxford what they are in the life of men — a home of "sound learning and religious education," of intellectual honesty and search for truth, of practical efficiency and sanity of outlook'.[3]

---

2   The first women in England to be awarded degrees graduated from London University in 1880. In Scotland, the first female students matriculated at Edinburgh in 1869, the same year that Girton was founded; however, no female Edinburgh students were allowed to graduate until 1893. Oxford started awarding degrees to women in 1920.

3   Emily Elizabeth Constance Jones, *As I Remember: An Autobiographical Ramble* (London: A. & C. Black, 1922), p. 69.

Rather surprisingly, for someone who was more oriented towards action than reflection, Margery chose to study Moral Sciences. The only extant comment we have about this in her own words is found in a letter to her mother from Girton, dated 7 February 1909, in which she says that she loves Moral Sciences because it is about how people feel and think. Perhaps she was also influenced by the Mistress who was, herself, a distinguished philosopher who had gained a first in her Tripos exam in the late 1870s. Miss Jones was known for her interest in, and kindness to, students and had begun her teaching career while she was a research student, giving logic classes to prepare students for the 'little-go' exam (the preliminary exam that students had to pass). In his introduction to her book, Dean Inge wrote of her: 'it is hard to say whether she was more admired for her brains or beloved for her heart'.[4]

Jones's memoir describes the contents of the Moral Sciences Tripos in 1875, which, at that time, included: political philosophy, psychology, metaphysics, ethics, logic, physiology, aesthetics and economics.[5] The only piece of direct evidence for Margery's studies is an essay she wrote in 1908 on higher education for women. Surprisingly, given her heritage — her aunts' part in the fight for medical education for women and for women's suffrage — as well as her own independence of mind, the argument of the essay is that men and women are different and should be differently educated. Women need a much broader education than men, she writes, because their most important role in life is to be intelligent companions to their husbands and to educate their own children. The 'equal but different' and 'women's place in the home' arguments seem such an unlikely attitude for her to take that the reader can only wonder whether she was writing tongue-in-cheek or whether she had been set an assignment to argue for something she did not believe in. However, there is no indication that this is the case.[6] Perhaps the essay reflects a general dissatisfaction with the Tripos curriculum. Perhaps, also, Margery's generation of students was showing its disillusion with the fierce aspirations to equality of the first Cambridge women: it is true that the fight for equality of women students with men

---

4   Ibid., p. v.
5   Ibid., pp. 52–53.
6   Among suffragists there was a wide range of views about women's place: Millicent Fawcett, for example, disapproved of state assistance for women on the grounds that they might feel it absolved them from their responsibilities for their children.

went through a quiet period between 1900 and 1914.[7] It may be, also, that there was an element of rebellion against the expectation of a life of public service: Margery was certainly determined to enjoy herself at Cambridge. However, if the views expressed in her essay were genuinely held by her at the time, she certainly did not live by them later: when she came to have children of her own, they were mostly brought up by nannies while she pursued a public life in which she worked tirelessly for the cause of less privileged women.

Perhaps, though, the most important aspect of university for her was just what Harry had predicted: the making of friendships, which went along with the loosening of ties to home, particularly to her mother. In Girton, she became part of a close-knit group, in which the most dominant figure was undoubtedly Eileen Power, later to become an eminent and ground-breaking mediaeval historian. Eileen was the oldest of three sisters born in 1889, 1890 and 1891 to a Manchester stockbroker and his wife. The emotional and financial security of her earliest years fell to pieces when her father was convicted of forgery and sent to prison. Under the huge shadow of this scandal, Eileen's mother Mabel and the girls were taken under the wings of Mabel's father and sisters. When Mabel died from tuberculosis in 1903, the girls remained with their maternal family, but moved to Oxford. This backstory, which Eileen rarely talked about, strengthened the ties between the three sisters and, perhaps, made them wary of marriage. All three were intellectually gifted and achieved distinguished careers.[8]

The best picture of the friendship between Eileen and Margery is found in the letters that Eileen wrote after they left Girton, particularly between 1910–1911, when Eileen was studying in Paris. She laughs at Margery, who having been slim as a child was now growing fat, addressing her by one of her nicknames — 'O hefty bargee' — and referring to her as 'Your fair & portly self' and 'you old comfort'.[9] However, Eileen also tells her she is the only person to whom she can say anything about anything. In the same letter she writes that she loves Margery's letters in spite, or perhaps because, of the 'ungrammatical sentences & ungainly phrases' and the 'luxurious labyrinth of mixed

---

7   Rita McWilliams-Tullberg, *Women at Cambridge* (London: Gollancz, 1975), p. 142.
8   Maxine Berg, *A Woman in History: Eileen Power 1889–1940* (Cambridge, UK: Cambridge University Press, 1996).
9   Eileen Power, letter to Margery Spring Rice, 7 April 1910.

metaphors'. While the letters are full of gossip about their friends, Eileen also discusses her difficulties with finding the right subject for her thesis and Margery's decisions — and indecisions — about the future. They also considered writing an opera together, lyrics by Eileen and music by Margery. When another of their Girton friends, Catriona (Kate) Robertson, becomes engaged to Margery's brother Ronald, Eileen gives a lively account of a rendezvous to which Ronald fails to turn up, leaving Eileen with a distraught Catriona on a station platform. Ronald eventually appears and Eileen writes that she still has a sore hand from his hearty handshake. Eileen thought that Margery's talents lay with people rather than with words: 'you have got lots of observation & a wonderful power of drawing lines'.[10] She appreciated Margery's gifts of 'combined sanity & sympathy',[11] her fearlessness, and her belief that 'valour is the better part of discretion'.[12]

The third person in the close triangle of friendship at Cambridge was Margaret Jones, who was studying history at Newnham. The story transmitted in the Garrett and Jones families to their grandchildren's generation was that large taxi fares were run up for the journey between Girton and Newnham as Margery and Margaret pursued their friendship. Margaret was the youngest but one of the eight children of Canadian parents who had met, married and settled in England. Mary Jones, *née* Ross, was the granddaughter of Robert Baldwin, lawyer and politician, and sister of Oscar Wilde's close friend and executor, Robbie Ross. There was plenty of money in the family thanks to the land grant made to the Baldwin family, an area that became the west end of downtown Toronto. Augusta Ross, Mary's mother, had brought her daughter to England in the hope that as an heiress she would make a good marriage, but Mary put paid to this plan by falling in love with a clever but impoverished captain in the Royal Artillery, Charles Jones.[13] Charles, who had been in his thirties when he married his teenage bride, came to suffer from

---

10   Eileen Power, letter to Margery Spring Rice, 15 August 1910.
11   Eileen Power, letter to Margery Spring Rice, 19 October 1910.
12   Eileen Power, letter to Margery Spring Rice, 18 August 1910.
13   The Joneses were Empire loyalists who had emigrated to Canada from the United States, leaving all their assets behind. The Rosses had come to Canada as economic migrants from County Antrim in Ireland. Robert Baldwin's grandfather (also Robert) emigrated from County Cork in Ireland partly for economic reasons but also because he was alarmed by the revolutionary unrest in Ireland at the turn of the eighteenth and nineteenth centuries.

diabetes and was advised to go somewhere with a warm climate since at that date (and until the isolation of insulin in the early 1920s) it was an incurable disease. He chose Algeria, but died there of pneumonia in 1896. When Margery came into their circle, Mary held matriarchal sway over her family in a large house — Jesmond Hill, in Pangbourne, Berkshire — which they had built in the last years of the nineteenth century. Margery was made welcome there and, in time, came to have a close relationship with Mary, in whom she found she could confide more easily than she could in Clara. The family — cultured, well-travelled and politically aware — were convinced suffragists,[14] which helped Margery to feel at home among them. They also had a penchant for nicknames: Margaret was called 'Puppy' (which later morphed into 'Pikey'), her mother was 'Muz', and it was the Jones family who gave Margery her nickname of 'Bargee' (which later became 'Margee').

The Joneses were (like Sam and Clara) not a religious family. When Margaret's sister Petica was married at the British consulate in Rome in 1909 to Donald Robertson, she got into a dispute with a cousin who berated her for not having a religious ceremony. She closed the argument by telling him firmly that she was an unbeliever. Although Petica, in particular, suffered from poor health, all the sisters enjoyed hypochondria to varying degrees and their letters are full of angst about minor health problems. Perhaps this was partly as a result of boredom: they were intelligent women who (with the exception of Margaret) did not have the opportunity of an excellent education — a gap which they dealt with in different ways. Petica's education was expanded by marrying an academic, while Lilian (known as Gil) was a voracious self-educator through her reading. Margery described Lilian as 'awfully clever, — no superficiality about it either'.[15]

Muz was a strong and self-willed woman who had caused two hiccups in her husband's professional career: once by persuading him to resign his commission because she was not prepared to go to India, and subsequently, by hating Newcastle, where he was working

---

14 At the time of the 1911 census, Margery was staying with the Jones family. She and three of the Jones sisters gave 'suffragist' as their occupation on the census form. For the suffragist campaign against the 1911 census, see: Jane Robinson, *Hearts and Minds: The Untold Story of the Great Pilgrimage and How Women Won the Vote* (London: Doubleday, 2018), p. 132; Jill Liddington and Elizabeth Crawford, *Vanishing for the Vote: The Story of the 1911 Census* (Manchester: Manchester University Press, 2014).

15 Margery Spring Rice, Diary 1910–11, 16 October 1910.

for Armstrong's, insisting they return to London where he obtained employment in Woolwich Arsenal, holding various roles there until he retired in 1880.[16] She did — at least up to a point — believe in education for her daughters,[17] although when it came to books she, herself, as her youngest daughter Emily (nicknamed Topsy) wrote of her, was 'a tremendous skipper, and all her life leafed through books without reading more than a paragraph here and there'. However, Topsy added, her mother was down-to-earth, intelligent, trustworthy, good-tempered 'and on the whole open-minded'.[18]

Margery fell in love with the whole family, but found Muz particularly sympathetic. As far as her own family went, she loved her father as deeply as he did her, but relations with her mother always had their tensions. Margery thought this a result of their marked differences as people: in her 7 February 1909 letter from Girton, in which she explains why she loves Moral Sciences, she says she thinks Clara (unlike herself) is not interested in individuals. For Margery, physical and emotional activity was much more important than intellectual. In 1907, one of her friends had written, in some unspecified crisis:

> All I can say is that you must not take anything your mother says too literally. Remember that her temperament and yours are totally different. She is extremely highly strung & apt to exaggerate all her emotions [...] with you it is different: & when you say a thing you mean it to the letter.[19]

While there may be some truth in this, it is also undoubtedly the case that Clara and Margery were alike in that they were both very strong-willed and opinionated, and that must have exacerbated the conflict between them. Margery was also trying to move away to some extent from the closeness of family life — she needed to separate herself from Clara. Sam recognised that relations between Margery and Clara were not always harmonious, but came down firmly in support of Clara. In May 1909, just as she was coming to the end of her second year in Cambridge, he wrote to her:

---

16 Charles's brother-in-law, married to his sister Mary, was Charles Wright Young, who also worked at Woolwich.
17 Petica, unlike Margaret, was not sent to university because Muz thought that she was pretty enough to make a good marriage.
18 E. B. C. Lucas, unpublished memoirs.
19 Violet Price, letter to Margery Spring Rice, 4 May 1907.

I am very sorry if I hurt you — but I had to do it. You argue your case
well [we do not know what case she was arguing] but it won't do. I am
very glad that you have determined to look at things in general through
the spectacles of people who are older, & who therefore unless they are
fools must be wiser, than yourself. I am sure that will conduce to your
happiness & comfort & well-being. What you say about Mother is very
sweet to me. She is as you say 'grand' in an emergency. You have it in
your power to make an immense addition to her happiness and I believe
I am justified in hoping that you intend to do it.[20]

While the strict rules of chaperonage at Cambridge pulled one way,
pulling in the opposite direction were contemporary ideas about personal
fulfilment for women, and if the rules discouraged the development of
relationships between men and women students that did not mean that
everyone abided by the rules. In Margery's case, such relationships were
described ironically by Eileen as a 'maelstrom of disgustful amours'
although we know little about what they actually amounted to.[21] In
1919, another Girton student, Florence Roma Muir Wilson (writing as
Romer Wilson)[22] was to publish a roman à clef, *If All These Young Men*, in
which a thinly disguised Margery ('Amaryllis') and Puppy ('Everett')
and four other Jones sisters all feature. Eileen certainly had no difficulty
in identifying all the characters when the book came out. For Margery,
however, although there were probably several fleeting affairs of the
heart at Cambridge, one of the results of her friendship with Puppy and
her introduction to the Jones family was that she fell deeply in love with
Puppy's brother Edward.

When Margery came down from Cambridge with an upper second
(she had only taken Part 1 of the two-part Tripos, but this was regarded
as a degree, and she was to obtain her MA in 1928),[23] she was uncertain
what to do. We know something about her life in the autumn of 1910
from a (very short-lived) diary that she kept. She had dithered about a
career, wondering whether to follow her brother Harry to art college but
eventually deciding to train as a factory inspector. However, the diary

---

20   Sam Garrett, letter to Margery Spring Rice, 2 November 1909.
21   Eileen Power, letter to Margery Spring Rice, 8 August 1910.
22   In a letter to Stella Benson dated 16 February 1930, Margery's second husband
     Dominick mentions Wilson's death and says that he had not seen her for eleven
     years 'because she was so nasty about Margery'.
23   Although a woman could not graduate, she could receive a 'titular' BA degree,
     which could be converted into an MA for a fee after a certain period of time.

suggests that she did not take this very seriously — singing lessons seem to have been more important than going to work. At this stage of her life, as is not unusual for a woman in her early twenties, she comes across as someone whose first priority was to enjoy her life and take as much as it offered her — relishing the arts, the opportunity to travel and her friendships. Although Eileen Power's biographer writes that Margery was 'like Eileen in her passion for causes. She took up crusades, and dominated and bullied her friends into matching her own energy in pursuing them', there is no evidence yet of any deep commitment to any particular cause.[24] Margery does not even mention the big suffrage demonstration that took place on 18 November, when Elizabeth Garrett Anderson and Emmeline Pankhurst led a deputation to H. H. Asquith, who refused to see them.

During October and November that year, Margery worked at the Industrial Law Committee as a preliminary to her training as a factory inspector. This resulted in her being asked to give lectures — firstly, on 23 November, to a group of women in East London; secondly, a few days later, to the Women's Liberal Association in Lewisham; and thirdly, on 6 December in Wembley (in this instance, Margery unfortunately does not tell us either her audience or her subject, only that she was 'dead-tired' when she got home).[25] Days, or half-days, of work were interspersed with lunch and tea parties, gallery-visits, singing or German lessons and lectures. In the evenings, there were sometimes dinner parties or trips to concerts or the opera — in the middle of October, she saw *Tristan und Isolde*, conducted by Thomas Beecham, with Puppy (who was working as a teacher in London) and Edward. 'It is impossible to write of Tristan. The last act is something too fine for words', she recorded, but she was disappointed by the singers being out of tune in the second act duet.[26] There were long weekends at Pangbourne, with the Jones family, and in Cambridge. By November, work seems to have faded even more into the background: she visits a sick woman referred to the Industrial Law Committee by the Home Office, but is dismissive of the woman's needs, as her husband is employed. On 9 November, she writes in her diary that work is interesting but that she finds it hard to concentrate. On 18

---

24 Berg, *A Woman in History*, pp. 41–42.
25 Margery Spring Rice, Diary, 6 December 1910.
26 Margery Spring Rice, Diary, 20 October 1910.

November, she heard that she was to be offered the part of a Valkyrie in the Spring Wagner Festival in Leeds: 'I am mad with excitement about it' (in the end, nothing came of this, though she attended a few rehearsals). There was also an unrealised plan to go to India. It is possible that at this stage of her life, she was reacting to the single-minded pursuit of more serious goals by older women in her family (her aunts Elizabeth and Millicent in particular) by determinedly pursuing social and cultural pleasures.

Much of Margery's social life was shared with members of the Jones family (particularly Puppy and Edward) but she gives no clue yet that Edward is anything other than a good friend. If anything, she seems more attracted to Kingsley Game,[27] another friend of Puppy's, of whom she says 'I could never have believed a man capable of such depth of understanding for a woman as he has. But then he adores me'.[28] The first real indication of Edward's importance to her comes in the entry for 4 December, when she was again in Pangbourne for the weekend. During a walk with Puppy and her sister Hilda, she and Edward 'split off, — came in awfully late for lunch, & had a perfectly glorious walk. We talked hard all the time[,] religion — politics, & ourselves, — subjects of eternal interest. I am inclined to believe that he is in love with me; I wonder. In the evening Puppy & I sat in Hilda's room & discussed It!!'[29] Early in December, she met Kingsley in Puppy's London rooms, with her permission, which makes it sound as though Puppy already regarded him with interest on her own account: she was to marry Kingsley in 1919 (and the ups and downs of their relationship crop up in Eileen's letters from time to time). On this occasion, Margery commented, 'he makes me appreciate Edward all the more'. She heard (she does not say from whom) that Edward had been discussing her with his sister Lilian: 'He does think of it, my

---

27 Arthur Kingsley Game, born 1890, had overlapped at Cambridge with Puppy and Margery, studying at Caius and graduating in law in 1911. There are persistent hints in letters and memoirs that Margery and Kingsley had an affair, which resulted in a long estrangement between her and Puppy, but I have not been able to date this.

28 Margery Spring Rice, Diary, November 1910.

29 Throughout her life, Margery was inclined to sprinkle her writings with commas followed by dashes: the habit, together with the vigorous handwriting that was characteristic of her from youth into old age, make the pages of her letters immediately recognisable.

God, — how exciting it all is'.[30] In a subsequent diary entry, Margery expresses that she 'can't help counting on it & dreaming of it',[31] though at this stage, she wants to keep it to herself, and hopes her parents are not discussing it.

Plans had been laid for Margery to travel to Paris in mid-December for a month to improve her French, learn cooking, and visit Eileen Power, who was studying there. On 14 December, she said goodbye to Edward, and two days later she set off to catch the ferry, only to be thwarted by a gale so strong that the ship was unable to sail. Knowing that there was a fancy-dress dance at the Slade that evening, to which Edward was going, she hurried back to London to persuade Harry to take her. Harry refused at first, on the grounds that there would be too many girls, but was eventually persuaded to agree. By the end of the party, in the small hours, Margery and Edward were engaged. A few days later, she travelled to Paris.

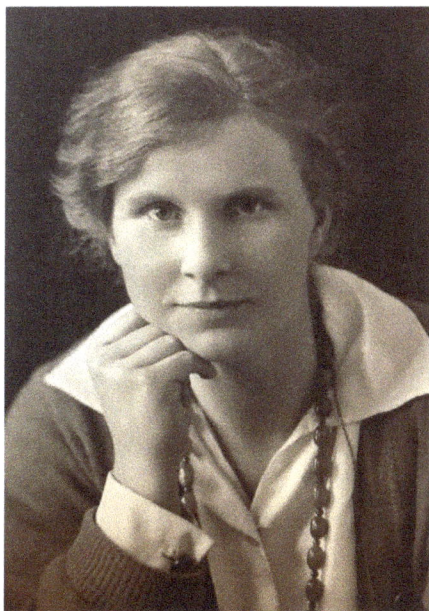

Fig. 7. Margery as a young woman, around the time of her engagement to Edward. Photograph: family archives (c. 1910).

---

30 Margery Spring Rice, Diary, 8 December 1910.
31 Margery Spring Rice, Diary, 9 December 1910.

Fig. 8. Mary Jones with seven of her eight children. 'Puppy' is the baby, Petica leans against Mary and Edward is on the far right. Photograph: family archives (c. 1888).

Charles Edward (always known by his second name), the fourth of the eight Jones children and the oldest son, adored by his sisters, was almost nine years older than Margery. He had started to study at Merton College, Oxford, in 1897: he passed his first-year Classics exams as well as the compulsory scripture paper and then switched to mathematics, but, for unknown reasons, did not complete his degree. He had held a commission in the Warwickshire regiment between 1900 and 1905, which had taken him first to Malta, then to a post in the camp for Boer War prisoners on Bermuda, and finally to Gibraltar, though he did not see active service. His great passions were walking and climbing, so he used his leaves for walking holidays in Spain and Sicily with his friend Ronald Rose. In 1905, when the regiment was due to be sent to South Africa, Edward decided to resign his commission (though remaining an army reservist) in favour of working as a bill-broker in the firm of Allen, Harvey and Ross in the city of London where his boss would have been his uncle, Muz's brother, Alec Ross.

Edward was a good foil for Margery — a man with a strong sense of honour and duty, and a quiet, reserved, steady personality that contrasted with her volatility and outspokenness. In his sister Lilian's words, 'he hides his light under a bushel & [...] it can only be discovered by the right people or person'.[32] The word that occurs more often than any other when his name is mentioned in letters is 'gentle'. Family and friends were generally delighted to hear of their engagement. Sam and Clara had set off a few days earlier for a holiday in Portugal, from where Clara wrote that Edward would get a 'good, devoted if somewhat headstrong wife'.[33] Sam was more expansive:

> Since I wrote you last a chorus in praise of Edward has reached me from those who know him much better than I do. So I am confirmed in my hope & belief that you have chosen wisely & well. I hope when we get home we shall give him as warm a welcome as his family have given you.[34]

Aunt Theo, in her down-to-earth way, refused 'to sing Glory Hallelujah' until she knew more about Edward and, even then, not until Margery had been married for a year and a day and was in a position to say that her husband improved on acquaintance.

One friend, writing in French, thought that Margery had 'trop d'esprit'[35] but also all the qualities needed for being loved and for making Edward happy. Another, Violet Price, who was living in Chile, was a little more uncertain: 'In spite of your level-headed remarks, I can feel you are genuinely fond of Edward. But [...] is this enough?'[36] Margery's own letters to Edward from Paris, however, are intense and passionate, and there is little doubt that she was deeply in love with him and felt she had found her soulmate. Writing to him on 20 December, she refers to herself as 'a conceited little Egoist', who 'wonders how you, — with your intense reserve, — your intense dislike of gush, — & your intense shyness of your own feelings, — would welcome the ineloquent, unvarnished, sincere outpourings of her foolish young soul'. Would Edward be shocked at her capacity for passion, she

---

32 Lilian Jones, letter to Margery Spring Rice, 3 January 1911.
33 Clara Garrett, letter to Margery Spring Rice, undated [December 1910].
34 Sam Garrett, letter to Margery Spring Rice, 27 December 1910.
35 Name illegible, letter to Margery Spring Rice, 31 December 1910.
36 Violet Price, letter to Margery Spring Rice, 14 January 1911.

wondered? Eileen showed her pleasure in the engagement by asking whether it would make her Edward's 'first fiancée once removed'.[37] She looked forward to following 'your matrimonial aeroplane circling round the Eiffel tower of convention till it totter bewildered on its foundations'.[38] As well as encouraging Margery's aspirations to remain independent and keep her own interests, Eileen wrote that she would never forgive Margery if she swore to obey Edward, but 'I think that you will always be happy (whatever you do) out of sheer force of character'.[39] Eileen recognised that she herself did not find it easy to make relationships with men, but she was generous in her recognition of Margery's happiness.

The exchange of letters between Margery, Clara and Edward over the Christmas period demonstrates that the engagement brought out all the old tensions and resentments between mother and daughter. Margery felt that Clara was expecting her to sacrifice all her interests to Edward's, just as (in Margery's eyes) Clara had sacrificed hers to Sam's and her children's. 'I have seen such an awful lot of it, — & it's so degrading' she wrote to Edward. She felt she was being treated like a child and that she and her mother had not 'an idea in common'. Clara did not value Margery's Cambridge experience and was completely out of sympathy with her liberal political views; this resulted in Margery's refusal to discuss anything important with her mother. 'There is not much spirit of compromise in either Mother or myself'. And yet, Margery recognised that she, herself, had behaved ungenerously in the past, 'when I was the vilest creature that ever stepped [sic] the earth'.[40] On a more mundane level, Clara and Margery's brother Douglas also assumed that she would return from Paris at once, to welcome Sam and Clara home from Portugal, when she was actually enjoying herself in Paris too much to be prepared to return early, in spite of missing Edward. Edward poured oil on troubled waters:

> I understand your being irritated by your mother's letter to you; but I think the attitude you say you have adopted the last two or three years is the only possible one. After all people can't help getting rather

37   Eileen Power, letter to Margery Spring Rice, 6 January 1911.
38   Eileen Power, letter to Margery Spring Rice, 23 April 1911.
39   Eileen Power, letter to Margery Spring Rice, 6 November 1910.
40   Margery Spring Rice, letter to Edward Jones, 25 December 1910.

old-fashioned as they grow older, & one of the signs thereof is a tendency to indulge in platitudes.[41]

When Margery suggested that after their marriage each of them should, on occasion, go away alone, he replied 'I absolutely agree with your idea about sometimes going away without the other. I am sure there is no greater mistake than the Siamese twins attitude!'[42] During their marriage, they followed the advice they had given themselves. 'I am not going to be a cabbage', she wrote in her diary on New Year's Eve.

Margery, who was twenty-three, and Edward, thirty-two, were married on 28 April 1911, at St Stephen, Walbrook, by Robert Laffan. She had written to Muz: 'I have dropped into a regular nest of dear people, whom I love for their own sakes, as well as for Edward's'.[43] Some compromises must have been made, in the light of Margery's view that showy weddings were vulgar and that the meaning of marriage was not to be expressed 'by orange-blossom & white satin & a priest'.[44] One Garrett relative was disappointed that there were no bridesmaids but appreciated the 'sumptuous banquet' given by Sam and Clara for family and friends after the couple had left for their honeymoon near Llanthony Abbey in Wales.[45] Margery's cousin Roger Gibb, who had a gift for teasing her affectionately, wrote: 'The City of London must mark this as a red-letter day. In a couple of hours you have been married and Balfour and Asquith have appeared on the same platform and spoken in favour of international arbitration'.[46] Not wanting to be 'Mrs Jones', Margery did not discard her own name, but added Edward's to hers.

It is fascinating to speculate whether, in a culture in which women were not expected to know much about their own bodies, Margery and her friends knew anything about sex. Marie Stopes' *Married Love*,

---

41 Edward Jones, letter to Margery Spring Rice, 29 December 1910.
42 Edward Jones, letter to Margery Spring Rice, 1 January 1911.
43 Margery Spring Rice, letter to Mary Jones, 22 December 1910.
44 Margery Spring Rice, letter to Edward Jones, 25 December 1910.
45 Clara Garrett, letter to Margery Spring Rice, 2 May [1911]. Elizabeth Garrett Anderson had been married 'without millinery and almost without cookery' (Jo Manton, *Elizabeth Garrett Anderson* (London: Methuen, 1987), p. 217): Margery may have emulated her as regards a hat, but certainly not as regards food.
46 Roger Gibb, letter to Margery Spring Rice, 28 April 1911. Asquith, Liberal Prime Minister, and Balfour, leader of the Conservative Party, both delivered speeches at the Guildhall in favour of President Taft's proposal for a general treaty between the US and the British Empire, concerning international arbitration. The treaty was signed in August 1911.

which offered a revelation described by Naomi Mitchison as 'a light in great darkness to many of us, though a light shining through a lantern which was possibly not in the best taste',[47] was not published until 1918.[48] There is no way of knowing whether Margery had read Henry A. Allbutt's popular pocket-sized guide for married women covering pregnancy and child-rearing, *The Wife's Handbook,* first published in the year of Margery's birth and in print for several decades afterwards. The forty-fifth edition, published two years after Margery's marriage, takes a patronising attitude to women and their sexuality: Allbutt advises, for example, that women in poor health should 'avoid too frequent sexual connections. Of course a little may be beneficial'. He includes a chapter suggesting various ways of preventing conception, such as inserting a quinine-soaked sponge into the vagina before intercourse, but the book also includes numerous advertisements for 'the best and most reliable Preventives' and a 'Descriptive Price List (Illustrated) of Neo-Malthusian Appliances and Hygienic Requisites'.[49] The emotional and psychological aspects of sex do not come into his picture.

We do not know, either, whether Clara had told Margery anything. Perhaps her aunt Elizabeth, who, by 1910, was at the end of her distinguished medical career, and to whom Margery always felt close, had spoken to her. However, Jo Manton, in her biography of Elizabeth Garrett Anderson, recounts that contraception was never mentioned at the London School of Medicine for Women: 'A young woman doctor, being interviewed for her first assistantship, was asked for her views on birth control. She replied tentatively that she had always thought large families rather jolly, and was relieved when this appeared to be the right answer'.[50] Margery had no sisters and neither of her two great friends

---

47   Naomi Mitchison, *Comments on Birth Control* (London: Faber & Faber, 1930), p. 31.

48   Simon Szreter and Kate Fisher, in their survey of sexual attitudes between 1918 and 1963, produce evidence that middle-class women were generally better informed about sex than working-class women: Szreter and Fisher, *Sex before the Sexual Revolution: Intimate Life in England 1918–63* (Cambridge, UK: Cambridge University Press, 2010), pp. 251–56, https://doi.org/10.1017/cbo9780511778353

49   Henry A. Allbutt, *The Wife's Handbook,* 45th ed. (London: George Standring, 1913), pp. 4, 40, 62. See also Kate Macdonald, 'Women and Their Bodies in the Popular Reading of 1910', *Literature and History,* 22 (2013), 61–79 (p. 73), https://doi.org/10.7227/LH.22.1.5. Macdonald points out that various newspapers and magazines carried coded advertisements for contraceptives, but again we have no idea whether Margery might have seen these.

50   Manton, *Elizabeth Garrett Anderson,* p. 284.

was married. Her eldest sister-in-law, Ethel, had married Squire Sprigge, a doctor and medical journalist, in 1905, but Ethel and Margery did not know each other well at the time of the latter's marriage. Another sister-in-law, Petica, had married a classical scholar, Donald Robertson, in 1909, but she and Margery did not become close until after Margery's marriage. Although there had clearly been flirtations and infatuations among her Cambridge friends, there is no suggestion that anything went further. Social attitudes and conventions made it difficult for a man and a woman to be alone together: even when they were engaged, Margery could have lunch in Edward's rooms, or go out to dinner with him, but could not have dinner in his rooms. That sex was certainly discussed among her friends is clear from hints in Eileen's letters: before the wedding, she asks whether Margery has found a woman doctor (possibly for contraceptive advice, although doctors themselves were often ignorant in that field, something Margery herself was to take up the cudgels about two decades later), and a few days after the ceremony, she writes 'Has IT come off yet?'[51] Margery appears to have told her that a Victorian bed and Edward's sore throat had caused a delay. Eileen may not have had personal sexual experience but she told Margery that it was hard to write about her thesis subject — Edward II's wife Isabella of France — without being obscene. Furthermore, on one occasion, she went with Edward's youngest sister Topsy (who was at school in Paris) to see a film about the white slave trade, commenting that it was lucky Topsy had not led a sheltered life.

Whatever the beginnings of the marriage were like, Margery became pregnant almost at once. Eileen hoped the baby would be a girl, but it is unclear whether Margery shared that view, although Eileen was to write later 'I know how much you always wanted a daughter'.[52] Charles was born in March 1912, and over the next three years, Margery bore two more children: Isabel in May 1913 and Ronald in June 1915. They were living in London, at 38 Brunswick Gardens (north of Kensington High Street and about two and a half miles from her family home in Nottingham Place) where she had at least two servants, a cook and a maid, in addition to a nurse or nanny. While her energies were expended on her children — although much of the hard work was

51   Eileen Power, letter to Margery Spring Rice, 4 May 1911.
52   Eileen Power, letter to Margery Spring Rice, 21 July 1914.

done by the nurse — and her social life, she also found time to be an active member of the Women's Liberal Federation[53] and to join her aunt Millicent Fawcett in suffrage activities. From 1912 to 1914, she was on the executive committee of the London Society for Women's Suffrage. Early in 1912, she was one of twelve members of the Garrett family to be present at a National Union of Women's Suffrage Societies fund-raiser in the Albert Hall.[54]

Fig. 9. Edward Jones with Charles. Photograph: family archives (1912).

Although as a teenager Margery had declared herself a socialist, this was based on an abstract idea of socialism and constituted an act of rebellion against her family, and she quickly returned to the Liberal fold. While she had a social conscience, it was to be another two decades before she found a cause that truly exercised her capacity for hard work and

---

53 This was an umbrella group linking local Women's Liberal Associations. It had been founded a few years before Margery's birth, by Sophia Fry, and aimed (not very successfully) to appeal to working-class as well as middle-class women. Krista Cowman, *Women in British Politics, c.1689–1979* (London: Palgrave Macmillan, 2010), pp. 80–81, https://doi.org/10.1007/978-1-137-26785-6

54 Elizabeth Crawford, *Enterprising Women: The Garretts and Their Circle* (London: Francis Boutle, 2002), p. 260.

organisational skills, her ability to persuade or cajole other people into action, and her empathy with those whose lives presented an enormous contrast with her own. At the time of her marriage in 1911, the war that was to change lives in unimaginable ways was only three years over the horizon.

3. Loss (1912–1916)

Social historians suggest that in the early twentieth century, middle class parents became more aware of the benefits of fresh air, rest, play and exercise[1]. For Margery, however, this was nothing new as she had been brought up in a family that regularly went to Aldeburgh for holidays by the sea, by a mother who loved cycling and had a strong belief in the benefits of fresh air. Margery certainly inherited this belief of Clara's: into her old age, she was passionate about it to a fault, sometimes driving friends and family to distraction by throwing windows open even in the coldest weather, exclaiming 'There's a *dreadful* fug in here!'. She loved the sea and, for several summers when they were small, she took her children to Saunton Sands in Devon where she shared a house rented or borrowed from a friend[2] with her sister-in-law Petica, whose two sons were born in 1911 and 1913.

Margery's attitude to her children caused some tension with her in-laws, particularly her sister-in-law Lilian (known as Gil). In Margery's view, the Jones family had a tendency to fuss about children and she was irritated when Gil implied that she did not fuss enough. Three letters from 1914, from Gil to Margery, survive with lengthy discussions of their different views and justifications of her own. Gil admitted that: 'It is a good thing maiden aunts can't run everything their own way — I do realise that', but she nevertheless made it clear that she did not think the nurses employed by Margery were experienced enough and that the children were not kept warm enough.[3] She pointed out that on one occasion, when Charles was

---

1   E.g. Jose Harris, *Private Lives, Public Spirit: A Social History of Britain 1870–1914* (Oxford: Oxford University Press, 1993), p. 82.
2   The house, called The Cleeve, and owned by Arthur Cardew, civil servant, pottery collector and friend of Oscar Wilde, overlooked the sand dunes of Braunton Burrows. Margery also stayed in a house in that area called Spreacombe Manor.
3   Lilian Jones, letter to Margery Spring Rice, 12 February 1914.

    https://doi.org/10.11647/OBP.0215.03

staying with Petica and both Charles and his cousin Martin were unwell, the doctor had suggested their room was too cold. This could hardly have been Margery's fault, since she was not there, but perhaps Gil was trying to be tactful by being oblique. Petica herself held back: she wrote to Margery in January 1914 that when Muz had taken her to task for sitting in judgment on other people's parenting, she had felt it to be just and learnt the lesson. What is clear is that both Charles and Isabel were delicate children, often ill, and that Margery was also determined to live a life of her own, a principle that her in-laws (in spite of their doubts) recognised and supported. In accordance with what she and Edward had agreed before their marriage, Margery sometimes took holidays without him: in early 1913, for example, she travelled with a woman friend to southern Spain.[4] But when Gil wrote that if Margery could not be with her children herself, 'which I do not think is anybody's business except yours', she ought to employ a good nurse, Margery read it as criticism, perhaps because, at some level, she knew that the criticism could be justified.[5] Yet, although she handed over much of the day-to-day care of her children to others, she did not always find the relationship with nurses and nannies easy given her own strong views on child-rearing: and at least one left her employment owing to differences over the children's upbringing.

However we balance the various sides in this, there is no doubt that Margery loved her children deeply. In the spring of 1914, she suffered a huge blow when Isabel died from meningitis. A letter survives from Ruth Dalton, a Labour politician and wife of Hugh Dalton,[6] praising her 'fearless clear thinking' in the face of unimaginable grief. She goes on to say that Margery, as 'someone so completely living up to the principles which I hold — which are so easy in theory & so agonisingly hard in practice', is the person Ruth would choose to come to in times of trouble. In an attempt to help her recover (and leaving Charles behind in the care of a nurse, in his grandmother's

---

4   In 1912, Eileen Power commiserated with her over being criticised for going on holiday without Charles, saying that it was important for a mother to have a cultivated mind.

5   Lilian Jones, letter to Margery Spring Rice, 20 February 1914.

6   Ruth Dalton, letter to Margery Spring Rice, 6 May 1914. Ruth Dalton was briefly a Labour MP, but more importantly a long-serving member of the London County Council. Hugh was a Labour MP and post-1945 Chancellor of the Exchequer.

house in Aldeburgh), Edward took her on a walking holiday in the Alps on the Italian-Austrian border, and that was where they were on 28 June, when Archduke Ferdinand was assassinated in Sarajevo, although they had no access to news and for some time were unaware of what had happened. On 28 July, Gil wrote Margery a long letter from Switzerland, where she and her sister Hilda were on holiday, sympathising with Margery in her evident distress at a critical letter from Aunt Theo: 'I never have and unless you alter very much never shall accuse you of not doing all you possibly can do which to the best of your belief is right & necessary for the good of your children'. Neither Gil nor Margery seems to have been in a hurry to get home, in spite of the prospect of war. Gil's only comment in the same letter is: 'Isn't the prospect of a European war too horrible for words? I can't believe that it will really happen — we shall have to cease to consider ourselves civilised at all if it does'.

Almost exactly fifty years later, one of Margery's grandchildren recorded her telling the story of the next few weeks, so we have it in her own words. The exact timing is not always clear, and memories are bound to contain inaccuracies after that length of time, but it stands as a vivid account of what happened to her and Edward between June and August of that terrible year. They had left some luggage in Munich before crossing into Italy to go walking, intending to collect it on their planned route home through Germany, Belgium and Holland. During their exertions in the mountains, Edward began to suffer great pain from piles (in her retelling of the story, Margery remembered him as having injured his back, but in a letter to her mother-in-law of 28 July 1914 she wrote that Edward was in bed upstairs after an operation for piles).[7] As they walked down towards Cortina, where there was an inn and they hoped to get medical help, they were stopped and questioned by four soldiers. They were allowed to go on but were alerted to there being something unusual happening. Finding a doctor in Cortina, they received the advice that they should go to the hospital in Munich; once there, Edward was operated on and Margery installed herself in a hotel.

---

7   There are only a couple of letters surviving from this period, but they make it clear that Margery misremembered some of the details of what happened.

Fig. 10. Edward's passport, 1914. Photograph: Sam Garrett-Jones (2010).

The first sign that warned her of the seriousness of the situation was that she was unable to obtain their daily copy of *The Times*. Very soon, they ran into difficulties because they did not have enough cash to pay the hotel or medical bills, so, finding she could not get money transferred from England, she went to the British consul and managed to persuade him to lend her a small sum. They did have their tickets home, and the hotel keeper was urging them to leave, even though Edward was still convalescing. On 3 August, the day before Britain declared war on Germany, the British consul in Munich issued a passport to 'Charles E. C. Jones, a British Subject, travelling on the Continent, accompanied by his wife Margaret'. Margery recalled 'the frightful journey home, the train stopping at every single little station', picking up soldiers all the way. They had to spend the night in a waiting room at Nuremberg station (about 100 miles from Munich), with Edward in great discomfort and with very little food. Continuing their journey, they reached Cologne, where an official from the American consulate was attempting to round up any Britons and Americans arriving by train. Several people who were desperate to get home, including Edward and Margery, refused to go with him but boarded the next train towards Holland. At each of the many stops, foreigners were made to alight and show everything they had with them — not much, in their case, as they had left a large trunk in the hotel in Munich: 'there the trunk as far as I am concerned still is, with a lot of nice things in it — my clothes and Edward's clothes'.[8]

After several changes of train and constant searches, which left Edward in a very weak state, they arrived in the town of Kleve, near the border. In the same situation was a family from Glasgow, a couple with their small baby and a nurse. In Kleve, two Germans who had also been in the train fell into an argument, each promising that they could get the English across the border. The Scots chose one of the two, and Edward and Margery the other, whose name was Buchbinder. However, it turned out that Buchbinder could not deliver: he tried several times to take them with him on a bus or tram across into Holland, but they were always refused entry, until eventually they gave up and returned to the hotel where they were staying where, among others, two Americans with their German courier and a Canadian doctor with his young daughter were also stranded. The courier went every day to the border town of Emmerich, ten miles away, to try to make arrangements. After a few days, he told them that he had managed to hire a 'wagonette' to take the group into Holland, but because Edward had remained in bed upstairs, he had not known to include his name on the list. When Margery said that she could not go without Edward, the courier expressed his

---

8   Margery Spring Rice, fragmentary memoirs, recorded by Sam Garrett-Jones 26 August 1965, transcribed April 1997 by Sam Garrett-Jones.

conviction that Edward's only option was internment, since he was of fighting age.

At this point the Canadian doctor came to the rescue: having visited Edward, he suggested that the sick man should be treated as his patient. In Margery's words: '"I shall swear on my oath that you are my patient, and the Germans won't keep you back; you're a sick man, I'll make you look sicker still". And I think he put some sort of white thing on to Edward's cheeks, and he said "you must travel in your pyjamas and your dressing gown and be wrapped up in a rug, and you will occupy the whole of one seat in the charabanc"'. When the Americans were informed of the scheme, they were angry because they felt it would put the whole plan in jeopardy, and also because they thought that one person taking up a whole seat would mean discomfort for everyone else, but they were overruled by the Canadian. At the customs point all, except Edward, got out of the coach and were given permission to pass. The official insisted on getting into the coach to see Edward, who 'played his part very well; he hardly spoke above a whisper, and so on and so forth. And then the man came back, and I heard him saying to one of his companions, "oh well, that's all right, he'll never fight again". And there we were, across the frontier. And that's the end of the story. Except that we got home to an almost weeping family. My father had been telegraphing all round Europe to know where we were. And of course we hadn't received any of these telegrams, but we just turned up'.[9]

The eventual success of their escape from Germany was something Margery would later desperately regret.

They returned, of course, to a Britain at war. Not only Margery's husband, but also her brothers and brother-in-law, were of fighting age, and all, apart from Douglas, who was already married and a father, were called up or were quick to enlist. Both Margery's brother, Ronald, and Petica's husband, Donald, joined the Army Service Corps and served on the western front. Harry enlisted in the Royal Engineers and received a commission in the East Yorkshires where he trained as a gunner. Geoffrey joined the navy; Brian Thornbury, who had been brought up like a brother to Margery, was already serving in the navy; Edward's brother Willie was also already a serving naval officer; his brother-in-law Squire Sprigge, married to his oldest sister Ethel, was in his fifties

---

9   Ibid.

on the outbreak of war. Margery's dearly loved cousin Roger Gibb was asthmatic and in generally poor health, but served nevertheless in the Friends Ambulance Unit. Edward, whose sense of duty overcame the strong anti-war feeling that he shared with Margery, volunteered and re-joined his old regiment, the Warwickshires, as a signaller. By October 1914, he was writing home from a camp in Andover; he left for France in July 1915, just after the birth of their second son Ronald[10] in June, an occasion on which he received a few days' leave. Donald and Margery's brother, Ronald, were already in France (in September, Edward was able to meet both of them there for dinner).

To return to August 1914: on their return from Munich, Margery and Edward were at Gower House in Aldeburgh, Sam and Clara's house. Douglas, for reasons that are unclear, did not join up at the beginning of the war (he did so in 1917, when he served with the Royal Naval Volunteer Reserve in west Africa), but, to Margery's amusement, he was set on ensuring the safety of the citizens of Aldeburgh by taking charge of preparations for 'the defence of [its] dozen miles of shingle beach'. Under the authority of the Navy League[11] (rather than the coastguard), as Margery wrote to Muz on 16 August, he tried to dragoon volunteers to patrol the shore. The territorials were also involved, but were a 'confounded nuisance' — managing to combine apathy, impudence and inefficiency. She added that Muz was not on any account to worry about them, as 'when the Germans do land here, — I shall have a great reserve fund of strength to draw upon, & shall be able to defend my invalid husband & helpless child with very little assistance from these gentlemen of the beach'. To his credit, Douglas could see the humour of the situation, unlike Geoffrey, who 'quiver[ed] with indignation' when Margery asked him what would actually happen if a German ship were to be sighted offshore at night. No official firearms were provided so it was clear that, had there been a landing, the volunteers would have been fairly helpless. The domestic comforts of the patrols were catered for by

---

10 Ronald was named after Edward's friend Ronald Rose, who had been killed on the western front in October 1914. Margery's brother Ronald wrote: 'Kate tells me it is a boy & that you had been hoping for a girl. I am sorry you have been disappointed, but you have the consolation, for what it is worth, that boys will be at a premium in this old world after the war'. Isabel's death was still very raw. Ronald Garrett, letter to Margery Spring Rice, 3 June 1915.

11 Founded in 1894 to support and emphasise the importance of British naval supremacy.

'a sculptor [who] has provided a wife, who has been commandeered to live somewhere between the lighthouse & point B. on the map,[12]—in a leaky tent, with only salt water marsh & shingle round her'. Luckily, though rather to the irritation of Douglas (who believed in encouraging a serious attitude in the volunteers), the sculptor's wife treated the whole thing as a delightful picnic. Margery also commented to Muz that the gardener at Gower House had replaced flowers with cabbages in one bed so 'That should complete our sense of security'.[13]

In June 1915, Geoffrey was wounded in the Dardanelles: Harry wrote to Margery that he was doing well in hospital in Malta, and that 'a wound must not be too bad but it must be bad enough!'.[14] Roger Gibb echoed his words, relieved that Geoffrey had been wounded seriously enough not to be able to fight again, but not seriously enough to be crippled for life. In July, Edward left for France and Harry was sent to the Dardanelles. August was a terrible month: on 9 July, Brian Thornbury was lost when his ship HMS Lynx struck a mine and was sunk off the Moray Firth, and on 31 July, when Margery was at Saunton, Sam and Clara received a telegram to say that Harry had been killed on 22nd in the battle of Suvla Bay in the Dardanelles.[15] Margery wrote to Muz about Harry on 4 September: 'he so loathed the thought of dying [...] he was a most awfully nice person, & even I, who have so much else to fill life out, shall feel an emptiness where he was. I am hoping at any rate that Mother & Father are finding some consolation, — for what it is worth [–] in the thought that his death has not been in vain. It is really a comfort that everybody does not share my feeling about the uselessness of all this sacrifice of life'. Three days later, she wrote again, thanking Muz for going to see Sam and Clara to offer her condolences, and adding: 'Poor dear old Harry — I can't get him out of my mind — the horror to him of these last few weeks must have been unspeakable'. She was relieved that in one respect, their refusal to wear mourning, she and Clara were of the same mind.

---

12   The map represented the shingle spit that runs south from Aldeburgh, dividing the River Alde from the sea, and point B was at its southern end. For a map of the area, see Figure 18 below.

13   Margery Spring Rice, letter to Mary Jones, 16 August 1914.

14   Harry Garrett, letter to Margery Spring Rice, 17 June 1915.

15   Two other grandchildren of Newson Garrett were killed in France in 1915, Claud Garrett Salmon and Louis Garrett Smith; two more followed in 1917, Louis' brother Godfrey Garrett Smith and Maurice Cowell.

A letter from Sam to the Master of Pembroke College, Cambridge, after Harry's death refers to the donation to the college of a stained-glass panel made by Harry. Unfortunately, there is no further record of this and it cannot be identified. There is, however, a stained-glass panel depicting St George and the dragon in place on what is now N staircase of the college, in the former Master's lodge, but we have no way of knowing whether this is Harry's.

From the beginning, Margery's view of the war was at odds with that of her family, though Harry, who had been appalled by conditions in the Dardanelles (particularly the lack of fresh water for his men to drink) was more in sympathy with her than the rest. Remembering him in her old age, she recalled his description of 'soldiers lapping up the small streams full of mud and filth'.[16] He had written to her in June[17] that, in spite of enjoying his work training gunners, he had hated the war for a long time; however he still thought that she was wrong in wanting peace at any price because 'Something spiritual [is] at stake'. While sharing her horror at the loss of life, he had nevertheless speculated that, in a hundred years, people would look back and think it had been worth it — a sad irony from today's point of view. For her brother Ronald, the defeat of German militarism was paramount: 'You must change that opinion of yours that any peace is better than this war', he wrote.[18] Clara too was deeply patriotic, in a way that was true to her military background, and could not understand Margery's attitude: 'the loss of life is not as horrible as the loss of liberty'.[19] On the other hand, as the war progressed, public opinion was moving more in the direction of Margery's views: witness (as one example) the change in tone between Rupert Brooke's poetry early in the war and that of Wilfred Owen towards the end. This is partly due to a change in the emotional environment as well as to the difference in temperament between the two poets and changing artistic responses to war.

Not long after Harry's death, Sam, with more understanding of their daughter than Clara, wrote to Margery from Kilninver in Argyllshire: 'I very much hope that a fortnight here will set us both up & enable us to

---

16 Margery Spring Rice, fragmentary memoirs, recorded 24 November 1968 by Sam Garrett-Jones, transcribed 12 January 2006.
17 Harry Garrett, letter to Margery Spring Rice, 17 June 1915.
18 Ronald Garrett, letter to Margery Spring Rice, 22 July 1915.
19 Clara Garrett, letter to Margery Spring Rice, 14 September 1915.

regain our equilibrium [...]. I am very glad that you wrote me so fully
& candidly of your feelings about the war [...]. What is quite certain is
that man (by that I mean males — I don't include women) is a fighting
animal & will so long as the world lasts fight to prevent himself being
oppressed'. But even he felt that Margery was putting the comfort of the
present generation above the long-term good. Harry's letters 'depicting
so vividly the effect of the horrors of war on his sensitive nature' forbade
Sam to belittle those horrors, and yet, Sam writes:

> there are things more horrible than death & even than the mental anguish
> which our dear boy went through — and I am perfectly certain that if he
> had known beforehand all that he would have to go through & how it
> would end he would have done exactly what he did & nobody who loved
> him — least of all his parents — would have wished him to do otherwise.
> Why? Because to do anything else would have been a dereliction of his
> duty.[20]

He asks whether Margery is not filled with pride at the way young
Englishmen were acting: earlier generations 'acted according to their
lights & if their lights were dim it was not their fault'. He counselled her
to try not to be embittered.

Edward's letters home from France constitute a plain and unemotional
account of his life as an officer on the western front. He was no stylist, nor
was he a man to easily express his feelings: there are few endearments,
other than the snatches of baby talk that they habitually used to each
other (he calls her 'littol Bargee') and messages of love to his sons. On
the other hand, despite his reserve, he wrote in September 1915 that he
could not bear Clara's 'principle of not discussing anybody'.[21] In this
letter, he was worrying about how his mother was being looked after:
he felt that some of her daughters were in danger of sacrificing their
personal lives for her, and that this was not something that should be
silently accepted.

Until the spring of 1916, Edward did not experience real action on
the front line so he found himself able to be fairly detached about what
was happening. Well aware that he might be killed, he wrote that he
had got used to the idea and that Margery must not grieve too much if
it were to happen. He was excited by action, but able to remain calm:

---

20   Sam Garrett, letter to Margery Spring Rice, 12 September 1915.
21   Edward Jones, letter to Margery Spring Rice, 18 September 1915.

watching a plane shelled by Archibalds,[22] he describes it as coming down like a dead leaf. The flies and mosquitoes were terrible, and the horrible weather made trench conditions wet and cold. His men had not had a bath for three weeks and mostly suffered from lice. The mud was appalling: on one occasion, when a man got stuck it took an hour and a half to pull him out. When Margery sent him some bottles of 'scent' (perhaps eau de cologne), he found them useful for masking the smell of corpses. In the autumn of 1915, he was optimistic that the Germans might be at the end of their tether, but by 1916, he was longing for the war to end.[23] Like her brothers, he felt that it was essential to defeat Germany but he agreed with Margery in disliking the exaggerated hatred of Germans that she was encountering at home. This was not an attitude prevalent among his men: at Christmas 1915, he was glad that 'the spirit of wanting to be friendly'[24] existed, even if he suspected that their main motive was personal safety. The letters contain few details of his activities, but in October 1915, he writes that he and some of his men had looted bicycle wheels from a ruined village with a view to making a handcart for moving signalling equipment around, but that, unfortunately, a lack of tools had hampered the cart's construction.

Even if officers were as vulnerable as men, Edward's letters do make clear the difference in their conditions: on 31 October 1915, he was able to have a bath in a copper cauldron usually used for transporting medical supplies, and he mentions a champagne lunch with his commanding officer as well as a good new year's eve dinner in Béthune. Officers were allotted beds or mattresses on the floor, while the men had to sleep in barns. In one billet, the hostess offered a bed to their messman, but when he found out it was in the same room that she and her husband slept in, 'he fled in terror out of the house and back to the barn!'. Edward told Muz that the only way to take life in the trenches was to treat it as a romance, which he tried to do, though at times 'I am seized with a fit of depression & then I can only think of the horrible part of it'. He was

---

22 German anti-aircraft guns.

23 He may have shared the view of Margery's brother Ronald, who in July 1916 wrote hopefully though mistakenly to Margery 'I think the days of the war are numbered. Before next spring we ought all to be happily at home & at peace again'. Edward Jones, letter to Margery Spring Rice, 20 October 1915; Ronald Garrett, letter to Margery Spring Rice, 8 July 1916.

24 Edward Jones, letter to Margery Spring Rice, 26 December 1916.

afraid that he would be in 'a devil of a funk'[25] if he came under fire. He found his skill in speaking French very useful as it allowed him to have philosophical discussions with the local curé and their free-thinking interpreter. He received boxes of apples and tomatoes that were very welcome, as well as gingerbread, cheese, porridge oats and boots, and, on one occasion, foie gras. A periscope (which might have been home-made) sent by Muz proved a splendid acquisition. He asked for socks, tobacco, shirts, vests, handkerchiefs, magazines (but not books — he had plenty to read), lavatory paper (a few sheets in every letter if possible), dates, Devonshire cream (when Margery was in Saunton), figs, senna, mouth wash, envelopes, chocolate, torch batteries, gloves. It is not clear if all these requests could be fulfilled! In return, he wished he could send Margery a German entrenching spade: they are 'nice little things, very handy for gardening'.[26]

Margery, meanwhile, moved between London, Aldeburgh, Sunningdale (about thirty miles from Muz at Jesmond Hill) and Saunton. In London, she usually stayed with her parents at Nottingham Place — the Brunswick Gardens house was let and later put on the market. Charles suffered from various ailments, including a tubercular gland in his neck, and both children had measles. In July 1915, she wrote to Muz from Saunton that Edward's letters sounded cheerful, but that the thought of what he might go through on the front 'wrings tears from my heart'. She knew the odds but was determined that neither she nor her family must allow 'black imaginings of what the <u>worst</u> might bring'.[27] Her happiness in the last few years would be something to look back on 'when the days of positive emptiness arrive'. Muz's reply to this letter expresses the closeness between them, something Margery had never achieved with Clara:

> I have always known since your marriage that dearly as I love Edward and much as I think him 'worthy' he had a wife in every way good & noble & highminded as he is — I do think he is the best & truest man I ever knew except his own father [...] He has known the joy — & so have you dear, of a perfect marriage[,] the best thing that can come to any man or any woman & as you say the memory of that happiness nothing

---

25 Margery Spring Rice, letter to Mary Jones, 21 August 1915.
26 Edward Jones, letter to Margery Spring Rice, 12 October 1915.
27 Margery Spring Rice, letter to Mary Jones, 23/24 July 1915.

can take from you whatever happens [...] Thank you dear for the love & happiness you have given my son & for your kindness & love shown to me always. Caring for you as I do & knowing that you love me is of such help & comfort.[28]

Clara tried hard, and it is difficult not to feel a little sorry for her. Writing to her 'dearest dear child' she pleads with her daughter:

I am so sorry for you Marjorie with all your worries & anxieties & I do appreciate the quiet way you have borne all & the resolution with which you have tackled your difficulties — turn to me when you can — you don't know how eager & anxious I am to help you [...] I can't bear to think of my dear hopeful daughter being miserable & looking at things in [sic] through black glasses. Remember that in spite of some misunderstandings I am still your mother who loves you dearly.[29]

In another (undated) letter she wrote: 'I am deeply conscious of your great love, your <u>real</u> devotion — and if I ever want consolation I should turn to you'. However, there were faults on her side as well: Ronald senior recognised that 'Dear Mum does not seem to be able to accord to her daughters (including in-laws) the same liberty of thought & action she allows to her sons, & she will keep interfering in their private affairs'.[30]

Margery was still in Saunton in October, wondering whether to spend the winter in London, and if so, where she would stay. Her struggle with anxiety was made worse when she was alone — something she did not normally mind. But in spite of all, 'If anything happened to Edward now I would still be happier than if I had never married him'.[31] Always more comfortable with herself when taking action than when sitting still, she was not prevented by troubles (like the children's illnesses) from following up on an idea she had conceived with Edward's support — that they should take up farming after the war, even though Edward would need to stay in the city at first for financial reasons. To this end, she parked the children and their nanny with grandparents and, with the help of Millicent Fawcett, apprenticed herself to Katherine Courtauld (a member of the textile family) at Elms Hall, Earls Colne,

---

28 Mary Jones, letter to Margery Spring Rice, 29 July 1915.
29 Clara Garrett, letter to Margery Spring Rice, 4 May 1916.
30 Ronald Garrett, letter to Margery Spring Rice, 2 March 1917.
31 Margery Spring Rice, letter to Mary Jones, 18 January 1916.

Essex.[32] She was there when Edward wrote on 16 May 1916: 'My own darling Bargee,/ Of course I don't think it's selfish of you to tell me about how you're feeling. I can quite understand & sympathise with you. If it wasn't for a certain amount of interest & excitement attached to being out here I should probably get just as depressed as you are'. He was impressed with how well she was coping with the long strain. In June, he wrote that he longed to see her ploughing.

Margery was on the farm when the battle of the Somme began on 1 July 1916, with the loss of 20,000 British soldiers on that first day. On 9 July, she wrote to him: 'My darlingest darling boy. You don't know how much I have thought & thought of you the last week & wondered, till I was sick [...] where you are'. Having read in the press that the Warwickshires were in the thick of it and had sustained heavy losses, she speculated that if Edward had been in battle he must have 'hated it all so dreadfully' and loathed the fact that she could not take a share of the burden of horror he was enduring. 'There's something so terribly casual in cleaning a pig-sty or milking [a] cow or making hay when people are doing things like you a few miles away'. She recorded having a conversation with Charles, who had said that killing Germans was a naughty thing to do: 'There are[,] you see, the elements of pacifism in him already'.

On 11 July, Margery received a telegram from Clara: 'Bad news from War Office come up immediately Nottingham Place'. Edward had been killed a week earlier, on 4 July, before her last letter to him was written.[33] Sometime in the days that followed, she (uncharacteristically) turned to writing poetry, producing a poem entitled *In the Hayfield* that begins:

> They say that you are dead; how should I know.
> Your letter lies here at my heart, as though

---

32   Katherine Courtauld's family was of Huguenot descent. They were Unitarians and Liberals. Katherine took on the Essex estate bought for her by her father, set up and managed a mixed farm there and pioneered farming careers for women. She was a supporter of women's suffrage. She lived with a lifelong female companion, Mary Gladstone.

33   Edward's name is on the Thiepval memorial but he has no grave. One of his fellow soldiers, Captain Edward Briscoe, wrote to Margery on 6 July 1916 that he had buried Edward 'in a small field and marked his grave with stones and a cross', which is probably not too sanitised a version of the truth, as it is confirmed by Captain Albert O'Donnell, Edward's next-in-command, in a letter to Margery of 18 July.

You too were lying with me in the hay.
I do not know; it is so far away.[34]

Margery had become one of thousands of war widows, but one person's sorrow is not assuaged by the fact that other people have also suffered loss. However, as was to be the case all her life, her principal way of dealing with her grief was to throw herself into action: almost immediately after Edward's death, she began searching for work that would channel her abundant energy. What drove her was not only pain, but rage — all her life, she remembered her anger at the condolence messages she received that assumed her pride in Edward's sacrifice for his country, an attitude she fiercely rejected. Years later, her fury was still plainly visible to her grandchildren; it was one of the forces impelling her towards the several causes she was to pursue during the rest of her life.

The way that practicalities habitually intrude into the hugeness of grief is demonstrated by the letter Margery received from Edward's colleague Captain Albert O'Donnell, who took over the command of the company on Edward's death. Writing on 18 July, he follows heartfelt expressions of condolence and the assurance that Edward had died instantaneously with a request for a cheque for 112 francs to cover Edward's debts. He also mentions that he is sending home, among other things, the 'intrenching tool' that Edward had thought Margery could use in the garden — this was in the possession of their son Ronald until his old age, but its present whereabouts is not known.

Margery hated the conventional though often genuine sentiments expressed in many of the letters of condolence that she received, from her brother Geoffrey among others; it may perhaps have contributed to the coolness that characterised their later relationship when he wrote:

all I can hope [...] is that you may feel that Edward, in following the example of so many thousands of others[,] has not made this overwhelming sacrifice in vain. I am most certainly convinced that he has not; that he, with all the others, has helped to take the first great step towards finishing the war.[35]

Her siblings-in-law were more attuned to her view than Geoffrey. Edward's brother Willie, himself serving in the navy, wrote:

---

34   The poem is written on a loose piece of paper, in the family archives.
35   Geoffrey Garrett, letter to Margery Spring Rice, 12 July 1917.

I wish of the two that it was I who had gone. The life of 'frightfulness' (little as I approve of it) is not unsuited to my temperament when there is lots of work & no time for philosophic reflection. Anyway I know the old chap did his duty with a certain grim & philosophic determination which was one of his endearing characteristics.[36]

Aunt Theo, too, understood Margery better than Geoffrey did:[37]

I did so hope against hope that your Edward would be one of the returning army of men [...] He knew better than to believe — this way the good of Europe lies — and yet he gave all that he had [...] When will the military monsters in all the lands have done enough damage to satisfy the people they have done too much. When will the Civil powers [...] dare to talk of peace with reason [...] When shall we B[ritish] Empire people cease from being bumptious & selfrighteous. When will the women demand a ceasing of this murder [...] Will Edward have taught many a young man his ideas — I wonder?[38]

Many of those who had known Edward knew that he had fought out of his sense of duty and in spite of what Aunt Theo's son Roger referred to as his 'hatred of war and all the warlike theories of the fighting nations'.[39]

Sam showed again that he understood Margery better than many of her family; in his condolence letter to Muz he writes:

I have often said to my wife that [Edward] was exactly the sort of man that suited Marjory. She, poor child, is very brave as one knew she would be, but I much fear that her views on the war will make it still more hard for her to bear his loss. We who believe in the justice of our cause & the necessity of our joining in the war, at any rate can feel that our sacrifices are not in vain. Marjory I fear will not have that consolation at any rate at present. But her pluck & strength of character will carry her through this trial.[40]

His letter is a kind of mirror-image of the one Margery had written to Muz about the effect on her parents of Harry's death.

In the days after the news of Edward's death, Margery went to Jesmond Hill, where the Jones family closed round her in support.

---

36   William Jones, Letter to Margery Spring Rice, 22 August 1916.
37   Aunt Theo was to spend the last years of her life with a Quaker, Ruth Fry. Her sympathy towards pacifism may have started in World War I.
38   Dorothea Gibb, letter to Margery Spring Rice, 12 July 1916.
39   Roger Gibb, letter to Margery Spring Rice, 12 July 1916.
40   Sam Garrett, letter to Mary Jones, 11 July 1916.

His death drew her and Muz even closer, as they clung to each other through their grief. Both were comforted in some small way by believing that Edward had been killed instantaneously and by holding on to the memory of the happiness of his marriage. Margery was also helped through the immediate shock and distress by her Girton friend, Eileen Power, who took her off for a few days' tour to the Yorkshire abbeys, to which, as a mediaeval scholar, she was an expert guide. There must have been some comfort to be found among the Garrett family too, though there are no letters surviving between Margery and her parents from this time. There is also another gap in the extant records, shocking to today's sensibilities though perhaps to be expected at the time: who comforted the children, particularly Charles, who was old enough to remember his father? Did Margery or anyone from either family consider how they might have been affected or what their emotional needs might be?

Friends and family alike recognised Margery's courage and energy and her need to find work of some kind. Roger Gibb cautioned her — without success — against rushing into anything: 'Don't try and escape from yourself by overworking. Take it easy looking round for suitable jobs for your courageous energy to cultivate, for you and your kind are only too much wanted in the world today'.[41] Margery was not to be persuaded to take it easy: what she looked for now, apart from deadening her own sorrow, was to make some practical contribution to a better post-war world.

---

41   Roger Gibb, letter to Margery Spring Rice, 12 July 1916.

4. False Starts (1916–1924)

Margery wasted no time in beginning to look for work. In fact, although she wrote to Muz that she was in no particular hurry, there is a frenetic sense of urgency about her search that suggests she was using it as a desperate salve for the pain of her loss. On July 23, less than three weeks after Edward's death, Katherine Courtauld wrote an open letter of recommendation: 'I should think any work that she took up would be thoroughly well carried out [...] I have formed a high opinion of her character & ability'. Had Edward died in peacetime, she would probably have given this time over to organising the funeral; instead she was applying for administrative work with the Agricultural Organisation Society, for which Aunt Theo's husband, George Gibb (a lawyer turned railway manager),[1] wrote her a reference:

> I have known Mrs. Garrett Jones all her life, & can testify from personal knowledge to her having the highest character & great energy & capacity. She has quite exceptional power of mind & force of character. Her education at Girton & the keen interest & active part she has taken in many intellectual & social movements has given her an excellent & full equipment for any work of organisation or administration. I have not the slightest doubt that she would perform the duties of the post she is seeking with industry, efficiency, sense, & success.[2]

Nothing came of this, but Margery told Muz 'I haven't settled anything about work. I am leaving no stone unturned to find the right job, — & I expect I shall succeed'.[3] She wondered about going back to the factory inspectorship, but thought that the hours would be too long and the pay poor. Bedford College was looking for a secretary to its council, which

---

1 Gibb had been general manager of the North Eastern Railway and managing director of the Underground Electric Railway Company of London.
2 George Gibb, testimonial for Margery Spring Rice, 24 July 1916.
3 Margery Spring Rice, letter to Mary Jones, 25 July 1916.

    https://doi.org/10.11647/OBP.0215.04

she felt would have suited her exactly, but someone else ('a perfect dear of a girl who will be very good') was appointed. And yet, at the same time as longing for activity to fill the void, she also needed peace and quiet: with the help of her cousin Roger she 'warded the various sympathetic relations off more or less successfully'[4] from herself and the children.

In the immediate aftermath of her loss, Margery felt strongly that there was no longer any point in her generation hoping or striving for personal happiness, but only in working to save future generations from 'a repetition of this gigantic folly'.[5] Consequently, when the opportunity for Margery to be at the core of the work for peace soon presented itself, she seized it: she was appointed the first secretary of the League of Nations Society, again likely through the influence of George Gibb.

The League of Nations Society had begun in 1915, in what one of its historians calls 'progressive drawing-room circles',[6] but it began to flourish in the context of the expansion of anti-war literature after 1919, and the belief in the need for a way of preventing such a disaster from occurring again. Both intellectuals (for example Leonard Woolf and Gilbert Murray) and politicians (for example Aneurin Williams and Robert Cecil) were instrumental in bringing the Society to birth, but the research on which it was based had been done by Woolf under the auspices of the Fabian Society Research Department.[7] Its purpose was to work for the foundation of a post-war League of Nations that would provide a mechanism for resolving international disputes without resorting to war, using the court of arbitration in the Hague (established in 1899) for matters of international law and the League's own representative council for other matters. It was not specifically a pacifist organisation — though there was a strong pacifist element — but rather an internationalist one, and its founders insisted that when the League itself came into existence, it must include the defeated nations as well

---

4   Ibid.

5   Ibid. This constituted another cause of tension between Margery and Clara, who had written to Margery while Edward was in France that the only essential in life was love.

6   Helen McCarthy, *The British People and the League of Nations: Democracy, Citizenship and Internationalism, c. 1918–45* (Manchester: Manchester University Press, 2011), p. 2, https://doi.org/10.7765/9781847794284

7   Janet M. Manson, 'Leonard Woolf as an Architect of the League of Nations', *South Carolina Review*, 39/2 (2007), 1–13.

as the victorious ones. Although it has been suggested that there was a strong link with feminism, when the Society was founded its seventeen-person committee included only three women.[8] To this body, Margery was appointed organising secretary, a post that she filled for about two years. During that time, the Society grew from its drawing-room origins into a something with greater heft, a development that owed a lot to the advocacy of President Woodrow Wilson from May 1916 onwards. On 14 May 1917, just after the entry of the US into the war, its profile was raised by a big public meeting, at which one of the prominent speakers was the South African statesman Jan Smuts.

Margery remained in post for just two years. In her old age, she recalled that she had resigned after a comparatively short stint because she was about to remarry, but this may not have been the whole story. While the range of beliefs in the Society might have added to its strength, there were deep fissures over the question of pacifism, indicated obliquely by Smuts in his speech when he referred to the intense desire among millions to see a better way than war:

> And you see the result in a meeting like this, where you have not only gathered the dreamers and the idealists, the visionaries who are the salt of the earth, but also practical men, and even men of blood like myself.[9]

Eventually, in late 1918, the League of Nations Society and the League of Free Nations Association (which itself had only been inaugurated in September) amalgamated to form the League of Nations Union. A letter from George Gibb to Margery, dated 11 December 1918, implies that she was unhappy with the direction taken. He wrote that he was distressed to hear that she had resigned and felt that her influence would be much greater if she stayed: 'Don't do it [...] Stick to it and quietly work for your opinions if they are right'. She was not to be swayed, however, and her forthcoming marriage to Dominick Spring Rice was surely a factor in her decision.

---

8 Mary Macarthur (married name Anderson) of the Women's Trade Union League, and two women listed only by their husbands' names, Mrs Richard Cross and Mrs A.W. Claremont. There was one female Vice-President (out of seventeen), Mrs Walter Rea.

9 *A League of Nations: Report of a Meeting Held at Westminster Central Hall, 14 May 1917*, p. 5, in a collection of pamphlets entitled *Publications of the League of Nations Society, the League of Nations Union, and the League of Free Nations Association / League of Nations Society [and others]*, bound together in the British Library with no publication details.

The second annual report of the League of Nations Society paid tribute to her industry:

> Office staff. The Secretary of the Society is Mrs. Garrett Jones, who has been working for us since the beginning of 1917. She has given invaluable work in and out of the Office, and it is largely owing to her strenuous exertions that the Society has made such marked progress.[10]

An undated open letter from Aneurin Williams is a more personal testimony:

> I have pleasure in certifying that Mrs. Garrett Jones acted as Secretary of the League of Nations Society for about two years, including the whole time of its first public activity until its amalgamation with another Society to form the League of Nations Union. It was the wish of all those who had worked closely with Mrs. Garrett Jones in the old Society that she should continue to hold an important post in the new Society. We greatly regretted that she did not see her way to do so. In her work for the League of Nations Society Mrs. Garrett Jones showed great zeal & intelligence: she had much organising to do & she did it well. She was head of our staff & had much responsibility & freedom of action. I regard her as a woman of remarkably [sic] energy, ability, knowledge & character, & have very great pleasure in recommending her for any similar position.

She had not yet found the cause that would create the opportunity for her life's most important achievement but she did voluntary work for other organisations during the immediate post-war period. She was a member of the executive committee of the Irish Dominion League[11] and, in the 1920s, acted as honorary treasurer of the Women's Liberal Federation. However, she may well have become disillusioned with the Liberal Party — in particular its internal divisions over women's suffrage, over Home Rule, and over the direction of the war (and particularly over the issue of conscription),[12] as she had with the League of Nations

---

10   League of Nations Society, *Second Annual Report, March, 1917–March 1918, as Approved at the Annual Meeting, June 14, 1918* (London: League of Nations Society, 1918), p. 14.
11   Margery was, as Edward had been, in favour of Home Rule for Ireland. The Irish Dominion League advocated dominion status for Ireland and opposed partition; the chair of the London committee was Thomas Spring Rice, second baron Monteagle, a cousin of Margery's second husband Dominick, and the father of the Irish nationalist gun-runner Mary Spring Rice. With Molly Childers, Mary brought guns from Germany to Ireland in the Childers yacht *Asgard*.
12   As the Labour Party rose, the Liberal Party declined from the glory days of its landslide victory in 1906. Some women got the vote in 1918: householders, wives

Society. Aside from her concerns about work, Margery's private life was also making insistent demands on her time and emotional energy. She had emerged from the war as a widow with two young sons. In four or five years, she had lost not only Edward on the Somme, but her infant daughter Isabel to meningitis and her much-loved brother Harry at Gallipoli. In 1919, she married Edward Dominick Spring Rice (always known as Dominick), and they set up house in Victoria Road, Kensington.

Fig. 11. Dominick Spring Rice, 1932. Photograph: Lafayette (1932). © National Portrait Gallery, London.

Margery had known Dominick since the days of her first marriage: his line of work was similar to Edward's and he had also been on the fringes of the League of Nations Society as a member of its Press and Literature sub-committee. He came from an Anglo-Irish family, but had been born in London where his father, Stephen, worked. His mother, Julia, held strong suffragist views. According to a little anonymous booklet printed after her death:

---

of householders, owners of property with an annual rent of £5 and graduates of British universities.

An infuriated man once told her that if she persisted in her advocacy of Women's Suffrage he would no longer open the door for her, to which she replied that if he did as he said, she would no longer pour out his tea.[13]

Dominick was also a friend of Margery's in-laws: according to Martin Robertson (Edward's nephew and, later, Margery's son-in-law), Dominick was 'expected' to marry the youngest Jones daughter, Topsy, who consequently very much resented his marriage to Margery. This resulted in a coolness between Margery and her Jones in-laws, although, as things turned out, it was probably to Topsy's benefit that she did not marry Dominick. The situation was fictionalised by Romer Wilson,[14] a near contemporary of Margery's at Girton, in her 1919 novel *If All These Young Men* — in which Margery is thinly disguised as Amaryllis, Topsy as Susan and Dominick as James.

Although she later stated as a principal motive for her marriage her sons' need for a father, for the first few months[15] Charles and Ronald (aged seven and four) were sent away to Stratford-Upon-Avon to stay with Margery's old school mistress, who had a young grandson of a similar age, and, shortly afterwards, Charles went to school near Bristol. These arrangements suggest that she was aware from the beginning of her relationship with Dominick that there might be difficulties between him and his step-sons. Margery knew that Dominick was a heavy drinker, but was nonetheless strongly attracted to his charm and charisma, and, at the time of their marriage, she may already have known that she was pregnant again. Their son Stephen was born in early 1920, followed in 1921 by a daughter, Cecil.

Of the Jones family, Margery's sister-in-law, Gil, particularly struggled with her distress at the marriage. She was determined that contact with Charles and Ronald — who having lost their father might need their Jones relations more than previously — should not be compromised. In a letter to her sister Hilda, Gil wrote of how she had 'implored' their brother Willie and his wife, who were 'very much longing' to ask that

---

13   J. S. R.: *Sketch of a Background* ([n.p.]: privately printed, [n.d.]), p. 7.
14   Pen name of Florence Roma Muir Wilson.
15   When Julia moved out, it was to a house just round the corner, where she remained until 1935, when she married again; her new husband was her first husband's cousin, Francis Spring Rice, who was also her sister's widower; she went to live with him in Limerick and died in 1936.

Charles and Ronald go to live with them, to hold back and to avoid quarrelling with Margery at all costs. In the same letter, she continued in a more emollient manner:

> as Margee does <u>seem</u> to intend to have the children after six months with her, they think it might be better to leave it alone & avoid quarrelling. I am of course not encouraging them to offer, because I don't consider it a good plan & anyway M. would not accept I believe.[16]

In another letter to Hilda written a few days later, Gil asked:

> Can you manage to adopt a philosophical attitude about Margee? I hope you can. I have quite made up my mind that it is no use feeling tragic over it & that one may as well, within limits[,] give back some of the blows that are aimed. I am being much more restrained than I like, as I could so easily give very great pain but I have so much personal feeling for Margee — & I am too much affected by knowing that I could never have abused her to Edward — to let myself go really — but what I think is — Charles & Ronald can't be suppressed or done away with — they won't have an ideal life or childhood — but most people don't and they wouldn't have, even if Edward had lived. If Margee is an Elise (to use the name merely as an abbreviation)[17] it is better for the children not to be with her. Other arrangements of a comparatively satisfactory nature will be made such as Mrs. Garrett, or Kate,[18] having them at Aldeburgh, and 'visits' to Margee & to us I hope — anyway they won't be cut off from us.[19]

She went on to say that she had written to Margery but had received an answer from Dominick: it is a great pity that his letter has not survived, as it might have thrown some light on these complicated interactions.

Whatever the reaction of other people to the marriage, it ran into problems almost from the start. In the statement Margery wrote for the court ten years later, after she had obtained a judicial separation and was thinking of applying for custody of the two children of her second marriage, who had been made wards of court, she wrote that she had wanted a father for her sons, and that she had known that Dominick drank too much but had hoped to be able to change him. That statement has to be read in context — she was justifying her own

---

16 Lilian Jones, Letter to Margery Spring Rice, 12 August 1919.
17 Mary Ross's sister Elise Blake and her husband Dr Morgan Dix Blake had gone bankrupt and were much disapproved of by the rest of the family.
18 Margery's sister-in-law, wife of Ronald.
19 Lilian Jones, letter to Margery Spring Rice, 17 August 1919.

conduct throughout the course of the marriage — but there is no reason to doubt that she genuinely thought it would be a good thing to give her sons a father figure, or that at the time, even if she had hesitations, she was in love with Dominick and hoped he would make a good husband.

Dominick himself is something of an enigma, partly perhaps because he was deliberately obfuscatory about his life. He was born in 1891 (although this was one of the things he made a mystery of, possibly because he did not want to admit to being younger than Margery) to an Anglo-Irish family: his mother was a Fitzgerald from Valencia Island off the south west coast of Ireland, and his father came from Limerick. His father's brother was Cecil Spring Rice, a distinguished diplomat who was British ambassador to Washington from 1912–1918. Dominick's father, Stephen, worked in the Treasury in London. Stephen died (possibly from alcohol-related causes)[20] when his son was eleven, and when Dominick himself had just had an operation for appendicitis — perhaps these circumstances help to explain his neuroses. His mother Julia was a dominating personality and, according to Margery's 1929 statement, his relationship with her was always tense and difficult. Dominick was educated at Eton and King's College, Cambridge, where he studied Classics and, though he did not do particularly well academically, was intelligent, charming and witty. His father, grandfather and great uncle had all been members of the Cambridge Apostles,[21] but Dominick appears not to have been elected to this elite society. After Cambridge came jobs in the City of London, where he worked for the *Morning Post*, the Alexander Discount Company and, subsequently, for Grace Brothers, bankers. He wrote articles about employment and was honorary secretary of the Political Economy Club. An article in an issue of the *Financial News*[22] describes him as having a look of humorous contemplation as well as a physical and mental agility that might surprise a casual observer of his (fairly solid) build. Both the twinkle in his eye and the solidity of his build are evident in a series of photographs of him by the Lafayette Studio, now in the National Portrait Gallery in London (see Figure 13).[23]

---

20 This is what Dominick told Stella Benson. Stella Benson, Diary, 13 July 1929.
21 Several members of the Bloomsbury group, on the fringes of which Dominick lurked, belonged to this highly selective intellectual society.
22 'Men of Mark: Dominick Spring Rice', *Financial News* (8 April 1931), p. 3.
23 These photographs have a history that Dominick might have appreciated: the negatives were in a collection that was rescued from a skip in 1968 and stored at

In 1918–1919, in the aftermath of the Russian Revolution, Dominick went as financial advisor with the British delegation to North Russia led by Ernest Harvey. Francis Lindley, another member of the delegation, records in his memoirs that Harvey had a difficult time negotiating with the Russians, and 'it was well for him that Spring Rice, sent to help him by the Treasury, had to go home early in the negotiations. A break-down in health had taken the inconvenient form of openly expressed contempt for all foreigners'.[24] Presumably 'a break-down in health' is a euphemism for being drunk, although he did suffer from severe asthma and had not fought in the war for that reason. It is possible that he also had back problems: the *Abergavenny Chronicle* of 20 August 1915 records that Dominick and his cousin Lord Monteagle had been in a rail crash on the Irish Mail from Euston, in which Dominick suffered spinal injuries. After this incident, Dominick wrote two letters to James Strachey from Northampton General Hospital: in the second of them (postmarked 29 August), he says he is getting on slowly and hopes to be moved to London in a week or so, 'when also I hope to be able to totter about a bit'.[25]

Dominick was a fantasist. He told his son the improbable tale that during the Russian Revolution, he had enabled the ballerina Tamara Karsavina to escape by forging a passport for her and fixing a passage in a destroyer; and that he had once been to a fancy dress ball in the Albert Hall, had seen a rather lonely-looking girl whom he had asked to dance, and discovered that she was Karsavina. The chronology of these two events (or non-events) is unclear, though it is possible that there is a grain of truth in Dominick's account. In her memoirs, Karsavina writes:

Pinewood Film Studios. When they were rediscovered in 1988, Pinewood offered them to the Victoria & Albert Museum. About 30,000 were kept by the V&A and the remaining 50,000 handed on to the National Portrait Gallery.

24   Brotherton Library, University of Leeds, Leeds Russian Archive MS 1372/2 [Francis Lindley's Memoir]. After early 1918, there was no British ambassador in Russia. The North Russian Mission arrived in Murmansk in June 1918, with the aim of taking charge of British interests in Russia. Dominick's name is only mentioned once in the official report: when Lindley left Murmansk, Dominick remained there to 'assist General Poole in dealing with any developments that might occur'. D. Cameron Watt and D. C. B. Lieven, eds, 'Report on the Work of the British Mission to North Russia from June 1918 to 31st March 1919', in *British Documents on Foreign Affairs: Reports and Papers from the Foreign Office Confidential Print, Part 2, From the First to the Second World War. Series A, The Soviet Union, 1917–39*, vol. 1 (Frederick, MD: University Publications of America, 1984), p. 158.

25   London, British Library, Add. MS 60699, ff. 56–73 comprise Dominick's letters to Strachey.

The British Embassy [in St Petersburg] had left in February [1918]. I had to stay behind. Unexpected difficulties arose with our passports — it was the time of the British landing in the North. When we had almost despaired of ever getting out of Russia, my husband [H. J. Bruce] was called to the telephone. A woman's voice told him that a permit to leave would be sent round to him. She rang off quickly, and he never knew who his good fairy was'.[26]

Karsavina had been in London before the war, and could conceivably have met Dominick then.

Both Margery and Dominick enjoyed telling stories to impress. One of Margery's grandsons remembers her telling him when he was a small boy that she had been at a party in Dublin at which the Irish revolutionary Michael Collins was a fellow guest; when the authorities came searching for Collins, he managed to escape over the rooftops. The origin of this story may lie in the rumour attached to Glendalough House in County Wicklow, where Erskine Childers' family lived, that Collins had once escaped from pursuers via the priest's hole in the house. The Childers and the Spring Rice families knew each other, and Dominick certainly stayed in the house: it is perfectly possible that Collins had such an escape, but, if he did, whether Dominick — or Margery — was there is an open question.

One of the difficulties with getting a sense of what Dominick was actually like is that much of what we know about him is filtered through Margery's statement to the court in 1929, after their judicial separation — a statement that was the product of extreme distress and bitterness on her part. When later she gave this statement to their daughter Cecil to read, Cecil was astonished — having assumed that Margery was entirely in the right and Dominick entirely in the wrong — to find herself for the first time sympathizing with her father, of whom she had been frightened, and understanding how difficult marriage to Margery must have been.

There is one other source from which we have impressions of Dominick, the diary of the novelist Stella Benson,[27] who had been

---

26 Tamara Karsavina, *Theatre Street: The Reminiscences of Tamara Karsavina* (London: Dance Books, 1981), pp. 331–32.

27 Cambridge, Cambridge University Library, Add. MS 6762-6802 [Diaries of Stella Benson]. There are some brief but vivid glimpses of Benson in Winifred Holtby, *Letters to a Friend* (London: Collins, 1937), pp. 291–92, 345, 366–67, 454.

introduced to Margery by Brooks Henderson (a reader for the Macmillan Press in New York) during the war. Benson recorded her first impression of the two of them before their marriage:

> [Margery] talked a lot about 'yearnest' people with mockery but she is rather yearnest herself, I think, not so very much sense of humour. She is sec. of the League of Nations Society, rather a clever talker. A Mr Dominic Spring Rice (heavenly name) seemed to be a sort of tame cat of hers, or rather say tame terrier, quite an amusing young man, with a startling cynical memory for unexpected things like the thirty nine articles, & LCC byelaws.

Just after Cecil's birth, Benson records going to dinner with Dominick and Margery:

> [Dominick] seemed nervous and yet also a little frightening, he states things with such accuracy and firmness that your objections shrivel away and you feel so sure that he would scorn [them?] that you lose confidence in them.

A few days later, Benson went there again, to tea: 'Everybody there was a considerable talker I guess and we all burbled at once but Mr Spring Rice won'. He had a fund of stories, odd and witty but maybe not accurate. Some weeks later, Benson, Dominick and another friend went to a dance (perhaps Margery was not going out yet, although Cecil was two months old by this time):

> D. Spring Rice dances violently with obvious delight — in fact, although he was almost at times speechless with asthma his obvious delight in everything was conspicuous far and wide. He runs and slides and jumps through windows and quivers with energy all the time. Indeed that is his form of party manners, an eager ebullience which I thought very engaging if he was really feeling so bad as I should have felt with that amount of asthma [...] I got appallingly tired and was specially speechless with D. Spring Rice because I think one has to be in great spirits to keep up with him, and though happy I was certainly tired.

A big cause of friction in the marriage was Dominick's need to play sexual games involving elaborate fantasies of pretending, in which one partner had to play a subordinate part, for example one being a servant and the other an employer. Although in the statement Margery describes herself as being a reluctant participant in these games, it seems entirely possible that she enjoyed them at first, until other issues destroyed any pleasure. She had a great sense of fun and certainly, later in life, she described for her grandchildren with amusement and gusto some of the games they played outside the bedroom: for example, they would hire an expensive car and Margery would put on a chauffeur's cap to drive it while Dominick sat in the back; or, when invited to a dinner party, they would agree some unlikely words that they would try to make their respective neighbours at table say, comparing scores afterwards. But in a darker vein, Dominick drew up a code of punishments that he inflicted on Margery for minor infringements of rules, such as forgetting to wind the clocks, and this was reinforced by the purchase of a pair of handcuffs and a cane. Sometimes, she was shut up in a cupboard for an extended period. The system worked both ways: Dominick insisted on being punished as well as inflicting punishment. One has to conclude that he was a sadomasochist.

Other sources of conflict between Margery and Dominick were children, money and drink. The sons of Margery's first marriage were, from the beginning, a cause of problems for her marriage with Dominick, and one can only feel that they must have suffered badly not simply because their step-father resented and bullied them, but because of the way Margery herself behaved and her extraordinary obtuseness about her children's emotional lives. To send the children away for the first few months of the new marriage was hardly a recipe for their emotional adjustment to their new circumstances. In the long-term, while Ronald coped robustly with this awful beginning, Charles was more damaged by it. Such small compensations as the model railway set up by Dominick in the garden at Victoria Road, which Ronald at least loved, cannot have weighed much in the emotional balance. There were rows from early on, caused by Dominick's bullying of the children and by his attempts to prevent Margery from having contact with her mother and brothers, which also inevitably had an impact on the children's relationship with their grandparents. When they reached their teenage years, both Charles and Ronald were sent to Rugby School, which offered bursaries for the sons of officers killed in the war. Again, Ronald, though not positively happy there, was able to cope much better than Charles.

In the middle of her marriage going sour, Margery lost her beloved father. In April 1923, when Leonard Woolf, whom Margery probably knew from her time in the League of Nations Society, was about to return from a trip to Paris, he recorded:

> On the station at Paris I suddenly heard 'Mr Woolf, I dont [sic] suppose you remember me', looked round, & saw Mrs Dominic [sic] Spring-Rice, ex Mrs Garrett Jones, ex Miss Garrett. I had a long talk with her on the boat. At Newhaven I bought <u>The Times</u>, opened it, & the first thing that caught my eye was that her father had died yesterday. She certainly did not know. Ought I to have broken the news? At any rate, I didnt [sic].[28]

Aged seventy-two, having been retired from his legal practice for just a couple of years, Sam had suffered a cerebral haemorrhage. Margery had always been closer to him than to Clara and his sudden death must have shocked and grieved her deeply. What had seemed like a time of new beginnings had perhaps come to seem more like a time of endings.

---

28   Leonard Woolf, 'Letter to Virginia Woolf, 24 April 1923,' in *Letters of Leonard Woolf*, ed. by Frederic Spotts (London: Bloomsbury, 1990), p. 227.

5. Finding a Cause (1924–1931)

It was at this time, in the early years of Margery's second marriage, that the cause to which she was to devote so much in the way of skill, time and energy for more than thirty years presented itself to her. Perhaps it was partly thanks to the stresses at home that she was so alert to the opportunity when it came her way. In that period, as is still the case today, the borough of Kensington included some of the poorest as well as some of the wealthiest areas of London. Margery was struck by the desperate need for facilities to improve the health of women and young children, and, in particular, by the need for the provision of contraceptive advice in the most deprived areas. Before the establishment of the National Health Service in 1948, panel doctors were available only to those with insurance — in effect, to the very group (employed men) that was least in need of them. Poor women and children were likely to suffer from malnutrition and the biggest killer of young women was tuberculosis. Despite the boost to female employment during the war, in 1921 it was back at its pre-war level,[1] to the detriment of income levels in the poorest households whose women were likely to have access only to the most casual forms of paid work.

Years later, Margery recalled how her eyes were opened:

One day early in 1924 Mrs Margaret Lloyd & Mrs Margery Spring Rice, who both lived in Kensington, were comparing notes about the domestic burdens of their respective charwomen, both of whom came from the very poor district of Notting Dale. At that time there was very little industry in North Kensington, and a great many of the inhabitants had casual work, such as window cleaning, street hawking, portering at Paddington Station; and a great majority of married women were adding to the poor earnings of their husbands by taking in washing from or charring in the well-to-do homes [at the other end of the borough].

---

1   Peter Clarke, *Hope and Glory: Britain 1900–90* (London: Penguin, 2004), pp. 91, 95.

    https://doi.org/10.11647/OBP.0215.05

To their 'incredulous listeners' the two charwomen 'poured out their stories; they told us of the measures they had tried to limit their families, such as driving their husbands into the arms of another woman rather than take the "Saturday night risk"; jumping from a ladder during pregnancy' and going to back-street abortionists.[2]

Margery was horrified by the conditions in which such families lived, including the physical state of their housing. Although the houses themselves — having been designed for business and professional families in the mid-nineteenth century — were solidly built with large rooms, the facilities had not been increased to cope with multiple occupation. Often, they had only one lavatory and a water supply up to the first floor but no higher, and were owned by landlords indifferent to the squalor. In notes she wrote later, Margery refers to these landlords as 'well-to-do East-end Jewish tailors'; it is difficult to know now whether this is a statement of fact. Today we may well read it as anti-Semitic: probably neither Margery nor her audience noticed this. Food had to be cooked on open fires or a single gas ring, and slops were emptied from windows into back yards. Crucially, many women did not want more children, and were sometimes forced to resort to dangerous back-street abortions, something Margery's own charwoman had undergone. In terms of their general health, most working-class women had no insurance to enable them to see a doctor without worrying about the cost.

Birth control, as contraception was known at the time, was generally a dirty word. In 1834, a book by Charles Knowlton entitled *The Fruits of Philosophy*, containing some basic though not always accurate information about it, was published in Britain, two years after its first appearance in the United States. It seems not to have made a great stir at the time but, some forty years later, it led to a Bristol bookseller being convicted of selling a book with obscene illustrations. Angry at what had happened, Charles Bradlaugh, founder of the National Secular Society,[3] and his associate Annie Besant, set up the Freethought Publishing Company and brought out a new edition at a price that made it much more widely accessible. Bradlaugh and Besant were tried for breaching the Obscene Publications Act of 1857; although they were found guilty,

---

2   Wellcome Collection, SA/FPA/SR21.
3   National Secular Society, https://www.secularism.org.uk/

and Knowlton's work was judged to be calculated to deprave public morals, it was accepted that their personal motives were not corrupt and they were able to get the judgement set aside on a technical point relating to the wording of the indictment. As so often happens with trials of this kind, Knowlton's book received a huge boost in sales because of the extent of public interest in the trial.[4]

In the 1920s, when birth control clinics began to be set up, the very fact that contraception was almost a taboo subject was attractive to some of the middle-class women who became involved in the work. As Margery's younger colleague and friend, Nancy Raphael, recalled in an interview in 1978: she enjoyed 'the fun of the unmentionable'. But also, for her as for Margery, there was a 'burning sense of the wrongness' that for some women the natural expression of their love led, inevitably as it seemed, to poverty and ill health.[5] Some of the most impassioned statements on behalf of women in poverty come from a book by Lella Secor Florence, an American married to a British academic, who was instrumental in founding a contraceptive clinic in Cambridge in 1925.[6] Florence does not shy away from telling stories of the distress she encountered among parents who found themselves unable to support their large and increasing families. In the foreword, the physician and academic Humphry Rolleston writes that the book 'throw[s] convincing light on the pitiful plight of the multiparous mothers of the poor and of their unwanted children'. Additionally, in the introduction, another academic, F. H. A. Marshall, explains that the origin of the Cambridge clinic was neither scientific nor political but the realisation that one of the greatest needs of working-class people was 'some certain and simple way of regulating the size of their families and preventing the arrival of unwanted children'.[7]

However, the same book demonstrates the depth of opposition to the very idea of discussing the subject of contraception as well as the misogyny that ran through the debate (if indeed 'debate' is the appropriate word). As Rolleston writes:

---

4   Edward Royle, 'Bradlaugh, Charles', in *Oxford Dictionary of National Biography* (2004), https://doi.org/10.1093/ref:odnb/3183

5   Women's Library, London School of Economics, 8SUF/B/177.

6   Lella S. Florence, *Birth Control on Trial* (London: Allen & Unwin, 1930).

7   Ibid., pp. 4, 5.

Birth control is a difficult subject and arouses rather vigorous expressions
of condemnation from those whose convictions must be respected as
evidence of sincere anxiety as to its effect on public morals.[8]

He also refers to a 'not unnatural disinclination to discuss an unpleasant
subject': doctors themselves were far from immune to such an attitude.
Church members, who were a far larger constituency than is the case
today, were sometimes treated to highly-coloured rhetoric from their
clergy. Florence quotes the bishop of Guildford:

'It is impossible to adopt [contraceptive] practices without a coarsening
of sensibility. I believe that any pure-minded girl, uncorrupted by
sophistry, shrinks from these methods with an instinctive repugnance'.[9]

When the Cambridge clinic opened, the Catholic bishop of Salford
urged people to 'smash' it and bricks were accordingly thrown through
its windows.[10] Raphael remembered that Margery was one of those who
handed out leaflets at the premises of the Cambridge clinic, in the face
of Catholic opposition. It was probably in support of her sister-in-law,
Petica, one of the founders and the assistant treasurer of this clinic, that
Margery took such action.

Despite some recognition by government that maternal and child
health was an essential part of public health policy,[11] birth control
did not figure as part of this. After the partial success in 1918 of the
campaign for women's suffrage, women were realising that they did not
only want a say in the political life of the country, they also wanted to
be able to control their own reproductive lives. The first contraceptive
clinic in the world had been set up in Holland in 1881, the second by
Margaret Sanger in the United States in 1916.[12] It was in this environment
that Marie Stopes founded her Society for Constructive Birth Control
in 1918, opening her first clinic in Holloway, north London, in 1921.[13]

---

8   Ibid., p. 3.
9   Ibid., p. 136.
10   Audrey Leathard, *The Fight for Family Planning: The Development of Family Planning
     Services in Britain 1921–74* (London: Macmillan, 1980), p. 32. 'Smash' is Leathard's
     word.
11   A Maternity and Child Welfare Act was passed in 1918, which began to bring
     maternal and child welfare under the local authority umbrella.
12   Barbara Evans, *Freedom to Choose: The Life and Work of Dr Helena Wright, Pioneer of
     Contraception* (London: Bodley Head, 1984), p. 125.
13   It later moved to Tottenham Court Road.

Thanks to the fact that advice there was given by a midwife rather than a gynaecologist, this clinic attracted hostility from the medical profession, although, as a profession, doctors were hardly in the forefront of providing contraceptive services. In the same year, the Malthusian League,[14] founded in 1877, opened the Walworth Women's Welfare Centre, south of the Thames near the Elephant and Castle. Sessions took place on two afternoons a week, one providing infant welfare services and the other birth control advice. To this clinic too there was strong opposition: for example, volunteer helpers were apt to find themselves pelted with eggs. Both clinics were aimed primarily at women, although, at Walworth Road in 1922, the medical officer began to give lectures to both men and women on sexual hygiene and related subjects. A pressure group, the Society for the Provision of Birth Control Clinics, was set up in 1924 and took over the Walworth Road clinic.[15]

Fig. 12 Birth control clinic in a caravan, est. by Marie Stopes. Photograph (late 1920's). Wellcome Images, CC-BY 4.0

14   The Malthusian League saw birth control as a socio-economic question rather than an individual one; its purpose was the reduction of poverty: Sheila Rowbotham, *Dreamers of a New Day: Women Who Invented the Twentieth Century* (London: Verso, 2010), pp. 86–87.

15   For the history of these clinics, see Clare Debenham, *Birth Control and the Rights of Women: Post-Suffrage Feminism in the Early 20th Century* (London: I. B. Tauris, 2014); Leathard, *The Fight for Family Planning*; Lara V. Marks, *Metropolitan Maternity: Maternal and Infant Welfare services in Early 20th Century London* (Amsterdam: Rodopi, 1996).

North Kensington had one of the worst infant mortality rates in London, with many malnourished babies and children dying of bronchopneumonia, gastroenteritis or infectious diseases in particular. In a 1932 enquiry into infant deaths,[16] the North Kensington rate was found to be twice as high as that of South Kensington, with deaths from infectious diseases ten times the number. Since 1911, there had been a baby clinic in the area, founded in memory of Margaret MacDonald (wife of Labour Party leader Ramsay MacDonald) and of Mary Middleton (wife of Ramsay MacDonald's Assistant Secretary); some doctors also ran infant welfare centres. But what Margery and the colleagues she gathered round her realised was that contraception was a crucial missing piece in the jigsaw of maternal and child health and welfare. It would be easy to regard her as a middle-class do-gooder, as indeed she was: but from the beginning, Margery was both an exceptionally hard worker and an excellent manager, and she also empathised, without being patronising, with all sorts and conditions of women.

In 1924, it seemed (in Margery's own words) 'clear & easy what we [Margery, Margaret Lloyd and their friend Margaret Dighton Pollock] had to do'[17]—start a contraceptive clinic. They set about roping in other supporters, persuaded four people to guarantee £25 each, and found premises at 12 Telford Road, which had been a child welfare clinic and was therefore reasonably equipped.[18] Since the local Health Authority was vacating it, they were able to rent it for £50 per annum. Margery cajoled some of her friends to form a committee, among them the writer Naomi Mitchison[19] and Naomi's barrister husband Dick,[20] and her sister-in-law Ethel Sprigge (*née* Jones), whose husband was a doctor and editor of *The Lancet*.[21] The only paid member of staff in the new clinic was the doctor. Its first year's funding had to come entirely from voluntary contributions because the Minister of Health in Ramsay MacDonald's[22]

---

16   Marks, *Metropolitan Maternity*, p. 97.
17   Wellcome Collection, SA/FPA/SR21.
18   The building no longer stands.
19   Naomi had read Stopes' *Married Love* and found it a revelation: Evans, *Freedom to Choose*, p. 84.
20   Later a Labour MP, and from 1964 a peer.
21   Dr Samuel Squire Sprigge: Margery rather unkindly recorded that she found him physically unprepossessing, though she liked him, and thought him clever and amusing.
22   Ramsay Macdonald was insistent that contraception was not a political matter. Women in the Labour Party voted several times for birth control advice to be

government, John Wheatley (a devout Catholic), had sent out a circular forbidding municipal health officers to give contraceptive advice. In 1926, Lord Buckmaster (father of Margaret Dighton Pollock) attempted to get a resolution through the Lords allowing local authorities to spend money on giving advice to married women, but it had been defeated. In the same year, Kensington became the first council in London (and second in the UK) to campaign, at first with a complete lack of success, for a change in the law to allow contraception to be provided through local authority-run infant welfare centres. Even in 1931, after such spending was allowed, the Ministry of Health permitted advice to be given only in cases where the mother's health would be endangered by further child-bearing.[23]

In the early years, therefore, there was a huge dependence on volunteer work as well as voluntary financial support: 'The three Margarets[24] were the interviewers, dispensers & bottlewashers',[25] Margery recalled. They were not squeamish. Interviewing, for example, might mean going to see women in their own homes:

> Sometimes [...] when I have been foolish enough to visit a Clinic patient at mid-day, the stench which greeted me on the opening of the front door was something never to be forgotten; 8 or 10 'dinners' being cooked in the house at the same time, — and most of them on an open fire in an old-fashioned grate, or on one gas-ring.

Not surprisingly, Margery and Margaret Lloyd took a justified pride in what their hard work achieved: in 1964, at a speech to celebrate forty years of the clinic, Margery said:

> Forty years ago in this building, a puny infant was adopted by two enthusiastic young foster-mothers, whom you see before you. At that time

---

available in clinics, but were defeated at the party conference: Rowbotham, *Dreamers of a New Day*, p. 97. The Workers Birth Control Group, originating within the Labour Party, fought to try to change government policy.

23   Marks, *Metropolitan Maternity*, p. 149; Lena M. Jeger, "The Politics of Family Planning', *Political Quarterly*, 31 (1962), 48–58 (p. 51), https://doi.org/10.1111/j.1467-923x.1962.tb01919.x; Elizabeth Draper, *Birth Control in the Modern World* (Harmondsworth: Penguin, 1965), p. 324. Joan Malleson, who later worked at North Kensington, was one of the first doctors to provide birth control advice for a local authority (Ealing), once it was allowed: D. E. Martin, 'Malleson [*née* Billson], Joan Graeme', in *Oxford Dictionary of National Biography* (2004), https://doi.org/10.1093/ref:odnb/54690

24   Spring Rice, Lloyd and Dighton Pollock.

25   Wellcome Collection, SA/FPA/SR21.

the baby, whom we called 'Birth Control', had only two relatives, — a slightly seedy, but courageous one in Walworth, and a flamboyant one off the Tottenham Court Road, called Marie Stopes.[26]

From the start, Margery's vision for the clinic encompassed a much broader field than simply contraception. Services offered included help with minor gynaecological problems, children's ailments, marriage guidance and advice on infertility. Freda Parker, a trained social worker who was appointed in 1953/4 to the post of 'outside organiser' (liaising with patients and raising awareness in the community), was interviewed in the 1980s for a television programme and said:

> 'Because Margery Spring Rice, who was one of the amazingly good pioneers, realised that you — it's not enough just to give a woman birth control and send her away. There's a whole gamut of relationships and problems connected with that. So she wanted to set up a centre where, not only birth control, but sub-fertility and help with er, sexual problems in marriage and pre-marital advice and so on could be given'.[27]

In an article written sixteen years after the founding of the clinic, Margery wrote that its function 'had been originally to give scientific birth control advice to poor women who were unable to pay the fees asked by the very few doctors who at that time knew anything about this branch of medicine. We found to our dismay that well over 50 per cent. of our patients, *coming only for contraceptive advice*, needed treatment for post-natal conditions of some sort or another'.[28] These were poor women, whose poverty was partly due to their large families, and they tended to be ignorant about their own and their children's health. As time went on, it was hoped that facilities such as rooms for recreational activities, playrooms and a café might be provided.

The first task of the clinic was of course to get women to come. One crucially helpful factor at North Kensington was that the doctor (from 1927, Dr Helena Wright)[29] was a woman and, therefore, more able to put at ease patients to whom speaking about intimate issues of health

---

26 Wellcome Collection, SA/FPA/SR7.
27 Wellcome Collection, GC/105/30.
28 Margery Spring Rice, 'The Health of Working Women', *Eugenics Review*, 32 (1940), 50–54 (at 51).
29 Helena Wright was chief medical officer at North Kensington for some 30 years. She pioneered sex therapy. At the beginning of her North Kensington work, she was paid £2 per week: luckily, she had private means as well as a private practice.

and sex did not come naturally. It was not a simple task for clinics to address their reluctance and their natural desire to protect their privacy. Patients either heard about the clinic through word of mouth, or were referred by doctors, but, in either case, it took a considerable amount of courage for a woman to bring herself to set foot inside the door of a place that was still far from being considered respectable. Some women also faced objections from husbands who felt that contraception was their responsibility and some women came without their husbands' knowledge. A survey of attitudes to sex and marriage between 1918 and 1963[30] found that couples tended to have a very gendered view of marriage, in which, particularly for working-class couples, contraception was seen as falling within the husband's sphere. Both men and women might also see withdrawal or abstinence as more 'natural' than other methods. Kate Fisher describes a 'fluent and contingent' approach to contraception, which emerged in the context of couples' reluctance to openly discuss sex. In her survey, she found numerous examples of women 'who presented themselves as having been almost entirely dependent on their husbands for birth control information' because sexual innocence was an essential part of their identity.[31]

Freda Parker was scathing about the attitude of some husbands who thought giving contraceptive advice to their wives might encourage them to have affairs: 'As if a woman with four kids in a damp basement under four is gonna have it off with the milkman'.[32] Occasionally, husbands themselves might come to the clinic, but it was perhaps even harder for them, in the context of the time, than for their wives to step inside that world of women. Sensitivity and confidentiality were essential to the clinic's work; the importance of cups of tea is also not to be underestimated in making the place welcoming.

Perhaps the boldness required for a woman to step over the threshold, and the barriers to its success, are illustrated by the account of one untypical patient: Pauline Crabbe, who herself later worked for the Brook Advisory Centres, was interviewed for a television programme in the 1980s. Although it was some distance from her home, she had been a patient at North Kensington in the 1930s in anticipation of her marriage,

---

30   Szreter and Fisher, *Sex before the Sexual Revolution*, pp. 225–26, 238, 254.
31   Ibid., pp. 8, 60, 66–67.
32   Wellcome Collection, GC/105/30.

having been told about it by a more worldly friend. The worst part, she
recounted, was that it was near a bus terminal, so that you had to 'walk
past a group of busmen who were waiting for the next um, tour of duty
as it were'.[33] Once inside, she found some of the staff quite brusque and
was acutely embarrassed by the whole procedure. She said that she had
not learnt to use the cap properly, as a result of which her first child was
born nine months after her marriage. In her view, from the perspective
of the 1980s, it was hard for the clinic to attract the women who needed
it most: if you have a whole range of problems, she thought, birth control
may not come at the top of the list, and the middle-class women who ran
the clinic did not always recognise that.

Freda Parker echoed this: the volunteers who interviewed patients
were usually 'dominant' women, who were apt to forget what a
traumatic experience it could be for the patient. If you are not ashamed
of your own underwear, you may not recognise such shame in another.
Interviews needed to be conducted 'tenderly': 'it wasn't in a way a lack
of care, it was a lack of understanding, and training, cos one didn't train
voluntary workers'.[34]

Helena Wright, a determined and single-minded woman who had
decided to pursue a career in contraception, visited Stopes's clinic and
then North Kensington, where Margery recognised her potential. When
a vacancy arose, Margery offered Wright the job on the basis that she
would be free to make any changes she saw fit. The partnership was
to be an enduring and fruitful one, though not always easy: Margery's
daughter described it as a love-hate relationship, commenting that
the two women must have been the two 'least diplomatic women in
history'.[35]

Margery's own role was multi-faceted. She worked hands-on in
the clinic, alongside patients, who were encouraged to help with its
running; for thirty-four years she chaired its committee; and she raised
funds. In 1968, when a BBC programme about the clinic was planned,[36]
a friend commented that when something was proposed but there
was no money, Margery's reaction would always be 'We'll get it'. She

---

33 Wellcome Collection, GC/105/43.
34 Wellcome Collection, GC/105/30.
35 Evans, *Freedom to Choose*, p. 135.
36 This programme appears to have never been broadcast (the BBC Genome search
    engine does not find any evidence of the programme).

did everything she could to raise the profile of the clinic, particularly among influential members of society. In 1928, she was the moving force behind a dinner party that was held at the house of a distinguished doctor, Arthur Ellis,[37] at which the guest of honour was Lady Denman, Liberal, suffragist and president of the National Federation of Women's Institutes. Several academics, including Winifred Cullis,[38] were present, as was the secretary of the Birth Control Investigation Committee (1927),[39] Marjorie Farrer, who was to become a personal friend of Margery's as well as a fellow-campaigner.

The outcome of this gathering at the Ellises was the formation of the National Birth Control Council in 1930, with Lady Denman as chair (which became the National Birth Control Association the following year, and the Family Planning Association in 1939). On the executive committee of this body, which co-ordinated five existing bodies, were Margery, Eva Hubback,[40] Mary Stocks,[41] Marie Stopes and Helena Wright.[42] The secretary was Margaret Pyke, a woman of 'single-mindedness, integrity and good humour',[43] another who formed a friendship for life with Margery.

Nancy Raphael, who began volunteering at the Islington clinic in 1935,[44] the year after its foundation, described Margaret Pyke as a good-looking, intelligent woman who was good with money and had an attractive

---

37 Arthur William Mickle Ellis was a Canadian doctor who had settled in London at the end of the war.

38 Cullis was the first woman professor in a university medical school. She believed that biology teaching 'should not end at the waist': R. E. M. Bowden, 'Cullis, Winifred Clara', in *Oxford Dictionary of National Biography* (2004), https://doi.org/10.1093/ref:odnb/32661

39 This committee was set up jointly by the North Kensington and Cambridge clinics, perhaps partly owing to the connection between Margery and her sister-in-law Petica. Clive Wood and Beryl Suitters, *The Fight for Acceptance: A History of Contraception* (Aylesbury: Medical and Technical Publications, 1970), p. 169.

40 Suffragist, economist and, later, Labour councillor for North Kensington on the London County Council.

41 Suffragist, writer and social campaigner.

42 Wright had persuaded Margery that Stopes should be on the committee, but co-operation did not come naturally to Stopes, and she resigned in 1933: Evans, *Freedom to Choose*, pp. 143–44. Rowbotham describes how, when Stopes declared '"I'm not the Cabin Boy in this movement. I'm the Admiral"' 'The other women listened politely and carried on regardless': Rowbotham, *Dreamers of a New Day*, p. 98.

43 Leathard, *The Fight for Family Planning*, p. 46.

44 One of the 'daughter' clinics of North Kensington, run, according to Raphael, by idealistic but totally impractical 'Bloomsberries', all talk and no action.

personality.[45] Pyke and Denman made an excellent team and happily shared a house later in life, both having been in unhappy marriages. Pyke was perhaps not one of those to enjoy the thrill of the shocking: she was always anxious to defend the good name of the movement, both with the public and with the medical profession, although she was later involved with the Brook Advisory Centres, founded specifically to give contraceptive advice to young unmarried people in 1964. According to Raphael, her single-minded commitment to the mission of the clinics helped to build loyalty across the movement; on the other hand, her love of power led her to surround herself with people unlikely to challenge her and, as she got older, the size of the undertaking began to be too much for her. There were times when Margery did challenge Pyke's authority but, according to Raphael, she always lost, being an excellent organiser but a less adroit politician than Pyke.

The North Kensington clinic made an enormous difference to many lives, but its success with patients was patchy. Margery was not the only one to feel that not nearly enough follow-up was carried out, since patients often came once or twice and then dropped out. While this could have been because they had been happily supplied with contraceptives, it could also mean that they had given up on a method, such as the cap. Helena Wright laid great emphasis on the cap as helping a woman to get to know her own body, but it was not an easy device to use. In 1931, the clinic carried out a survey involving personal visits to 780 patients who had ceased to attend (one of the first systematic attempts to follow up drop-outs), and widespread dislike of the methods on offer as well as their unreliability were reported. It was recognised that there was a great need to find simpler as well as more reliable forms of contraceptive.

However, although the success of the clinic may have been intermittent in terms of its influence on the lives of individual women, if looked at in the larger context of social history and women's rights, the importance of North Kensington and the other pioneering clinics can hardly be overstated. In the long term, they changed the picture entirely.

While Margery was devoting her considerable skills to the work at North Kensington, her marriage continued to deteriorate. In 1924, she embarked on a brief affair with a man called Herbert Reade but brought it to an end because, she said later, she began to despise

---

45   Women's Library, LSE, 8SUF/B/177.

herself for it and hated the secrecy.[46] Much more significant was her affair with Dick Mitchison, a supporter of the North Kensington clinic, which began in 1926. Margery and Dick's wife, Naomi (known as Nou), had probably met through their public activities. In one of her volumes of autobiography, *All Change Here*, Naomi recalls how she went to a meeting of the League of Nations Society, of which, at that time, Margery was secretary: 'The then secretary, Margery Spring Rice, remembers me coming in with a silent duenna, perhaps my mother-in-law's personal maid'.[47] One of Nou's biographers, Jenni Calder,[48] says the two women met through the Women's International League, which is possible, although there is no record of Margery being a member of that body.[49] Dick and Dominick had overlapped at Eton, but Dominick was a few years older (Dick was about seven years younger than Margery). Whatever the exact circumstances of the first meeting between them, a close friendship grew between the families, founded not only on the personal affection between the women but on their shared interests: left-wing politics, feminism, internationalism, Irish politics[50] and the birth control movement. Soon, the two couples were dining together at least once a week and taking shared holidays at Varengeville[51] in Normandy. For a period, they and another family owned a cottage in Bledlow Ridge, Buckinghamshire, where, according to Naomi, Margery did most of the cooking. In 1928, Margery went on a sailing holiday in the Aegean with Dick, Nou, and other friends.

The Mitchison family had moved, in 1923, into a house in Rivercourt Road in Hammersmith while the Spring Rices were in Victoria Road,

---

46 She may also have had an affair with Margaret Jones's husband Kingsley Game, but this is likely to have been before 1919, the year in which she married Dominick and Margaret married Kingsley. Much later, she told her daughter that she had slept with five men in the course of her life.

47 Naomi Mitchison, *All Change Here: Girlhood and Marriage* (London: Bodley Head, 1975), p. 153.

48 Jenni Calder, *The Nine Lives of Naomi Mitchison* (London: Virago, 1997), p. 68.

49 This had its origins in the 1915 women's peace conference in the Hague.

50 Mitchison recalled, in *You May Well Ask: A Memoir, 1920–40* (London: Fontana, 1986), p. 183, how the two women had marched together in a demonstration for Irish independence.

51 On one of these holidays, Margery introduced Benson and Nou to each other, and they became friends. One scholar believes that their friendship had a Lesbian element (Catherine Clay, *British Women Writers 1914–45: Professional Work and Friendship* (Aldershot and Burlington, VT: Ashgate, 2006), https://doi. org/10.4324/9781315261256), but her evidence does not necessarily bear this out.

Kensington; later Margery moved to St Peter's Square, a few minutes away from Rivercourt Road.[52] Arthur Ellis, who had been instrumental in publicising the work of the North Kensington clinic, and his wife Winnie, lived nearby on Chiswick Mall. When Margery's brother, Douglas, was advising her around the break-up of her marriage, he referred despairingly to the bad influence on her of the 'Chiswick milieu'. Dick and Naomi had agreed to have an open marriage: Dick had three significant affairs[53] in the course of it and Nou had a long amitié amoureuse with the classical scholar H. T. Wade-Gery ('Widg'). They were not unlike the Bloomsbury group in their passionate belief in the importance of friendship and of sexual freedom. It is unfortunate that we do not have Margery's letters to Dick, but there are extant letters from him and Nou to Margery. As far as Nou is concerned, what comes through is the huge difficulty of living up to the ideal of not being jealous: she loved Margery deeply, and completely accepted the affair between her and Dick, but still struggled at some level, particularly as it is clear that she was not getting everything she wanted from Widg. In one undated letter, she writes that she would like to experience the kind of passion that Margery and Dick have for one another, which she has never had. When Dick's affections shifted from Margery to Tish Rokeling, Nou and Margery shared confidences with each other about it. Margery felt that Nou was the one who held them all together.

Often Dick and Nou wrote to Margery by the same post, with their letters in a single envelope. Nou expresses enormous affection for Margery, though her struggles for equanimity do show through. In an undated letter addressed to 'Margy, my own darling', at a time when Dick and Margery were evidently together, she writes that necessary readjustments have to be made, which is 'a little bit uncomfortable at the moment'. Unlike Dominick however — she wonders whether he is doing his readjusting 'in the dark' — she is 'in the full light, and can examine the machinery and say how nice I think it is [...] Kiss [Dick]

---

52   15 St Peter's Square, bought by Margery soon after the separation, was partly tenanted to start with, but once she had the run of the house it became both an architectural project and a place where she was able to cultivate a gift for gathering round her all sorts and conditions of people. In the late 1920s, Robert Graves was also living in St Peter's Square, in a flat he referred to as 'Free Love Corner': Virginia Nicholson, *Among the Bohemians* (New York: William Morrow, 2002).

53   With Margery, Tish Rokeling and Margaret Cole.

Fig. 13. Eric Ravilious (1903–1942), *River Thames at Hammersmith* (1933). Watercolour and pencil on paper. Image Towner Eastbourne. At the time this painting was done, Margery, the Mitchison family and other friends were living near the Thames on the Chiswick-Hammersmith borders.

at once from me. It seems to make it all the realer that I should love you both so completely'. On 30 December 1926, from a holiday in Avignon, Dick writes that:

> Nou sometimes doubts whether you and I are happier for loving one another, as things are. At least, I don't think she really doubts — only intermittently. And anyhow, we are happier, aren't we? I like writing your name. And I kiss your hair & throat, your cheeks & lips, my dear, dear love.

Dominick's position in the relationship with the Mitchisons, like so much else about him, is hard to pin down. In the statement to the court that Margery made in 1929, when she was considering asking for custody of the children, she wrote 'I do not think that either Dick or D[ominick] have ever had a closer friendship with anyone else than they had with each other',[54] but the extant letters do not quite bear this out. It is unclear whether he knew about the affair from the start, as Nou did, though

---

54   Margery Spring Rice, Statement to the court, October 1929.

Margery alleges that Dominick encouraged it. In the undated letter to Margery already referred to, Nou writes that Dick has told Dominick 'the essential fact, that he is completely in love with you'; she has given [Dominick] opportunities to talk, but he has not taken them. In another letter, she writes:

> Dominick and I had a long walk yesterday and a short but very exciting one today — through the original slough of despond, I should think. I've never seen such completely muddy mud. D., I think, enjoyed it (subject always to every possible reservation!) and the week-end altogether. But he does make me muddled in my mind; sometimes I think I must be half-witted not to be able to understand him at all — for often I can't — when he says he's being perfectly normal. Is he really the normal, the natural and proper thing, and are we all quite unreal? Are we quite outside ordinary life? — or is he?'[55]

Over the course of the affair between Dick and Margery, however, and as the Spring Rice marriage went from bad to worse, the Mitchisons were definitely on Margery's side. Nou thought that Margery was (naturally in the circumstances) blind to many of Dominick's good qualities, but when they eventually separated, she wrote 'I wish I was driving a steam roller and could run over Dominick'.[56]

The two families supported each other through various crises, children's illnesses and Margery's marital problems, but, in July 1927, the Mitchisons faced a terrible loss — that of their eldest son Geoff, who died after an operation on his mastoid. Nou was distraught: part of her distress was that she thought she bore some responsibility for Geoff's death, a view openly and cruelly expressed to her by her brother, Jack Haldane.[57] Their misery was compounded when, in the winter of 1927–1928, there were terrible floods, causing the Thames to break its banks. Two of the fifteen people drowned were servants of the Mitchisons. It was a time when Nou and Dick relied on Margery for both emotional and practical support. Nou, in her turn, supported Margery through the end of her affair with Dick. In another undated letter to Margery, probably written in spring 1928, Nou wrote:

> All decent people make themselves bread for their friends to eat [...] At present you and Dick and I have none of us got much bread to spare.

---

55 Naomi Mitchison, letter to Margery Spring Rice, undated.
56 Naomi Mitchison, letter to Margery Spring Rice, undated.
57 Calder, *The Nine Lives*, p. 80.

> And we want food desperately [...] Last summer Dick and I ate you — I
> particularly; after all, you probably saved my life [after Geoff's death].
> Since then, you've wanted feeding worse than any of us.

The end of the affair with Dick caused Margery great distress. She
expressed her misery about losing him to Tish in a letter dated 17
October 1928, probably never intended to be sent as the envelope
is marked 'To be burnt unopened, if lost, — or in case of accident',
though such instructions are always ambivalent. She could easily have
destroyed the letter herself. Dick and Margery remained friends but the
two families were never so intimate again, partly because, under the
terms of a judicial separation from Dominick, Margery was required
by the court to promise not to bring the children into contact with the
Mitchisons. Like all his ex-lovers, she used to receive a case of wine from
Dick every Christmas, until near the ends of their lives (they were to die
within a few weeks of one another).

Stella Benson remained in contact with both Margery and Dominick,
though she was often away in China with her husband James (or
Shaemas) Anderson. Although Benson had a clear-sighted view of the
difficulties of being married to Dominick, she did not warm to Margery
as she did to him. In October 1928, she wrote in her diary:

> Margery lunched with me today and talked a great deal about her
> affaire. I am not spontaneously sympathetic with Margery because she is
> always so <u>right</u> [...] She also doesn't view her own side with that touch
> of cynicism that makes for just observation of one's own point of view.
> Nevertheless it would be unbearable, I admit, to have a fundamental
> liar, poseur and irresponsible like Dominick for a husband — still worse
> to have him as a domestic enemy as well — and as for his mother, she
> seems, by Margery's account to be a poisonous old adder. But yet I feel
> sorry for Dominick, though he is by far the most in the wrong.[58]

Benson had come to understand well that that there was another
side to the exuberance that she loved in Dominick. In 1929, she was
writing 'Dominick so seldom allows anyone else to show off', and
there are numerous comments on his drinking — Benson's father
was an alcoholic, so she knew something about what that meant for
a person's nearest and dearest. On one occasion, according to Benson,
Dominick was 'hopelessly fuddled and very tiresome — staring at one

---

58   CUL Add. MS 6762–6802.

with that dreadful blank unblinking smile', and on another, he 'was most disturbing — continually trying to light my nose, thinking I had an unlighted cigarette, & exclaiming & singing from time to time [...] It really is heartbreaking — so clever and so kind a person so imprisoned'. At one point, she thought he might have been 'paying spies' to inform him about Margery's activities. In the summer of 1930, she went to Lords with him: 'My withers were rung [...] by the fact that Dominick knew so many people at the match, & strove to buttonhole them while they all, painfully obviously tried to escape'. Benson recognized that while Dominick had 'almost unlimited potential intellectual understanding', his emotional intelligence was far behind. She was also irritated by the way he overplayed his Irishness.

However, at the same time, she was enthralled by his wit and the speed at which he lived life. Two extant letters from Dominick to Benson[59] convey something of the qualities she loved in him and bear out her feeling that people had to run to keep up with his mental agility. The first letter, written in January 1926, ranges over politics, Ireland, China (where Benson was living at the time), culture, scandal,[60] his work and family news. He describes a car journey they had taken: the car, known as 'Hotenpot' —

> began to run backwards down hill so that even when Margie had checked her by steering into the bank she was only saved from turning turtle by a swift movement of my vast bulk to her outside edge. Every time I go in a motor car I dislike it more, but Margie is keener about, and better at, driving than ever. Nor has she been hailed to Bow Street again, so she appears to be learning cunning as well as caution.[61]

As the state of her marriage deteriorated, Margery increasingly felt that things could no longer continue as they were, and eventually, she confided further details of the situation to her friends Arthur and Winnie Ellis. The Ellises already knew about Dick, and had been instrumental in persuading Dominick to sleep in a separate room from Margery. In

59   Cambridge, Cambridge University Library, Add. MS 8367, ff. 308 and 346 [Dominick Spring Rice's letters to Stella Benson].

60   Jack Haldane came close to being dismissed from his post at Cambridge University when he was cited as co-respondent in a divorce case.

61   Margery had evidently had a brush with the authorities: later in her life, she was notorious among friends and family for her cavalier attitude behind the wheel.

August 1927, just before Dominick left for an extended visit to America,[62] he and Margery went together to see the Ellises and Margery stated in front of them that she could no longer live with him. However, when he came home earlier than expected, in November, she felt that she needed legal advice and turned to her brother, Douglas. Since Douglas kept diaries over this period, the turbulent relationship (and its culmination in an application to the courts for a judicial separation) can be seen from a different perspective.

As the oldest of the five Garrett children, Douglas provided a wise and steady foil to Margery's more adventurous nature. There was clearly great affection between them even though he strongly disapproved of what he regarded as her irresponsible behaviour and she was sometimes deeply irritated by his conventionality. With regard to her marriage, however, she recognised that he was invaluable, and he was generous with help and advice. After Dominick's return from the US, he records:

> there were interviews with both of them, I trying to hold the balance & get them to put a face on it & continue keeping house together. But I fear this attempt has now broken down.

He referred each of them to a solicitor: 'I am satisfied they could not be better looked after, & hope that I shall now be left out of it more or less'.

Predictably, it was less rather than more. In June 1929, he wrote:

> <u>Marjorie & Dominick</u>'s affairs culminated in a separation deed executed in (I think) July 1928. This was followed by an arbitration last autumn, principally on the question whether D. was entitled to deduct income from the allowance paid by him under the deed from July till the end of Sept., when 55 Victoria Rd was given up, and on other minor matters. The award was in M.'s favour, with costs. They still squabble over every conceivable thing, whenever there is an opening for doing so. M. has taken 15 St Peter's Square, Hammersmith. At present she only has possession of half the house, & until she gets her tenant out next March the house will not be in the least suitable for her requirements. She still seems as thick as ever with the M[itchison]s, to my regret; and is still very restless and emotional. The whole thing is a miserable business, and from the end of 1927 till the deed was signed (and, to a less extent, since then also) I had a very worrying time of it between the two of them, as

---

62   Bizarrely, on the passenger list his country of future permanent residence is given as Ecuador: a mistake? Or Dominick's joke?

I have tried to keep on reasonably good terms with D., though of course supporting her generally.

Another friend who was supportive — but at a distance, because she was mostly abroad in China and elsewhere at the time — was Eileen Power, who wrote in a letter to Margery on 22 October 1927:

> I really am extremely distressed over what you told me yesterday: not at your separating from Dominick, but at your having had such a bad time for so long. You were so loyal in not speaking of your married life, & I (as you know) never ask questions, that I had thought you happy until the last year. I then thought that you were four friends trying to carry on on a new basis (owing to your being in love with Dick), and that you were bound to break at the weakest link, which was Dominick, who I did not think a large enough person to manage it: but last summer I thought he seemed to be behaving well about it, though I did not think he would be able to keep it up. I had no idea that you had been unhappy with him for so long (I had persuaded myself that I was quite wrong in not having wanted you to marry him), & I wish I had known in the summer, because I should have tried to see more of you, just to show you how devoted I am to you & I should certainly have come on the yacht! I cannot bear to think of your having had such a miserable time & having been forced through the sort of scenes which I know you detest. You deserve to be happy all the time without stopping & it is a shame.

The deed of separation was signed in May 1928. Dominick agreed not to drink alcohol other than beer or cider, though this was not a promise he was capable of keeping. Their two children, Stephen and Cecil, who were sent to boarding school in the autumn of that year, were made wards of court and were to see him one day a week at his mother's house and to spend half of the school holidays with each parent. Margery moved out of Victoria Road to St Peter's Square, and Dominick moved to De Vere Gardens (the next road parallel to and east of Victoria Road). In the statement Margery made the following year, she wrote that she thought the matter of the separation 'could be made not to seem a very important one to [the children]' — when Cecil, as an adult, read this extraordinary pronouncement, she simply added two exclamation marks with her initials in the margin. Margery also asserted that Dominick had become a Catholic,[63] in spite of his previous scorn for all

---

63   As members of the Irish Protestant Ascendancy, Dominick's father's family was nominally at least Church of Ireland; his mother's family, the Fitzgeralds, had been

forms of religion; it is unlikely that he ever took this step, but he was certainly attracted by the drama of the mass. Stella Benson recalls going to the Russian Easter service with him, where he 'wallowed in excessive worship' leading her to wonder whether 'drunkenness has any direct connection with religious fervour'. They also attended high mass at Westminster Cathedral together where he, again:

> positively wallowed in devotion, almost washed himself all over in the font full of holy water. All showy offy, poor darling, the kind of showing off that strikes inward for he really feels a great excitement in his theatricality.[64]

Stephen also, in a letter to Margery from his preparatory school, mentions being taken to Westminster Cathedral by Dominick; and the head of Cecil's preparatory school reported that Dominick objected to Wycombe Abbey School as a possible destination for Cecil on account of its Protestant atmosphere.

The separation by no means ended the troubles between Margery and Dominick. In 1931, Douglas wrote in his diary:

> Marjorie's affairs are still unsatisfactory. Dominick has, to all appearances, left the City & is believed to have been sacked from his post as manager of Grace Brothers (whether for drink or not, nobody knows certainly). He has announced, through Withers (his solicitor) that he is now earning nothing, & accordingly the prospect for M. is that after April next he will pay her nothing under the deed. How the education of his children is to be provided for after that I don't know.[65]

In due course they both won scholarships, Stephen to Eton and Cecil to Wycombe Abbey, so that worry was greatly reduced: both schools were extremely generous in their financial provision.[66] According to the statement to the court, Margery had made a will on her marriage leaving everything to Dominick — something that would not have been unusual at the time — but it had become apparent that he was obstructive

---

Catholics but had become Protestant in the eighteenth century. However, I have only been able to trace a baptismal record for one of Julia's ten siblings. This does not mean that none of the others had been baptised, but it is a surprisingly low number. For Julia's father's relationship with the (Protestant) Church of Ireland, see Nellie O'Cleirigh, *Valentia: A Different Irish Island* (Dublin: Portobello Press, 1992), pp. 12, 47.

64   CUL Add. MS 6762–6802.
65   Douglas Garrett, Diary, Vol. 1, p. 110.
66   Cecil was awarded a scholarship of £150 p.a.

about everything to do with money; since he was unable or unwilling to contribute anything to Charles and Ronald's maintenance, Margery was worrying about how she would continue to pay fees for Ronald at Rugby and future university costs. In February 1930, Dominick wrote to Stella Benson 'meanwhile it's hard to educate children & oneself[,] pay taxes & pay £860 a year to Margery'.[67]

In the circumstances, it must have been extremely distressing for her to receive two highly critical letters from Aunt Theo early in 1931.[68] It is unclear whether Theo was referring to something specific, or to Margery's lifestyle in general, or whether the outcome caused a breach between them. Nonetheless, they were corresponding about Clara in a friendly way the following year, and in later years they were close. Margery had sent Aunt Theo a calendar, and, in a letter to Margery, Theo wrote:

> But, dear child, I cannot hang it up on the wall — the very sight of it makes me almost too sad for tears when I think of the tears & sorrows your mistakes & mistaken opinions on Life & Conduct have made for yourself — your children & your mother[,] brother & me as one of the least of these. So I tore it up — & wished with all my heart that your life had been built on opinions like your father's — it wd then have been happier & more useful.[69]

Theo admitted that her generation had landed the world in 'the most revolting war in history' but saw 'purity & duty' as essentials for the future — the word 'purity' crops up again and again. With her own deep Christian faith, she felt that she had not done her duty as Margery's godmother. A second letter, dated 10 April, continues in the same vein:

> My poor God-daughter — who has lost her way & cannot see that she has taken a wrong turning — Dear Child, of course I have loved you dearly for yourself's sake & also for your very dear Father's sake — and also for your mother's.

---

67 Dominick Spring Rice, letter to Stella Benson & Shaemus Anderson, 16 February 1930.
68 There is an implication in a letter from Gil Jones to her sister Hilda in 1919, at the time of Margery's second marriage, that Aunt Theo had also been very critical of Margery over Isabel's death.
69 Dorothea Gibb, letter to Margery Spring Rice, 6 January 1931.

She accused Margery of betraying 'all the great causes of Liberty & Peace that you uphold with one hand and tear down with the other [...] You have cut yourself off from me & my house'. Such statements must have heaped coals on the burning pain that Margery was already enduring.

From 1924 onwards, Margery had been spending a huge amount of time on the North Kensington clinic. In the midst of all her personal difficulties, she threw herself with even more vigour into her public activities while the children were either at school, at home in the care of the nanny, at Aldeburgh with Clara, or spending their allotted periods with Dominick. In the early months of 1930, she travelled to the United States on a lecture tour, on which Dominick's comment to Stella Benson was: 'I don't know why but I suppose to spout Free Love & Birth Control & find a rich man'.[70] Margery's work at North Kensington had put her in touch with Margaret Sanger,[71] American birth control campaigner, and the main purpose of her tour was to meet Sanger and other pioneers in the field and to give a lecture entitled 'English Women in Private and Public Life'. The press comments printed in the flyer for her Seattle appearance refer to her 'charm and graciousness', her philanthropy and her 'fluent discourse'. Contraception was a hugely controversial subject in the US — as Margery recalled many years later, there were states in which, she was told, she must not even mention it. The trip was not all work: she enjoyed herself too, spending time in New York and Boston, as well as in California, where she went with Sanger to a tea party hosted by the socialite, socialist and philanthropist Kate Crane Gartz, and also took particular delight in meeting Charlie Chaplin. Both at Gartz's tea-party and at the Los Angeles breakfast club, at which she was a guest,[72] she found that her English sense of humour was at odds with that of her hosts. On 2 March 1930, while she was away, Ronald, aged fourteen, wrote to her:

---

70 Dominick Spring Rice, letter to Stella Benson & Shaemus Anderson, 16 February 1930.

71 Sanger was the founder in 1921 of the American Birth Control League, which became the Planned Parenthood Federation of America. She was later much criticised for her views on eugenics.

72 Another guest was Prince Friedrich Leopold of Prussia. Margery was described by the *Los Angeles Times* (26 February 1930) as 'Lady Margaret Spring-Rice, famous English feminist leader' (p. 14).

> You seem to be quite far-famed in America already! I now have a mother
> visited daily by reporters, photographers, etc. Why on earth are they so
> keen on you, and how did they get to know about you so quickly?

At home again, she somehow found the emotional and practical
resources to support friends in their marital difficulties — the artist
Paul Maze and his wife Margaret[73] (a cousin of Naomi Mitchison's)
and David and Ena Mitrany. David Mitrany, an academic economist,
was teaching at Harvard in the early 1930s, while his wife Ena, who
had suffered some kind of mental breakdown, was being treated in a
residential setting by the psychiatrist, Eric Strauss. Margery acted as
intermediary between the couple and Strauss, as well as going to visit
Ena. Despite the agonies of her marriage, the late 1920s and early 1930s
were not entirely unhappy years for Margery, not only because of the
two years of joy Dick gave her. She had a great gift for friendship,
which blossomed particularly among the many Germans and Austrians
she became friends with at this time, offering practical and emotional
help in the shadow of the rise of Fascism. In the second half of her life,
Margery's capacity to gather communities of friends around her was to
be one of her defining characteristics.

---

73   The Mazes were to divorce in 1949.

6. A Single Woman (1931–1936)

Family life was not always easy. Margery's relationship with her children was complicated. She loved them dearly, and wanted the best for them, but she never let their presence interfere with her own activities, in either her private life (which included holidays without them), or her public work. Of course, she was not at all unusual for her time and class in leaving nurses and nannies to bring them up, but she perhaps allowed this to happen to an even greater extent than many of her peers. The situation was also more complex because, from the late twenties, she was in effect a single parent. In contrast to this semi-detached way of parenting, she was, at the same time, deeply emotionally invested in her children and found it extremely hard to let go (particularly of her sons) as they grew into adulthood, or to allow them to make their own decisions about careers and marriages. While this took the form of trying to help in any way she could, it caused some difficulties for them in making independent lives.

Charles and Ronald were both sent away to Rugby School, which offered bursaries for the sons of officers killed in the war. Both boys were unhappy there, though Ronald coped better with school life than Charles. In 1930, following a summer in Germany, Charles went from Rugby to Trinity Hall, Cambridge. However, university life did not suit him any better than school had done. He stayed at university for two years, helped by a girlfriend, Lilli.[1] However, Margery, Muz and other relations regarded her as unsuitable (to some extent at least from class snobbery, and almost certainly also from a degree of anti-Semitism), and arrangements were made for Charles to go to Toronto, where his Jones grandfather had studied, to finish his degree. This choice was

---

1   Lilli Bronowski, sister of Jacob Bronowski. She graduated from Girton with a first in 1933.

    https://doi.org/10.11647/OBP.0215.06

perhaps partly made with the aim of loosening Charles's ties to Lilli. Douglas confided to his diary that Lilli was:

> a clever, but common, young Polish Jewess [...] we met her at Aldeburgh this summer. She is I believe genuinely in love with Charles (tho' I doubt whether he is with her), & she is a girl of a good deal of character; but she is quite definitely not 'out of the top drawer' and is looked at askance by M.L.S.R., & detested (unfairly) by Mother! We all hope that Charles will have enough gumption to break it off while he is in Canada. Lilli's father is supposed to know nothing of the affair, & to be capable of turning her out of his home if he did — such are his strict Jewish principles.[2]

The affair did indeed peter out but Charles hated Canada and came away still without a degree. He had no idea what he wanted to do with his life: in a letter to Margery in 1933, Ronald reported that Charles was thinking of acting (he had done some at Cambridge) or bookselling, and, later, journalism was mentioned.

Charles was struggling to break away from Margery, but a lack of enthusiasm for her children's choice of partners was to become a pattern over the next few years. However, to her credit, she did recognise the problem herself, writing to a friend that she had agreed with Arthur Ellis that it would be good for Charles to have some distance from her. As well as consulting Ellis, she asked other friends and acquaintances if they could help in terms of finding him work. As he had been an enthusiastic collector of moths and butterflies since childhood, on 25 November 1934, Margery wrote (without success, as it turned out) to the entomologist Karl Jordan of Tring Zoological Museum to ask if there might be a place for him there:

> he has had a very difficult life. His father, my first husband, was killed in the War, when Charles was four, and it made a deep and lasting impression of horror on the child; and my second husband, (from whom I am separated, mostly for this reason) ill-treated him by a subtle and extremely cruel form of bullying. He has consistently thought himself, probably unconsciously for these reasons, less capable and successful than my other children.

At some point in the early thirties, to some extent no doubt as a way of escaping his upper-middle class origins, Charles joined the Communist

---

2   Douglas Garrett, Diary, 1, p. 127.

Party, of which he was to remain a staunch member until the Soviet invasion of Hungary in 1956. On his return from Canada, he met a young Swiss woman, Paula Reinhardt, with whom he set up house; they were married in April 1935, and Paula gave birth to their first child, Susan, in early 1936. According to Douglas, they lived in Battersea on a tiny income, Charles having cut himself off from family and friends in an attempt to sever all bourgeois ties, while he devoted his energies to working for the Communist Party. While this was true, the family did need support of all kinds — financial, practical and emotional — and Paula at least sometimes felt she had to ask for it, writing, after Susan's birth, 'Margie would you please help Charles to get a job? A paid job!'[3] Margery did continue to try to help as best she could, and if her interventions seemed very heavy-handed to the young couple, it is hard to see how she could have got it right. Gil (Lilian) and Hilda Jones, Charles's unmarried aunts, who always felt a big responsibility for their nephews, did their best to keep lines of communication open. Gil, feeling that 'the damned inferiority business' was behind Charles's troubles, wrote to Margery that it would be better to hold back rather than creating hostility by probing.[4] Margery's friend Rhoda Power (Eileen's sister), who spent a period around this time staying with and looking after Clara, also kept in touch with Charles and Paula and attempted to mediate between them when she could.

Ronald's path was easier, since he had not suffered nearly so badly from Dominick's bullying or from the miseries of public school, and he knew that he wanted to work in gardening or agriculture. With a very different temperament from Charles's, he was able to tease Margery: 'Excuse the two holes in the paper, if you do I'll excuse your short letter'; 'Are you taking up politics in despair of finding any land for your flats,[5] or is it merely that you can't bear to see the Liberal Party falling to pieces for lack of your support?'[6] He charted her imagined rise as a politician and suggested that after the 1931 general election she ought to become Minister of Transport. From his letters, it looks as if Margery was constantly inventing new projects, presumably as a way of dealing with

---

3   Paula Garrett Jones, letter to Margery Spring Rice, undated.
4   Lilian Jones, letter to Margery Spring Rice, undated.
5   What this refers to is not clear.
6   Ronald Garrett Jones, letter to Margery Spring Rice, 30 November 1924.

her personal unhappiness: at one point she thought about applying for a job at the International Labour Organization, at another, she thought of running a guest house near Dartington in Devon.

When Ronald left Rugby, he went to work as a farming apprentice in Essex and then to Denmark for a few months to extend his knowledge. After a period at the East London College,[7] he enrolled at Wye College in Kent and subsequently at Cambridge for a diploma course. By the time he went to Wye, he too, like Charles and for some of the same reasons, had joined the Communist Party, the beginning of a lifetime allegiance (though not slavish or dogmatic). It is possible that the adherence to Communism of both Margery's Garrett Jones sons was a contributory cause to the coolness between her and her brother Geoffrey, certainly after the outbreak of war in 1939 if not before. On 11 January 1940, Geoffrey wrote to Margery expressing his strong objections to the Communist Party of Great Britain, on the grounds that it slavishly followed instructions from Russia. He could allow for people holding their own views, he said, 'but I am <u>not</u> willing to tolerate people who <u>act</u> against the vital interests of the country at this time'. According to Douglas's diary, Geoffrey refused to meet either Charles or Ronald, though for how long this lasted is unclear.[8]

Stephen seems to have dealt reasonably well with his traumatic childhood, although his relations with Dominick were not without incident: on 31 January 1932, Ronald wrote to his aunt Hilda Jones from Rugby, 'I suppose you have heard that Stephen ran away from Dominick'. Cecil found it much harder than her brother, perhaps because Dominick was enormously proud of his son but had wished that Cecil too had been a boy: it may be that her name reflects this.[9] In the spring of 1933, Cecil was expected to spend the allotted time on her own with her father (because Stephen was away somewhere else) but she hated the idea, writing to Margery from school: 'Father says that he is going to take Stephen to France for Easter and then have me afterwards, but I'm not going to him by myself so what is going to happen?'.[10] She was afraid

---

7   Now Queen Mary University.
8   Geoffrey died in 1949.
9   It may also have been after Dominick's diplomat uncle Cecil Spring Rice, ambassador to Washington during World War I and author of the hymn 'I vow to thee my country'.
10   Cecil Spring Rice, letter to Margery Spring Rice, 26 March 1933.

of him and until, as an adult, she read Margery's statement to the court, she thought that she hated him. Stephen, though only just over a year older, was her protector against him. On 3 October 1934, Stephen (aged fourteen) wrote to Douglas from Eton to ask whether their stays with Dominick could be limited to no more than ten days at a time: 'it would save him trouble and expense, and would give us more pleasure. Cecil does not want to go to him at all, but she agreed in the end that the idea was all right'. Douglas's reply, dated the following day, is a model of clarity and kindness, and he ends by saying that he regards their correspondence as being between solicitor and client, and therefore, not to be shown to Dominick without Stephen's permission.

In 1934, Stephen had followed in his father's footsteps to Eton as a King's scholar. Although he was clever, academic work was never his priority and he cheerfully refused to revere his teachers, or, in various aspects of school life, to comply with what was expected of him. He did not believe in compulsory chapel and declined to be confirmed: 'I'm not being confirmed [nor] am I joining the corps. What a shock for Jeeves [nickname of his house master, Wilkes]! "you must do one or the other" he says'.[11] Having already built a small sailing dinghy at Aldeburgh, he spent a great deal of his Eton time building a sailing boat[12] in the workshop, not an easy thing to do when, as a scholar, he was expected to behave as part of the academic aristocracy:

> The boat is getting on very well. All the parts that I thought were going to be boring, such as sawing, drilling holes for nails etc. are quite fun here because of the marvellous tools, mechanical saws, drills, lathes. I can bore at least 15 holes for rivets through 1" oak per minute, whereas with a hand drill it takes more than ½ minute to do one.[13]

It says something for the comparative freedom of the school, as well as his own character, that he was able to evade some of the demands of school life in this way. Other than boats and sailing, his great interest was music, and he had a good tenor voice. He made two great friends at Eton, both also keen musicians, each with a wild streak to match

---

11 Stephen Spring Rice, letter to Margery Spring Rice, 25 November 1935.
12 A Sharpie, a small international racing dinghy. The river Alde demanded a good deal of skill from its sailors: Margery was very distressed by the drowning of three non-swimmers whose boat capsized in a squall in 1954.
13 Stephen Spring Rice, letter to Margery Spring Rice, undated (postmarked 20 October 1935).

his own. One was Christopher Ellis, who (according to an obituary in the *Bucks Free Press*),[14] at the age of sixteen, single-handedly sailed his father's yacht through the English Channel without permission; and the other was Anthony Gillingham. From the point of view of a schoolboy, Margery might easily have been an embarrassment to her son and his friends but Stephen seemed not to be worried by her eccentricities and Anthony positively loved them.

Anthony, two years older than Stephen, the son of an Anglican priest, was already something of a rebel when Stephen arrived. Under the influence of his godfather, Dick Sheppard, he was turning to pacifism but was finding that difficulties were put in his way when he tried to resign from the Officers' Training Corps.

> Then I met Margery Spring Rice, mother of my friend Stephen. She was short and round like Mrs Tiggywinkle, but certainly no domestic drudge. She came down to Eton in a battered old Riley amid the Rolls and Bentleys, in an old overcoat done up with string as a belt [...] In my first meeting with her at Eton she said in a very loud voice 'I hear you are trying to resign from the OTC. Congratulations: I hope you succeed.' I loved her from that moment; she was my first adult ally [...] But her support did me little good at Eton. They thought her a wicked woman because of her advocacy of birth control, and because she was trying to divorce her husband, an Old Etonian and brother[15] of the writer of 'I vow to thee my country' and who had turned Catholic in order to thwart the divorce.[16] The MIC [Master in College] even wrote to my father, warning of her influence over me, with dark hints of subversion, atheism and sexual perversion. She threatened to sue him, but as it was only a private letter and not published she was dissuaded by her lawyers: a pity, for it could have made a great *cause celebre*. [Friendships between boys in different year groups were frowned upon, but] of course, the only effect of such a threat was to make my friendship with Stephen more intense. It was now spiked with danger and romance. We had to arrange secret meetings in the churchyard or in cafes down town. It created a love between us which, however, remained entirely platonic. I went to stay with him and his mother every holidays where we indulged in sailing, boat maintenance and singing. He taught me sailing. I crewed for him in the schoolboy championships at Burnham, where he won two out of

---

14   *Bucks Free Press*, 28 February 1998, [n.p.].
15   In fact, Dominick was the nephew of Sir Cecil Spring Rice.
16   This is probably not true, though it may have been a threat used by Dominick as a weapon.

three races [...] Margy Spring-Rice put the fire back in my belly and I fought the good fight against the OTC with renewed vigour.[17]

Cecil struggled more than Stephen in her childhood. Although as a child she thought she hated Dominick, the better side of his character does come out in an incident that she later recounted to her own children. It was her birthday, and Dominick took Stephen and her out but said nothing to indicate that he remembered what day it was. They walked past a shop and Dominick, remarking that he thought they might be hungry, went in and emerged with a box or tin of biscuits that he gave to Cecil to open. When she did so, she found that in between the biscuits, all the way through, there were sixpences. More commonly, though, Dominick would take the two children out, disappear into a pub and leave Stephen to find their way home. They were largely brought up by their nanny — the diminutive, stern and much-loved Edith Best — who had a serious episode of mental illness in 1928 (probably not helped by the tensions in the household) and was admitted to Hanwell Asylum. Cecil, herself, was seriously ill with whooping cough in 1927 and also suffered from severe hay fever, undergoing various treatments, some of which she found more distressing than the allergy itself. Like Stephen, she was sent away to boarding school quite early. While she loved her preparatory school, St David's at Englefield Green southwest of London, she loathed Wycombe Abbey, where she won a scholarship in 1934. As she remembered it in adulthood, the aspect that most irked her was the lack of privacy. Her anxiety about Dominick was never far from the surface.

For all four children, their grandparents' house in Aldeburgh, Gower House, remained a haven for holidays — with its paradise of a garden, including ponds, an orchard and woodland, as well as a paddock complete with Brenda the horse. When Ronald was about eleven, a play shed was built for the children. Charles and Ronald also spent time with their Jones relations, while Stephen and Cecil had occasional holidays in the Lake District with Dominick's uncle Cecil Spring Rice and his wife Florence, or in Limerick with other Spring Rice relations. Besides these, there were family holidays shared with the Mitchisons at Varengeville

---

17   Anthony Gillingham, *Young Rebel: Memoirs 1917–39* ([n.p.]: privately printed, 2007), p. 50.

in France. But for none of them was it a happy or secure childhood, and the disastrous state of Margery's marriage to Dominick must have been a constant source of anxiety, the impact of which on them Margery was never really prepared to acknowledge.

However, parent-child relationships are frequently complex: when Ronald, in his old age, came to set down his memories, he wrote that Margery 'was unfailingly supportive of her children and their spouses & families, for which I and my siblings were immensely grateful even if our demonstration of this sometimes lacked'.[18]

Through the early thirties, Margery continued to devote time and energy to supporting the North Kensington clinic. She negotiated some difficult issues with the local authority, as well as trying to open as many lines of communication as possible: in 1933, for example, she tried to involve the Kensington Fathers' Councils.[19] As was the case for much of her work for women's health, her belief that fathers mattered too was ahead of its time. One of the obstacles to the work of the clinic was the lack of any contraception element in the curriculum for doctors in training and the lack of interest in providing it by many of those responsible for teaching medical students. After the First World War, doctors were more inclined to accept the use of condoms by patients because of their role in preventing venereal disease,[20] but Margery understood that much more needed to be done to educate the medical profession, and one initiative of North Kensington was to set up conferences for doctors.[21] Another pioneer, Dr William Nixon, teaching at St Mary's in 1934–1935, wrote to Helena Wright asking if he could bring some of his students to the North Kensington clinic for some training, but when he did so, he felt it necessary to arrive under cover of darkness! It was not until 1936 that the first lectures on contraception were given in medical school,[22] and even after the war when Nixon established a family planning clinic at University College

---

18   Ronald Garrett Jones, Memoirs, 1995.
19   The first Fathers' Council had been set up in Kensington by James Fenton, medical officer of health, in 1921, in the belief that fathers as well as mothers should be involved in decisions about children.
20   Jane Lewis, 'The Ideology and Politics of Birth Control in Inter-war England', *Women's Studies International Quarterly*, 2 (1979), 33–48 (p. 33), https://doi.org/10.1016/s0148-0685(79)93008-2
21   Wood and Suitters, *The Fight for Acceptance*, p. 169.
22   Leathard, *The Fight for Family Planning*, pp. 57, 98.

Hospital, it was known by the euphemism 'the clinic in the Records department', and was unique among the London hospitals. Nixon wanted his students to attend, but the medical school's ruling council would only agree on the basis that the clinic took place on a Wednesday afternoon, which was traditionally the students' free time for sports. In 1966, things had barely changed: Nixon reported that his students were clamouring for education in contraception, but that he was fighting against uninterested or sometimes antagonistic colleagues.[23]

In 1933, a group of eleven voluntary bodies set up the Women's Health Enquiry Committee to investigate the health of married working-class women: Margery was the representative of the North Kensington clinic, and wrote *Working-Class Wives*, the report that was the outcome of their study.[24] The committee's findings were based on a survey of 1,250 responses to a questionnaire — this had two parts, the first, factual, the second, designed to elicit women's own feelings and perceptions of their lives, and in particular of their health. Although the committee had hoped to use control samples of unmarried women and those of a higher social class, too few replies were received from these groups to make this worth-while. The administration of the questionnaires was carried out mainly by health visitors, who were often familiar to the respondents, which helped to encourage the addition of supplementary information. There was no suggestion that the sample was chosen in any scientific way, but the final publication, which includes many quotations from the women's responses, gives a vivid and moving picture of some very bleak lives. Many of the women in the sample displayed cheerfulness and fortitude in appalling circumstances, and were upbeat about their health, in spite of the fact that 'For many of them, good health is any interval between illnesses, or at best the absence of any incapacitating ailment'.[25]

Under the Health Insurance Act of 1911, manual workers — and those earning less than £160 per annum — paid contributions that gave

---

23 Nixon was ahead of his time in many ways: he was, for example, 'an early advocate of the doctrine that women should govern the destinies of their own bodies'. Geoffrey Chamberlain, *Special Delivery: The Life of the Celebrated British Obstetrician William Nixon* (London: Royal College of Obstetricians and Gynaecologists, 2004), pp. ix, 55. See also Wellcome Collection SA/FPA/SR5.

24 Margery Spring Rice, *Working-Class Wives: Their Health and Conditions* (Harmondsworth: Pelican, 1939; repr. London: Virago, 1981).

25 Ibid., p. 72.

them access to unemployment and sickness benefits, and to the services of 'panel' doctors. Although this did not extend to their dependents, there was a maternity grant. Between the wars, legislation was gradually introduced to give local authorities more responsibility for maternal and child health and welfare, but it was discretionary rather than mandatory, and contraceptive advice was minimal. As Margery's daughter wrote in the introduction to the 1981 reprint of *Working-Class Wives*:

> It would seem [...] that when respondents in this book quote a doctor or nurse as advising less child-bearing, for at least three-quarters of them — if they heeded the advice at all — what was on offer was abstinence or coitus interruptus, either of which demanded maximum co-operation on the part of husbands.[26]

Time and again it came up in the completed questionnaires that women were being given advice about health that they were either unable or unwilling to follow. They tended to be extremely mistrustful of hospitals, which were in any case often too far away for them to get to; they frequently did not have the money, the skills or the cooking facilities to eat a better diet; the 'rest' that doctors often suggested was an impossible dream. Sometimes the advice was not advice at all — one woman with severe backache was told by a doctor '"all women get backache round about 40, so why worry"'.[27]

The impact of *Working-Class Wives* is due, on one hand, to the mass of anecdotal evidence it includes (the picture that women paint in their own words of the details of their lives) and, on the other, to Margery's larger vision. She understood that, alongside relieving poverty and ignorance, much more could be done:

> so to lighten [these women's] work that they would have time [...] to make contacts with the outer world, and to enjoy some at least of the cultural and recreative pursuits which would release them spiritually as well as physically from their present slavery.[28]

The survey demonstrated that the start of a woman's ill-health often coincided with the birth of her first child, because perinatal care was not good enough, and that the degree of ill-health often correlated with the

---

26   Ibid., p. xi.
27   Ibid., p. 45.
28   Ibid., p. 106.

number of pregnancies (including miscarriages, stillbirths and perinatal deaths), because women became worn out with constant child-bearing and -rearing.[29] The experience of working on the book reinforced Margery's view of the importance of contraceptive and childcare advice, preferably given in local, multi-functional clinics staffed by women:

> parents should be in a position to *decide* how many children they can have. That such knowledge should not be available to women in the circumstances of the 1,250 under review is a serious indictment of the care given by the State to the mothers and children of the present generation.[30]

The unequivocal message of the book was that the problems endured by the women in the survey were due, above all, to poverty and were not of their own making.

***

In 1936 (the same year in which Wallis Simpson incurred opprobrium for divorcing in order to marry the king), Margery and Dominick were divorced because he wanted to remarry.[31] The year before, on 30 June, Stephen had written to Cecil from Eton with some glee:

> He's taken a flat with Peggy Ritchie! The rest is left to the imagination.......!
> He's done it quite openly, so that Margee should hear of it. She has, and two days ago filed a divorce petition, which is exactly what Father wants. If Margee doesn't withdraw her petition, (she may have to, because I think the court knows about Dick etc. in which case her petition would not be valid) the decree nisi (a sort of provisional divorce for 6 months) will be given in November and the decree absolute in May. Father told me all this quite proudly yesterday; there are other complications, but I'll leave Margee the fun of telling you these; I've had my go.

---

29 Ibid., p. 49.
30 Ibid., p. 56.
31 It is possible that Dominick's mother Julia disapproved of his separation from Margery or of his new relationship: we know very little about how he got on with her, but she was a formidable woman, and may have cast quite a long shadow. When she remarried in 1935 and returned to Ireland, where her family came from, the dynamic between her and Dominick may have changed, possibly allowing him to feel freer to divorce and remarry. Julia's religious views are unknown, but her own mother came from a Catholic family. One of her ten siblings was baptised in the Church of Ireland. Julia died on 9 May 1936, between the decree nisi and the decree absolute.

Douglas recorded that at the divorce hearing:

> M. made the most wonderful witness — Ernest Bird, her solicitor, told me in court that he had never seen a better witness in his whole experience — in spite of having a difficult and painful story to tell [...] [The judge said] that he had seldom had a witness before him whose complete candour and honesty carried such conviction to his mind, and he had no hesitation in granting the decree.[32]

Divorce at that date was far more unusual than it is today and carried much more of a social stigma. Until the Matrimonial Causes Act of 1923, proof of adultery or violence was required, and, in the case of adultery, only a husband could petition. Even after that Act, which allowed a wife to petition, there was a heavy burden of proof. It was not until 1937, the year after Margery's divorce, that a broader range of grounds (including drunkenness) was allowed. The big change in numbers came at the end of World War II: in 1936, there were just over 5,000 divorces compared to 60,000 in 1947.[33]

On 12 March, the day after the divorce was granted, Clara Garrett (Margery's widowed mother) died in Aldeburgh, aged eighty-nine. Margery had been with her earlier but had had to go back to London because of the court case; Douglas's wife, Frieda, and Clara's youngest son, Geoffrey, were present. The last time Douglas saw her, she had told him that she had been for a walk in the garden but when she had gone only a few steps, her heart—

> 'began to jump about and give [me] pain [...] So I stopped, and I said to my heart "Now then, I have had no exercise yet, and I need exercise. Get on, damn you, get on!" And it went on.'[34]

According to Anthony Gillingham, Clara 'was a tough old atheist. On her death-bed she was asked if she wanted a priest: "Priest be damned" she said, "Give me a cigarette" and died quite serenely half an hour later'.[35]

---

32   Douglas Garrett, Diary, Vol. 2, p. 46.

33   The high 1947 rate reflects the fact that many wartime marriages ended when couples were reunited. The rate dropped again after that (to about 23,000 in 1958), and then rose sharply.

34   Douglas Garrett, Diary, 2, p. 43.

35   Gillingham, *Young Rebel*, p. 50. I have not seen any other evidence that Clara smoked.

Dominick's new wife was a doctor, Margaret Ritchie, known as Peggy, who came from an Indian army family and was a descendent of William Thackeray. Her medical partner, Eric Strauss, probably moved in the Mitchison circle, and this may have been how they met (Margery and Strauss had been in contact over Ena Mitrany). Peggy was a supportive step-mother to Stephen and Cecil. Stephen particularly spent a good deal of time with Peggy, playing chamber music and singing. In 1940, Dominick died of heart failure and nephritis. On his death certificate, his age is given as fifty-one even though he was, in fact, forty-nine. Of course, he cannot be held responsible for the mistake, but it seems entirely characteristic of him to have continued beyond the grave to lie about his age. In 1957, Peggy married Hugh Meredith, an academic economist known to his friends as 'Hom', who also moved in the Mitchison circle. In an ironic twist, there is a faint suggestion that there had once been a tendresse, if nothing more, between Hom and Margery.

Another sad loss had occurred a couple of years before Clara's: early in 1934, Margery received a letter from Stella Benson's husband, Shaemus Anderson, from China, giving her the news of Stella's untimely death at the age of forty-one.[36] Although Margery had not seen much of Stella, on account of her living in China much of the time, and although Stella was quite critical of Margery, Margery certainly regarded her as a close friend. Shaemus wrote:

> I was with her for a day and a night before she died [...] I think she died in her sleep. She suffered of course, but not more than she often did with a bronchial chill. The day before she died she promised me most resolutely not to die. And she all but came through. It was her heart that failed. You never saw such courage. I wish I had a little of it.[37]

Since 1932 or earlier, Margery had been thinking about leaving London to return to Suffolk and had been looking fruitlessly for a suitable house. The opportunity came in 1936, just after her divorce and Clara's death, an appropriate moment in that Gower House would no longer be available to her as it had been previously.

---

36 Muz also died in 1936, a few months after Clara.
37 Shaemus Anderson, letter to Margery Spring Rice, 23 January 1934.

7. War Again (1936–1945)

1936 was a turning point in Margery's life. For about four years, she had been looking for a place in Suffolk, but nothing had been quite right. In the year that saw her divorce, her mother's death and the consequent sale of Gower House, she wanted more than ever to leave London and return to her beloved county. A farmhouse (which she had had her eye on since 1932) in the tiny village of Iken, on the river Alde just below Snape — the site of the maltings built by her grandfather Newson Garrett — was at last available to rent from a local landowner, Bernard Greenwell. It was exactly what she wanted. She would never own it, but she was to live there for twenty years, and it became the place where her great gift for friendship and hospitality flowered. Douglas was to describe it in his diary as 'a menagerie of friends & foreigners' — an apt description if you ignore the slightly xenophobic tone. She welcomed people of all ages, nationalities and walks of life. Friends came back again and again. Sometimes they came and stayed; those who came as strangers often left as friends. Margery offered sanctuary to a large range of people in all sorts of circumstances, and if she could be autocratic, she was also immensely generous. Stephen's friend, Anthony Gillingham, borrowing the house once with his family in the 1950s when Margery herself was away, described her in the visitors' book as 'a generous and loving despot'. Yet at the same time she was capable of giving her guests, especially young people, enormous freedom.

Margery did not sell the house in St Peter's Square which continued to be let or lent to friends (often refugees from Germany or Austria). One of these was a young Berliner, Leni Nörpel, daughter of a trade union official, who came to study dressmaking in London, and remained a close friend even though she returned to Germany; later, she became a much-loved and wonderfully glamorous visitor for Margery's grandchildren. In about 1930, Margery had taken Charles and Ronald on holiday to

    https://doi.org/10.11647/OBP.0215.07

Fig. 14. Iken Hall, c. 1918. Photograph from the Sudbourne Estate sale brochure.
Courtesy of Ben Johnston.

the Salzkammergut, where they had stayed in a baronial pile owned by Willy and Myra Gutmann. Here, they met Myra's sister Bettina Bauer, a children's book author and illustrator, who married the sculptor Georg Ehrlich that year. They also met the violinist Fritz Rothschild (no relation of the banking family) and his wife Tilde, for whose quartet Margery acted as London agent for a period. The Ehrlichs and the Rothschilds[1] were Jewish and, after the Anschluss, Margery was able to offer them sanctuary while they established themselves in Britain. The friendship between Tilde and Margery lasted until Margery's death.

Another person to whom she offered help was Anya Zisserman, born in Harbin in China in 1923 to an Austrian Jewish mother and a German father who had been a landowner in Russia. Her parents had escaped

---

1   Always referred to by Margery as 'the Rothschildren'. Fritz was not a very good violinist, but as a pioneer of authentic performance, he is unjustly neglected. The quartet was also innovatory in initiating the practice of making recordings with one part missing, so that amateur players could play along with them.

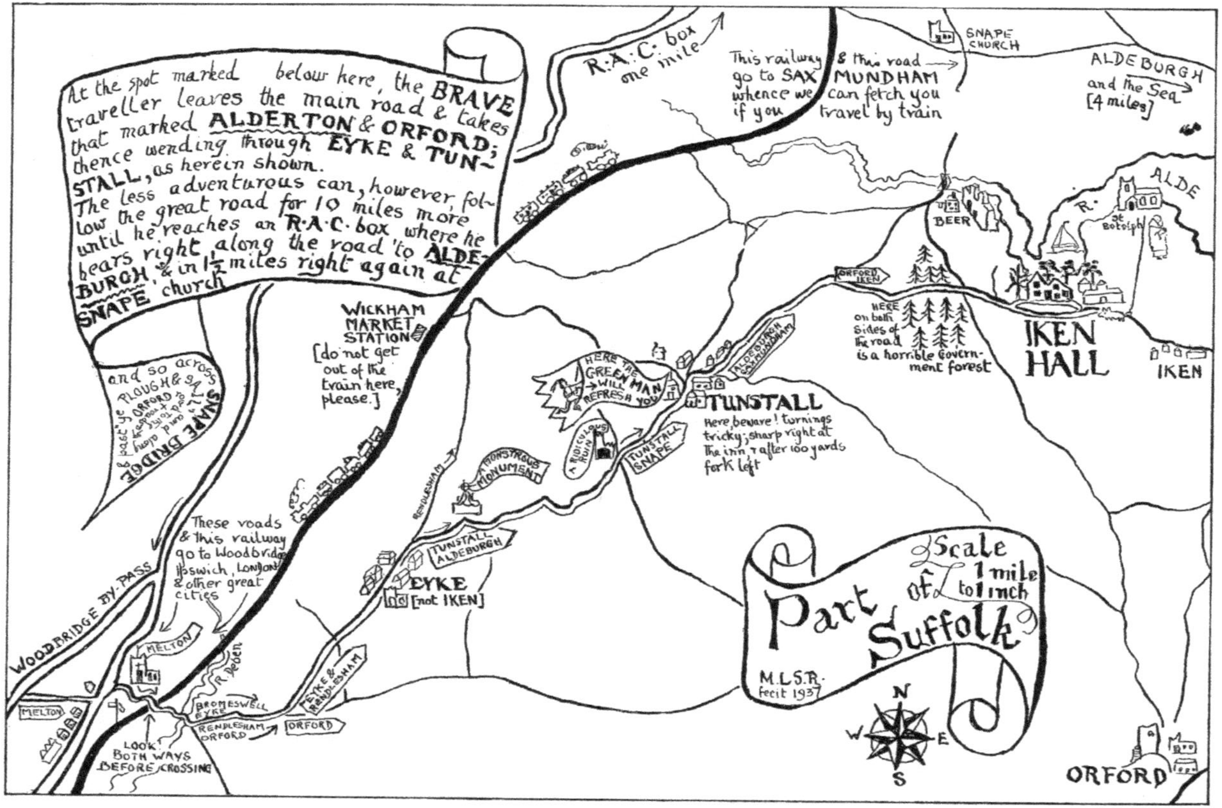

Fig. 15. Margery's map for visitors to Iken, 1937. Photograph: the author (2020).

to China at the time of the Russian Revolution, but in 1936, Anya and her mother returned to Vienna. In the following year, Margery, a friend of a friend, escorted the teenage Anya from Vienna by train to Britain to spend a few weeks learning English. It was quite a journey, as the beautiful teenager attracted plenty of attention, including a proposal of marriage from an Egyptian fellow-passenger. Anya spent time with Cecil and Stephen, with whom she got on particularly well, both in St Peter's Square and at Iken. In 1938, after the Anschluss, Margery sponsored Anya so that she could come to England permanently, later welcoming her mother as well. Anya's first impressions of Margery were that she was an extraordinary mixture of upper class, Cambridge-educated Fabian who was 'frightfully wah wah wah' and yet 'talked all the time about equality and labour': 'she was absolutely weird, I had never seen anything like it [...] She had had a very chequered sexual career [...] and she had lots of what she called "luvaahs"!'[2] New to English society, Anya could not at first fathom its oddities: when she went to the cinema with Stephen and some of his Eton friends, the audience stood up to leave at the end, but when *God Save the King* was played, to her amazement all the boys promptly sat down again and started laughing. Anya's mother and Margery did not get on well, but Anya herself became a friend for life of Margery and her children.[3]

Now settled at Iken, Margery and her family and friends took to Suffolk life with gusto. On one occasion, when Anthony and Stephen sailed down the river Alde in a Whitewing,[4] they went aground on a shingle bank as they left the river mouth. Stephen told Anthony to jump out to refloat the boat, which happened so quickly that Anthony only just managed to grab on to the stern while he was towed into deeper water. Luckily, Margery had insisted he take a change of clothes. They anchored in the mouth of the river Stour and slept under the stars; as they sailed back up the Alde the following day, the wind dropped, and they arrived home in the small hours. Anthony expected Margery to be

---

2   Anya Berger, unpublished memoir.

3   Anya's family (she had four brothers) were separated for many years, with her father in China and her mother in Vienna, but the parents were eventually reunited in Britain. After Anya's marriage to Stephen Bostock (which produced two children) broke up she lived for many years with the artist Peter de Francia, and subsequently with John Berger, with whom she had two more children. Anya was a gifted linguist and translator.

4   A class of 23′ sloops based on the river Alde/Ore.

frantic with worry and full of recriminations, but she simply welcomed them with hot soup and an enquiry as to whether they had enjoyed themselves. Perhaps Stephen's easy nature, in contrast to Charles's more anxious one, helped to make such freedom possible.

Margery's son Ronald described Iken Hall[5] as 'a slightly self-important 1850ish 3 storey block, built onto the west side of a much earlier, lower house. It was comfortable, if hard to keep warm when cold east winds blew'.[6] It was large — seven bedrooms, a huge double reception room and much else. There were two staircases as well as a box room, cellar, attics and passages, making a three-dimensional jigsaw of a place that later gave great delight to the grandchildren. Water was pumped from a well, and until 1950, there was no mains electricity: the house was lit by oil lamps. The location was stunning,[7] with common land covered in bracken sloping gently down north of the house to what is known as Iken Cliff (although it can hardly be said to deserve the name, being less than ten metres high at its highest point). A row of ancient oaks grew along the cliff top. The beach — sandy at high tide, when it was lovely for swimming, and muddy at low tide — was at that time almost private, except to those arriving by boat. There was a seventy-five-foot long wooden jetty extending from the beach into the river.

The Alde estuary, which is tidal from its mouth to Snape (the highest navigable point), widens out at Iken and then narrows again where a spur juts out into it. The medieval church of St Botolph stands as a landmark on this spur, with its Victorian old rectory beside it. Part of the wider area of the river, known as 'the lagoon', was a field that had been permanently flooded — the boundary walls still visible at low tide.

Iken Hall had an extensive garden with lovely mature trees (mainly beech and pine) and a range of outbuildings, including a large boat shed where Stephen could indulge his pleasure in building and repairing dinghies. Margery took to gardening with enthusiasm, following in Clara's footsteps and with the help of Ronald's horticultural expertise. They planted hundreds of daffodils round the lawn on the south side

---

5 'Hall' is a title given to many substantial but not grand East Anglian houses.
6 Ronald Garrett Jones, Memoirs, 1995. The house Margery lived in no longer stands: it was burnt to the ground (possibly in the late 1950s or early 1960s, though there are differing accounts, but certainly after Margery had left).
7 One of the few disadvantages of its situation so close to the river was the prevalence of mosquitoes.

of the house, which multiplied over the years to make a wonderful display in spring. They also created a fruit cage on the river side of the house, and in 1938 or 1939, with a view to self-sufficiency, broke up an area of waste ground — sheltered on three sides by outbuildings, farm buildings and a high wall — to make a vegetable garden. The only thing that disturbed the peace, from the early 1950s, was the roar of United States Air Force jet-engined aircraft, based at Bentwaters airfield nearby, practising low flying over the river.

For many years from about 1948, those who arrived at Margery's front door were greeted by a painted ship's figurehead, made of wood, whom Margery named Annabel Slyboots Lee. The *Slyboots*, a sailing vessel of about 100 tons, had been washed ashore in Slaughden, at the southern end of the town of Aldeburgh, in about 1903. She had run aground on the Shipwash sands, and after her crew had been taken off, a gale drove the wreck on to the beach, where she broke up and was pillaged. Some remains were sold off at auction, including her figurehead, which was bought by a cousin by marriage of Margery's. At an auction after this cousin's death, Margery bought Annabel Slyboots Lee, had her repainted in bright colours (she had been painted grey to imitate stone) and set her up on the Iken Hall doorstep.[8]

In the spring of 1937, Margery was struck down with scarlet fever and had to go into Ipswich isolation hospital. Her live-in domestic help at the time was a woman with a young daughter. Ronald, who was staying in the house, remembered the difficulty of being left alone to get the child to bed, but history does not relate why this task fell to him. Perhaps the mother was also ill. However, this was only a blip: leaving London did not mean that Margery lessened her range of activities in any way. She remained active on the committee of the North Kensington clinic, writing articles and giving speeches.[9] By early 1939, her book *Working-Class Wives* (with a statistical element contributed by Cecil), which amply demonstrates how broad her concern was for the health and well-being

---

8   She was repainted in 1952 by Anya Zisserman's then partner Peter de Francia. Margery eventually gave the figurehead to her GP Dr John Stevens and his wife: she is still cherished in that family, but has moved indoors.

9   In 1941, Margery's daughter described hearing a lecture of hers to the National Union of Students on '"Sex education" not, as she endeavoured unsuccessfully to make the audience believe, to be confused with "sex"'. Cecil Spring Rice, letter to Stephen Spring Rice, 3 May 1941.

Fig. 16. Annabel Slyboots Lee. Photograph: the author (2016).

of young families in poverty, was ready for publication. She was always prepared to stand up for the importance of attending to the needs of deprived families, even when many people were putting the emphasis elsewhere. When the war came, with her pacifist tendencies still strong, she was determined that the work of the clinic did not deserve to suffer. In an article in the *Eugenics Review*[10] in 1940, she wrote:

> I can imagine no more evil a confusion of thought than to see in the problematical victim of an air raid a patient more worth treating than the present victim of tuberculosis or an underfed pregnant woman. One of the most dangerous and insidious effects of war is that the effort

---

10 Many of those involved in the birth control movement were members of the British Eugenics Society between the wars. Eugenics was academically respectable, with doctors, scientists, writers and politicians among the members of the Society, and the subject did not have the bad connotations that it inevitably and justly acquired after its association with the Nazis; it was seen as being positive rather than negative. Even before World War II, however, there was a division between those who accepted the influence of environment on a person's physical and mental state, and were therefore open to the potential benefits of welfare programmes, and those who did not. But, of course, the fundamental objection to the idea of eugenics is that it allows someone other than the potential parents to decide who is 'fit' to reproduce.

needed for its immediate prosecution is allowed to destroy what is most worth saving.[11]

In the late 1930s, and through World War II, there was concern about the falling population, leading to a Royal Commission on Population appointed in 1944, which carried out a sample family 'census' in January 1946. Birth control campaigners worried that this would have a negative impact on the clinic's work, but Margery had always taken a broad view of what its remit should be, emphasising that it should help women to have wanted children as well as allowing them not to have unwanted ones. In a letter of 12 December 1938 to the Kensington Medical Officer of Health, she had written that she was 'an unrepentant believer in voluntary parenthood'. The best thing a married couple could do was to bring up 'as large a family as their health and resources allow'.

Much more controversial was the question of contraceptive advice to unmarried women. Margery, along with some of her colleagues (medical and non-medical), took a liberal view on this but had to tread carefully at a time when sexual activity outside marriage was widely frowned upon. In today's more liberal atmosphere, at least in the UK, it is hard to remember that contraception itself was something of a taboo subject, let alone advice to the unmarried. Even in 1964, Elizabeth Draper[12] was writing in *The Times* about the embarrassment and uncertainty still surrounding the subject. Pointing out that ignorance was widespread, and that those who sought advice often did so furtively, she urged the need for change in the medical profession, the churches, schools and universities. But only in 1967 did the Family Planning Association allow its clinics to give advice to the unmarried, and only in 1970 was the policy rolled out nationally. In the 1920s and 1930s, the situation was much worse. In 1938, Dr Joan Malleson[13]—who was in charge of the treatment of sexual difficulties at North Kensington for many years — referred a 14-year-old, pregnant after being raped by five off-duty British soldiers,

---

11   Margery Spring Rice, 'The Health of Working Women', p. 53.
12   Elizabeth Draper, 'Birth Control in the Modern World', *The Times* (26 February 1964). See also Draper, *Birth Control in the Modern World*.
13   Malleson and Helena Wright have been described as '[making] birth control both respectable and available': Evans, *Freedom to Choose*, p. 145. In 1950, Malleson was appointed head of the contraceptive clinic at University College Hospital in London, the first such unit in a British teaching hospital. Her own marriage to the actor Miles Malleson had been unconventional.

to gynaecologist Aleck Bourne. He performed an abortion and then informed the police what he had done, in order to get clarification of the law: his subsequent trial and acquittal set an important precedent for such cases.

The innovative medical officer of health in Kensington, Dr James Fenton, had close ties with the clinic and may have been privately more sympathetic to Margery's view than he was able to be in public. When invited to become a member of the clinic's committee in 1936, he tentatively refused, stating in a letter to Margery that he thought it 'unwise' for someone in his position 'to be actively associated with the [birth control] movement to the extent of being a member of your council'.[14] Fenton felt that neither he nor the clinic could afford to antagonise members of the public, when the Council made a grant to the clinic 'derived from contributions to the rates made by people with all shades of opinion'.[15] In 1933, a disagreement had apparently arisen over the clinic's Prospectus. The Prospectus itself does not survive, but Margery, as chair of the committee, wrote to Fenton:

> I am asked to tell you [...] that we fully understand your point with regard to the paragraph about unmarried women in our Prospectus. The committee wishes to point out that this paragraph is meant to apply only to teaching young women the principles of the care of their health, particularly with a view to their future task of bearing healthy children. I venture to think that if the prospectus is carefully read and if the context and wording of this specific paragraph are taken into account, it would not be possible for anyone to think of it as applying to Birth Control.[16]

In 1938, the question of advice to the unmarried came up again. On 25 November, Fenton wrote a letter to Margery that was intended to be a record of a conversation that they had had earlier in the day:

> I asked whether you were giving any birth control advice to single women. You said it was against your usual practice but that it did happen occasionally when young women were on the verge of marriage and as a rule their mothers came with them. You were pretty clear in your own mind that these were the only cases but you undertook to look into it.

14　Wellcome Collection, SA/FPA/NK87, James Fenton, letter to Margery Spring Rice, 8 April 1936.
15　Ibid., James Fenton, letter to Margery Spring Rice, 25 November 1938.
16　Ibid., James Fenton, letter to Margery Spring Rice, 8 May 1933.

> I asked if you would be good enough to consider whether you would
> give me an undertaking that you would discontinue entirely the practice
> of giving birth control advice to single women or whether you felt
> compelled to continue it. You offered to look into the cases carefully and
> let me have a report in due course.[17]

Two or three weeks later, Margery reported back: all the unmarried
women who had been seen in the clinic had subsequently married.
She also mentioned that no woman with an income of more than £5
per week was accepted as a patient — such women were referred to
private doctors: income may seem to have nothing to do with morality,
but there is an implication that perhaps better-off unmarried women
might be more inclined to try to get access to contraception. The
unmarried women who were accepted as patients, Margery continued,
are 'the type of young woman who has made up her mind that she
does not want to have a child in the first year or two of marriage', but
official policy was to dissuade them from this. For herself, she wrote 'I
[...] firmly believe that the power of deciding the number and the times
of [children's] birth is a direct and powerful stimulus to parenthood'.[18]
The words she used to Fenton were carefully chosen to reassure him
of the clinic's compliance: they do not necessarily express the whole
truth of her own views.

Fenton's uneasiness about who was treated by the clinic continued.
Reporting in 1939 on a meeting between his staff and the clinic staff, he
was anxious to make sure that the clinic's patients were the 'lowest strata
of North Kensington women, that is the very debilitated ones with large
families' rather than the 'better type of working class young women'.
He remained concerned about the possible reputational damage of
advice being given to the unmarried, although the outbreak of war was
to change his perspective to some extent. In 1940, when there was some
unease about the falling birth rate, he was writing that he understood
that in wartime the country needed more births.[19] To her credit, Margery,
who tended to be outspoken and was not over-endowed with tact,
managed mostly to keep her temper, though sometimes her irritation

---

17   Ibid., James Fenton, letter to Margery Spring Rice, 25 November 1938.
18   Ibid., Margery Spring Rice, letter to James Fenton, 12 December 1938.
19   Ibid., report of meeting between James Fenton's staff and clinic staff; and James
     Fenton, letter to Margery Spring Rice, 6 March 1940.

shows. Around this time, when there was an influx of Czech refugees asking for advice, Margery wrote to the superintendent of the clinic, Stella Wylson: 'I am sure that even our most squeamish subscribers and Borough Councils do not want to flood the country with illegitimate English-born children who will be a burden on their rates!'[20] The sarcasm was surely intended, but one cannot avoid the feeling that there is an element of xenophobia in Margery too.

In April 1940, she told Fenton that the clinic had decided to give advice to single women who were about to be married 'as we believe that a young married couple may have excellent reasons for wishing to postpone for a year or two the birth of their first child'. To be eligible, they had to have an income of less than £3 per week. She also pointed out the obvious — that they could not prove that a woman was about to be married, nor could they prove that someone was already married, except by asking them to show a marriage certificate which was not North Kensington practice (although it was the case in some clinics). She recognised that young women with husbands serving in the forces might well wish to take up work outside the home, and she raised the spectre of abortion:

> We all agree with you that the country was never in greater need of more babies [...] you are aware that I, for one, believe in large families[, but a woman without contraceptive knowledge] is often driven to a desperate and terrible remedy which may permanently impair her efficiency as a mother.[21]

In the pre-war period, she was also offering a safe haven to friends and refugees at Iken as well as in London: on 21 August 1937, Ronald wrote to his aunt Hilda 'Our international colony is flourishing. We have scored so far 2 Austrians, a White Russian and 3 Germans'. From July to December of that year, Roger Gibb's wife, Lorna, and their small daughter, Rachel, were also living with Margery while Roger was away. The 1939 Register records a couple called Josef and Emma Crusser living at Iken; he is described as 'Refugee seeking work (sheet metal worker)' and she as 'house worker'.

---

20   Ibid., Margery Spring Rice, letter to Stella Wylson, 27 February [1940].
21   Ibid., Margery Spring Rice, letter to James Fenton, 26 April 1940.

Fig. 17. Margery, her children and her two eldest grandchildren, Iken, c. 1939. Left
to right: Margery, Cecil, Maurice, Charles, Susan, Stephen, Ronald, Paula.
Photograph: family archives (c. 1939).

In the autumn of 1939, just as war was declared, both the Spring Rice
children went up to Cambridge to study maths — Stephen to King's
College and Cecil to Girton. Ronald, who tended towards pacifism,
was in the event able to stay in civilian jobs throughout the war (since
agriculture was a reserved occupation) but, at this time, he was
struggling to find work. He had become involved with a pharmacist
called Mary Jacoby, a relationship which caused both Margery and his
Jones aunts serious concerns: they did not think Ronald was happy,
and Margery and Mary clearly disliked each other from the start. Gil[22]
tried to be tactful, writing to Margery that there was nothing to be done
'except to avoid making it more acute by arousing Ronald's opposition
& chivalry as her protector against a wicked world of relations',[23] but
such tact did not come naturally to Margery, and although she seems to

---

22 The coolness between Margery and her Jones in-laws had reverted to its old
     friendliness.
23 Lilian Jones, letter to Margery Spring Rice, 4 December 1938.

have tried, she was only intermittently successful. On 6 April 1938, after
a visit to Iken, Mary had written:

> I should have written to you before, but the attitude you took towards
> me — of which, I think, you were quite well aware — makes it
> extraordinarily difficult to know what to say to you.

On 26 September 1939, Hilda wrote to Margery, thanking her for having
her to stay (and promising to send strawberry runners — they shared
their love of gardening):

> I enjoyed every minute of it except the deplorable Mary who I have
> awful quakes about. I much admired the way you were dealing with the
> situation & I hope your tact & forbearance will be rewarded by her failing
> to hook Ronald — it would be a disaster.

Ronald had been looking for a way out, since he had fallen in love with
someone else,[24] but Mary was pregnant and had put pressure on him to
marry her (in Margery's view she had deliberately allowed herself to
become pregnant for that purpose, but there is no evidence that this was
the case). The marriage took place in Sutton Coldfield in October, with
Margery and Mary's father Henry as witnesses. In November, Ronald's
aunt Petica saw them both in Cambridge:

> I feel utterly miserable about it as I think that poor Ronald is terribly
> unhappy & I cannot see that there is any chance of his life with Mary
> J being anything but a failure [...] she has an injured tragedy queen
> attitude I think towards him & he is clearly exasperated by anything she
> says & does [...] Naturally M. J. was showing off for my benefit though
> there was one moment when I felt her to be utterly genuine when she
> admired my foxfur in a <u>longing</u> way which made me feel she had always
> been <u>starved</u> of all the things she wanted & that really clothes & a good
> time were what she was pining for poor girl![25]

It may well have been a totally unsuitable match, but one can only feel
sorry for this poor young woman with such a weight of opposition
against her.

---

24 In a twist that sounds more like a novel than real life, his new love was Mary Hope
    Rokeling, daughter of Dick Mitchison's lover Tish.

25 Petica Robertson, letter to Margery Spring Rice, November 1939. Mary came from a
    professional background: her father was an electrical engineer.

The crisis came in November 1939, as tragic as it was unexpected. Margery wrote to Douglas on the eleventh asking him, in effect, if she could buy Mary off. Margery's anger and distress jump off the page:

> I would also ask you to remember that none of my sons has had the benefit of the shadow of a father. My devotion to them and theirs to me, I am convinced of. But till someone has tried to do the work of both father and mother to a family of four children, they have not the ghost of an idea of the difficulties and dangers.

Douglas, as always, tried to calm her down, and proposed that once Mary had paid a planned visit to Iken he should talk to Ronald and draw up a deed of separation. He stressed that Margery must not, on any account, offer Mary money. Mary came to Iken on 17 November for a few days as arranged; on 22 November, she stayed in bed until late afternoon before she, Margery and Lorna went to the cinema in the nearby town of Leiston. When they arrived home, around ten o'clock in the evening, Margery and Mary went for a walk down by the river — an odd thing to do on a November night — but according to Margery's written account, Mary had been sleeping badly and Margery thought a stroll in the fresh air would help. It was a fine, dry, moonlit night. At some point, Margery went to check whether her dinghies were securely tied up, suggesting Mary sit on the jetty to wait for her. Reading between the lines, one wonders whether they had had a row and needed to cool off. There is some confusion about the timing of what happened next: Margery registered a splash but 'did not associate it with a person falling in the water'.[26] Hearing a voice, she called Mary but became alarmed when there was no reply. She walked out to the end of the jetty to shine a torch into the water, but could see nothing, so she climbed down and saw something floating down the river. High tide that night was at around 10 pm, so the tide would have been on the turn, which perhaps explains why such an object had not already been carried away out of sight. Margery was a strong swimmer: she jumped into the river, caught what turned out to be Mary, got her head out of the water and dragged her, at first struggling and then limp, on to the beach twenty to thirty yards downstream of the jetty.

---

26 Margery had been completely deaf in one ear since her youth and found it difficult to identify the direction of sounds.

She tried artificial respiration, of which she had no experience, calling out all the while in the unlikely hope that somebody would hear. Eventually, she returned to the house, where Lorna rang for the doctor, Dr Robin Acheson, who arrived at about 11.15 and confirmed that Mary was dead. In his witness statement to the coroner, Acheson explained that he had seen Mary two days earlier and found she was very anaemic, which could have made her dizzy and caused her to lose her balance when she was standing on the jetty. By the time he arrived, the water at the far end of the jetty was nearly five feet deep (it would have been six at the height of the tide). The jetty, which was licensed by the Board of Trade, was in good condition, though according to the police constable who arrived after Acheson 'the planking whips considerably'. Mary had been wearing shoes with medium heels, and there were no signs of violence on the body. The constable took statements: according to Margery's, Mary was anxious about Ronald's lack of a job, but was otherwise cheerful. She had no financial worries, was looking forward to the baby, and had not threatened suicide; Lorna's statement described Margery and Mary as being on good terms. The constable returned to Iken beach the following day to inspect the jetty by daylight and found a piece of recently broken wood hanging by a nail on the end. The coroner's verdict at the inquest held on 24 November was accidental death from shock and drowning.[27]

In addition to the tragedy of this event, it is an uncomfortable story. The statements are certainly economical with the truth and leave a number of unanswered questions; although it is possible that relations between Mary and Margery had improved over the five days that Mary had been at Iken, was her death simply an awful accident? Was it suicide? Or was Mary trying to give Margery a fright? As there were no witnesses, we will never know. At that time, the coroner would have been unwilling to return a verdict of suicide if he could avoid it, since it was still a crime in UK law. One or two of Margery's friends subsequently joked that maybe Margery had pushed Mary — this demonstrates that her friends viewed her as someone unafraid to act, and unafraid of what people thought of her, but it seems highly unlikely that she would actually have done such a thing. If they really thought it might have

---

27   The coroner's report is in the Suffolk Record Office (EC1/2/17/121, A348/5/2/37).

been the case, they probably would not have joked about it. Perhaps the most uncomfortable element is that, of course, for Ronald, it was undoubtedly a release from an unhappy marriage. However it is looked at, it must have been a traumatic experience for all of those involved. On 25 November, the day after the inquest, Petica, whose house in Bateman Street in Cambridge was like a second home to Stephen and Cecil, wrote to Cecil at Girton:

> Margie rang up at lunchtime as she wanted you & Stephen to know that everything was over & that the Jacobys were there & behaving admirably. She said she was terribly tired but quite all right.

Lorna's entry in the Iken visitors' book a couple of weeks later — 'Five unforgettable months' — is an understatement!

***

Both Stephen and Cecil were restless and unhappy in the autumn of 1939. In Stephen's case, it was because he felt unable to pursue his education when the country was at war, knowing that he had nautical skills that could be of use, not to mention his natural sense of adventure. Before he had been at university for more than a few weeks, he had joined the Royal Naval Volunteer Reserve, and, by the beginning of December, had accepted a convoy job. He soon decided to go into submarines (joking to family and friends that that way he would avoid the seasickness from which he suffered severely); promoted rapidly, he was already training at the navy's submarine school in the autumn of 1940 when he and Cecil attended Dominick's funeral. He served for a few months on the submarine *Ursula*, operating out of Malta and Gibraltar, and then on P615 on exercises in Scotland. From May 1942, he was second in command of P48, a newly-built submarine, first in trials in Scotland where one of his girlfriends recalled a party on the submarine when it was in Holy Loch, and then with the tenth flotilla, based in Malta. Stephen's zest for life made him many friends and the camaraderie of navy life suited him. He enjoyed submarines because there was no room for shirkers — everyone had to pull their weight. At the same time, not surprisingly when he was so young himself, he struggled with the man-management aspect of his job and he did not think highly of P48's captain, though he did not mention this to his immediate family.

At the same time as Stephen was going through the process of joining up, Cecil applied from Cambridge to the Women's Royal Naval Service. Petica, who did not agree with this decision, and who had not had the benefit of a university education herself, wrote to her with admirable restraint:

> I absolutely understand your feelings about not coming back [to Cambridge] to go on, all though [sic] I do actually feel that people should if possible finish their education but it must be a matter for each to decide & if ever there was a person I should trust to know what it was best for herself I think it would be you.[28]

Cecil thought that she had been offered a job in the Women's Royal Naval Service but, for reasons that are unclear, this did not materialise; she later told her children that the authorities had taken the same view as Petica, sending her back to Cambridge to finish her education.

As for Margery, early in the war she became involved, along with any members of the family or friends who happened to be around,[29] in cleaning up and equipping some empty cottages in the village to house women and children evacuated from London because of the prospect of air raids. This scheme did not last long, not only because the expected raids did not happen, but also because the Londoners tended to loathe the isolation and quiet of Iken and could not wait to get back to the city. In August 1940, Margery lost her old friend Eileen Power, who died suddenly aged only fifty-one. In February 1941, an even more awful blow fell, landing particularly heavily on Stephen and Cecil — Petica was killed on fire-watching duties when a bomb exploded in Cambridge. She was in her fifties and left behind her husband, Donald Robertson, and two sons. She had been a pacifist until the outbreak of war in 1939, when she felt there was no alternative but to fight Fascism, so had become an Air Raid Warden. Another warden observed what happened from further down the street: Petica had seen a light from a badly fixed blackout, and was hurrying to deal with it, probably all the faster because she could hear a plane. The aircraft may

---

28   Petica Robertson, letter to Cecil Spring Rice, 19 June 1940.

29   In the 1939 Register (29 September 1939), thirteen people are recorded as staying in the house, including several members of the Gibb family, three (probably) of Margery's children, and three servants (there are three closed records, i.e. redacted names of people under a certain age, who could still be alive, so it is impossible to be exact).

have been over the Midlands but the pilot had evidently been unable to launch his bombs there so, having seen the same light that Petica had seen, decided to launch them over Cambridge to make it easier to get his damaged plane back across the North Sea. Petica went to deal with the bomb that fell near her, but it exploded in her face, killing her instantly. She had been close to both Stephen and Cecil: 'I dote on them both', she had written to Margery during their first term in Cambridge. On the morning after her death, Cecil found a pencilled note in her pigeon hole at Girton that read 'Prof. Robertson rang up to say that Mrs Robertson was killed by a bomb last night instantaneous'. It seems a particularly brutal way of breaking bad news.

After the petering out of her first wartime project, Margery undertook a much bigger and more successful one: under the auspices of the Waifs and Strays Society (later the Church of England Children's Society), she set up a residential nursery for a dozen or so under-fives who were evacuated from London during the Blitz. The reason she gave for doing this is that it justified staying on in such a big house, and that it enabled her to avoid 'maddening little village activities' and gossip (she always liked a broad canvas). She obtained permission for the nursery from the Ministry of Health[30] in the early summer of 1941, but permission was withdrawn after the ministry consulted with the regional military authorities. However, Margery was not to be daunted. According to a report produced by the Women's Voluntary Service (WVS), probably for circulation to WVS branches (which has all the signs of being written by Margery herself, although she speaks of herself in the third person):

> Mrs Spring Rice however returned to the attack, and as a result of various interviews and explanations of the peculiar immunity of that particular tract of country[,] cut off as it is from the sea and from all military objectives[,] she finally got her way in the matter.[31]

---

30 The Ministry of Health delegated the running of the scheme to the Waifs and Strays Society, which selected the children, employed most of the staff, and oversaw the accounts. It was funded by the American Junior Red Cross, together with the WVS and the Ministry. Some funds also came from Canada.

31 Royal Voluntary Service Archive and Heritage Collection, Iken Hall War Nursery Report. Iken may have been comparatively safe, but Aldeburgh a few miles down the river was not: an air raid in December 1942 killed twelve and injured thirty. The Hospital in Aldeburgh High Street was badly hit, but according to Douglas's diary some patients were moved to Gower House close by for safety. Even at Iken, in July 1940 Margery, Miss Best and the children (presumably Charles's children

Fig. 18. Orford and Sudbourne battle area. Ordnance Survey Second World War map, 1940, sheet 87. OS © Crown copyright (1940). Courtesy of Brian Boulton.

She achieved something of a triumph when, in July 1942, most of the village (together with the neighbouring village of Sudbourne) was evacuated to create a battle training area[32] to be used for tank training in preparation for the Normandy landings, and since Iken Hall was right on the edge of the designated area, she managed to persuade the authorities to allow her and her nursery to remain.[33] On 12 October 1942, she wrote to Charles with characteristic chutzpah that she was 'getting the army under control'.

In all, about one hundred and twenty such nurseries were established over the course of the war, although the greatest number functioning at any one time was ninety-eight. Some house-owners simply allowed their properties to be used, taking no part in the running of the nurseries; others actively helped to a greater or lesser extent.[34]

The first Iken children, four pairs of siblings chosen by the society, arrived in October 1941, and over the next two and a half years, a total of fourteen children (mostly under six) spent time at Iken. Margery did the catering and organising herself, with the help of a succession of staff mostly chosen and employed by the Waifs and Strays Society. She was much helped by a young woman called Heather Masterman,[35] who came as a probationer nurse from the beginning of 1941 until August 1942,

---

Susan and Maurice), the only occupants at the time, were sleeping in the cellar to avoid having to move if there were alarms. In October 1944, a doodle-bug hit Snape, luckily without causing any casualties.

32 This was a triangular area of land the borders of which were the Tunstall to Iken road and the river Alde on the north, the river Alde on the east, and a line from just north of Orford back to the Tunstall/Iken/Snape crossroads on the south west. A guard post was set up at the crossroads, preventing access to Sudbourne and Orford. Although the battle training area has been written about, the continued existence of the nursery seems to have been wiped from the record.

33 Two or three other families remained in Iken throughout the war, in the cottages near the river, on the Snape side of Iken Hall. The story in Margery's family was that when the battle area was established, she simply refused to follow orders to move: it seems unlikely that she could have done that — but when, in 2019, the author met an ex-resident of Iken village, her first reaction to the name 'Margery Spring Rice' was 'Oh I remember her, she refused to move when the battle area was formed'.

34 Mildred de M. Rudolf, *Everybody's Children: The Story of the Church of England Children's Society, 1921–48* (London: Oxford University Press, 1950), p. 152.

35 In the late 1920s, Margery had been in contact with Lucy Masterman, widow of the Liberal politician Charles Masterman, first to ask her whether she would be interested in being Parliamentary Secretary for the Women's National Liberal Federation, and subsequently in connection with Masterman and her children renting the cottage in Bledlow Ridge. I have been unable to find out whether Heather was any relation, but it seems quite likely.

and again during the summer vacation in 1943, when she was training at Homerton College, Cambridge. Margery was nothing if not versatile: when she lost her nursery teacher, she was quite prepared to take that role on herself if it was easier to find a cook than a teacher. She also raised funds to support several of the children who were too old to be eligible under the official scheme. The WVS report mentioned above is designed to publicise the needs of the nursery, in terms of both staff and equipment; it was not always easy to find staff who could work happily with Margery and in such an isolated place:

> This is a reserved occupation and should make the strongest appeal to young women who want to combine war work of the greatest importance with a training which will be invaluable to them in later life.

There was a shortage of clothes and toys for the children: 'Magnificent parcels' were received from the Waifs and Strays, from the Women's Voluntary Service and from a working party in the local town of Southwold but there was still a great need for such items as warm pants for the boys, and indoor and outdoor games. Margery had received a consignment of chamber pots (presumably made of enamelled tin) but found them too small so she had the handles sawn off and the bowls converted into 'little washing basins, which have been set into specially constructed tables'. If they were small for chamber pots, they must have been tiny wash basins! Voluntary school took place in the mornings. The children slept in two large bedrooms, with a member of staff always on duty through the night. Visitors were welcome, but were asked to give prior notice, 'so that a cake may be specially baked'. At Christmas that year, seven parents or relatives of nursery children turned up to visit, five of them to stay in the house, with the result that Margery found herself cooking for twenty-four people.

Fig. 19. Margery with her nursery children. Photograph: family archives (c. 1941).

It must be remembered that the nursery was being run in a house where, of course, there was not only no fridge and no washing machine,[36] but all heating was by open fires, cooking was on a solid fuel stove, water was pumped from a well, and there was no electricity so lighting was by oil lamps. The amount of work involved was enormous— the oil lamps alone required frequent cleaning, refilling and wick trimming and replacing. Some of the vegetables were harvested from the garden or the surrounding countryside: one person who was a nursery child remembers nettle soup.

A couple of months after the arrival of the first group of children in the nursery, on 29 December 1941, Margery wrote to Paula that in the period since her own children had been small 'I had learned a great deal more about life, and knew far better than I did [...] what young children need for their own security and stability'. It is undoubtedly true that she gave her nursery charges an immense amount of loving kindness as well as good food, fresh air and stimulation.

Margery was given a petrol allowance for journeys to Ipswich, Saxmundham and Aldeburgh, but in the summer of 1944 (by which

---

36   At this date, only a tiny proportion of households had refrigerators or washing machines.

time the nursery had closed), the authorities caught up with her for a breach of her conditions. She was away in Oxford when (in Cecil's words) 'Temporary Acting Unpaid Detective Inspector Short of the Chelmsford Police turned up' at Iken, having been misinformed that Margery was driving over to see him. Cecil invited him to lunch, and he won the heart of her nine-month old daughter, going away 'swearing that he would do all in his power to let you off lightly'.[37] A report in the *Essex Chronicle* of 6 October 1944 explains all: Margery had been stopped by police at Margaretting, in Essex, on the way to London on 23 May with two women and a child (possibly the last nursery child) as passengers. Summoned before the magistrates, she told them that she had tried to get the three on to a train first at her local station of Wickham Market, and then at Ipswich, without success: 'The stationmaster would not allow the carriage doors to be opened, because the people jammed inside the train would have fallen out'. She was in a dilemma, and decided to make the journey by car. 'The Chairman said the bench realised the predicament the defendant was in, but there had been a breach of the regulations, and the fine would be £2.'

Many of the archives concerning residential war nurseries appear to have been lost. However, one remaining piece of documentary evidence is a letter dated 24 January 1943, from an official of the Ministry of Health to an unknown recipient, in response to a suggestion from Margery that other households should be actively recruited to run nurseries like hers. The writer is discouraging, on the grounds that it is difficult to find people 'so accommodating as Mrs. Spring-Rice':

> For example, some want only girls of 18 months, others boys who can walk, others won't have anything but orphans, others will only take the children of service men, and a number think how nice it would be to have four cot babies and break out into loud lamentations when they discover that a single nursery nurse cannot cope with the work!

All of this was very likely true but one can imagine Margery's scornful reaction to such wringing of hands. In July 1941 she had written three articles for the *Times Educational Supplement* about the needs of young children which were highly critical of the government's actions in this field. The articles showed that she was indeed more alert to the

---

37   Cecil Spring Rice, letter to Margery Spring Rice, 7 June 1944.

emotional needs of working-class children than she had been to those of
her own. Douglas expressed his admiration for what she was doing in
his diary in 1943:

> M. is still carrying on with her Govt. War Nursery, with a dozen evacuee
> children under 5, and with the battle-practice zone only 20 yards from
> her front gate! R[onald][38] & I saw the children who were, mostly,
> attractive little souls, and obviously enormously improved by their
> residence at Iken, in body, soul and mind; it was tragic to think they
> are destined — mostly — to return to dirty (often verminous) ignorant
> homes.

Whether he had any evidence for the latter statement is unknown.

One child, who arrived at Iken aged six in the spring of 1942 and stayed
for several months,[39] has provided some vivid memories of nursery life
(she also returned for holidays after the war). She recalls her fascination
with the soldiers she chatted to over the fence when the battle area was
established, how she watched the tanks roaring over the fields and
the bullets that whizzed across the roofs of the farm buildings. As she
remembers it, she spent most of her time running wild, climbing trees
and mudlarking rather than having any lessons, although Margery did
read aloud to the children a great deal. She also remembers the children
dressing up as 'red Indians' for some kind of entertainment. Benjamin
Britten and Peter Pears were frequent visitors — usually met with a roar
of welcome from Margery; one highlight was when they were all taken
out to a high tea of poached eggs on toast in a hotel in Aldeburgh by the
two musicians.[40] Another striking image is of a posse of 'Bohemians',
including visitors like the eccentric and wild-haired Ursula Nettleship
as well as Margery's son Ronald, bathing naked in the freezing river.

This family may not have been typical of the nursery children and it is
unclear how the connection with Margery was first made. The youngest
of the three children was an 'official' evacuee, sponsored by the Waifs
and Strays, but the two older ones were over five when they arrived and
therefore not eligible. On 10 November 1942, Margery wrote to the Waifs
and Strays Society 'as I showed in my financial statement, I have raised a

---

38   Margery's brother.
39   Her two younger brothers followed her to Iken in June 1942 and stayed on until
     September 1943.
40   For Margery's connection with Britten and Pears, and with Ursula Nettleship, see
     the next chapter.

private fund for Harry, as well as for the other over fives'. The three were the youngest of eight siblings: their mother was descended from Scottish landed gentry, but had fallen on hard times. Her husband, a doctor, had died in early 1941 in the middle of the Blitz in London, but she managed with extraordinary resourcefulness to provide for her children. In her diary of the war years, she records her first impressions of Margery as 'well born, untidy and tweedy [...] I took an immediate liking to her'.[41] In the spring of 1943 she came to spend the weekend at Iken:

> Harry and Sandy so well it was lovely to see them. Having taken my most ancient clothes and no stockings at all I was dragged off to a cocktail party given by the officers of the district so had to go in a tweed skirt and bare legs [...] I feel quite happy about Harry & Sandy being there, they could not be in better hands.

Two other children who joined the nursery for much of the time were Charles and Paula's, Susan, born in 1936 and Maurice (known as Toby in his childhood) born in 1938. Charles was deeply involved in political activities, but struggled to get work because of his lack of qualifications, and did not always hold down jobs when he did get them. Cracks in the marriage began to show early on. Paula's background is obscure; she had been brought up by a foster mother and may not have had much of a role model for parenting. Charles, of course, had lost his father when he was very young and also lacked examples of good parenting. Money worries did not help, nor the fact that Maurice had a series of health problems. Margery offered them a home at Iken, but her critical attitude was not easy to live with; they needed, but at the same time understandably resented, her help. Paula may have been afraid of her and Charles had, since childhood, found it difficult to move out of the shadow of her personality. For some months in 1939–1940, the family lived in a cottage owned by Gil and Hilda in Upper Basildon in Berkshire, the village where the two aunts also lived together. However, some kind of crisis occurred: in late March 1940,[42] Charles wrote to Margery 'We <u>must</u> park the children on you absolutely at once', and by the summer of that year, Susan and Toby were largely living at Iken, where they stayed on and off until April 1942. Paula seems to have moved house frequently, sometimes with Charles and sometimes on her own, sometimes taking

---

41 Eglantine Grey, unpublished diary; Joane Whitmore, private communication.
42 Charles Garrett Jones, letter to Margery Spring Rice, undated.

the children with her and sometimes leaving them at Iken for months on end without visiting. She missed the children while they were away from her, but thought it would be difficult to have them with her whilst she was employed in various jobs. Margery also found reasons not to send them back, writing to Charles that she would find it 'devastating and irreparable' to lose them.

Paula's foster mother in Switzerland, Rita Banderet, in spite of describing Paula as having an 'unbalanced, helpless character', wondered why Margery did not employ her to help in the nursery. Although such an idea seems to have been suggested to Paula, she declined, saying with justification that it would be too hard to watch Margery making all the rules about the children. The situation was complicated by the fact that, by now, there was someone else in Paula's life, as there would soon be in Charles's. In the summer of 1940, having been called up, he was expecting to be sent to a malarial field unit, possibly in India, Egypt or the Sudan. Before he left (for Egypt via South Africa in the event, and subsequently Lebanon) in March 1941, he offered Paula a divorce which she rejected. She also rejected the suggestion that she and the children could go to the US to stay with relatives.

In the autumn of 1942, Malta, where Stephen was serving, was suffering constant air-raids and both the civilian and the military population were enduring food shortages. Stephen, however, found plenty of opportunities to enjoy himself, from dinghy sailing (he even acquired his own dinghy) to singing and playing the clarinet, which he had taught himself. He was one of a group of RNVR officers who were expecting to be sent on their 'perisher' course, which would lead to getting their own commands.[43] To their mutual pleasure, his time in Malta overlapped with that of Anthony Gillingham, who was serving in the Fleet Air Arm, and also briefly with that of Christopher Ellis, who had joined the navy. For all three of them, their time on the island was hugely enhanced by the presence of the hospitable Price family, a retired naval officer with a Russian wife and a beautiful teenage daughter under whose spell they all successively fell.

Stephen and his family knew that the odds on a submariner's survival were low: Anthony recorded Margery's great and understandable

---

43 See Edward Young, *One of Our Submarines* (Harmondsworth: Penguin, 1952).

distress at his choice of that branch of the navy; Stephen, aware of the strain on his family, wrote to Anthony's wife Brenda of the need to insulate feelings from facts. When he was stationed in Barrow-on-Furness early in 1942, where submarines were built, waiting for P48 to be fitted out, he made friends with a young Anglican clergyman, Stephan Hopkinson. Stephan recorded in his memoirs:

> Sometimes officers, waiting for their ships to be commissioned, stayed with us at the Vicarage. One of them was Stephen Spring-Rice. He was a Cambridge mathematician by background, now second in command of a 'coastal class' submarine. There had been ten subs with him, he told me, in Valetta Harbour; eight of them were already lost. He worked therefore on the principle that every patrol would be his last, and a safe return would be an unexpected bonus. 'But it's occurred to me', he said, 'that it would be sensible to marry some nice girl. It's a pity that the marriage pension to a widow should be wasted'. 'But she might actually love you' I suggested. 'I know' he said, ' that's the drawback to the idea.' He didn't marry — and he didn't come back'.[44]

Submarine P48 was declared missing in early January 1943; in fact, it had been depth charged by Italian destroyers on Christmas day 1942 and probably lies somewhere off the coast of Tunisia. Margery continued for months to worry about what kind of death Stephen might have had to suffer: when she asked Dominick's widow Peggy, a doctor, what it would have been like to have died of oxygen starvation, Peggy did her best to reassure her, and one can only hope that this was not just out of kindness. Condolence letters cannot give a rounded picture of a person's character, since inevitably they concentrate on the good qualities, but those that Margery received after Stephen's death make it clear that not only was he deeply loved by many people,[45] but also that he had managed to pack a huge amount of activity into his twenty two years. And as Cecil wrote, 'something is left'. She expressed the sense many people had that Stephen was something special: 'I almost feel that if Stephen were one of my children I should hardly notice the others'.[46]

---

44 Stephan Hopkinson, *Encounters* ([n.p.]: privately printed, [n.d.]).
45 Four children were named after him in the next few years, including Cecil's eldest son, born in 1946.
46 Cecil Spring Rice, letters to Margery Spring Rice, undated and 14 January 1943.

In the third week of January, Margery's brothers Douglas and Ronald went over to Iken to see her. 'M. was — of course — admirably brave;' Douglas wrote in his diary:

> for half an hour after we arrived she talked to us of things in general without giving a sign of her grief. After lunch we walked down to the river & along the wall to Iken Church, and the sight of the river, the boats' moorings etc. were for a moment too much for her; as she said 'every turn of the channel & ripple of the water reminded her of him'. He was a brilliant, attractive boy and would have made his mark in the world, though not (I think) without giving his family and friends some heartaches.

Cecil had fallen in love with Petica's son Martin, ten years older than her, and married him in September 1942, soon after leaving Cambridge.[47] Margery, although she got on extremely well with Martin later, was at first quite ambivalent about the engagement: she never found it easy to accept her children's choice of partners. Cecil became pregnant just about the time of Stephen's death: the coming grandchild was perhaps a small consolation to Margery, who mainly dealt with her grief by working harder than ever to look after her evacuees. But she was to find Christmas a hard time for many years after Stephen's death. Since coming down from Cambridge, Cecil had been working at the Registrar General's office, but her job could only be kept open for her if she agreed to take a maximum of three months' maternity leave — which she was not prepared to do. Martin was in the War Office before being sent to Athens and Cairo for intelligence work, while Cecil went to Iken and so was able to provide another pair of hands to work in the nursery. The baby, a girl, was born in September. Although Margery had said — perhaps because of Stephen's death — that she hoped it would be a boy, she doted on her new granddaughter.

In the last two years of the war, Charles and Paula's marriage became increasingly fragile, neither of them able to commit either to staying in it or to leaving it. Charles was upset to be turned down for the Army Education Corps, though what he really wanted was a political career. After his demobilisation in 1945, he and Paula lived an on-again off-again marriage while he looked for work that would suit him and underwent

---

47   Margery gave them 15 St Peter's Square as a wedding present, though they did not
     live there until after the war.

some therapy. But in 1947, he fell in love with Daphne Lindner, whom he was to marry in 1951. In early 1952, Paula and the children sailed to Canada with her friend Bill Langford, in a move that turned out to be permanent.[48] It was a great sadness to Margery to be more or less permanently separated from these two grandchildren.

After the nursery came to an end, Margery pondered various other schemes (she thought about adopting two of the nursery children, and considered running a home for the young children of service personnel), but none of these came to fruition. In fact, by the end of the war, she was physically and emotionally exhausted and wondered whether she could cope with another winter in the isolation of Iken. She was also worried about being able to stay in the house as her landlord tried to evict her at various times, or to persuade her to leave, in order to sell. She investigated the possibility of buying either the old school house or the old rectory at Iken (Benjamin Britten also considered the latter at some stage), possibly with some land that Ronald might farm. Eventually, however, Iken Hall and some of the surrounding farm land was sold to another local farmer, Mann, with Margery as a sitting tenant. As she recovered from the stresses of the war and her work in the nursery, her natural buoyancy returned. As her sister-in-law Frieda had written to her on 27 November 1939, after the drowning of Mary Jacoby:

> Douglas always speaks of you when your troubles come as 'My dear old war-horse of a sister', and like a tried war-horse your wounds heal and you go forth to battle again to bring home once more some wounded warrior.

---

48 The passenger list for the *Empress of France*, sailing 26 March 1952, wrongly records Paula's date of birth as 1894 instead of 1913. Bill was probably a Canadian serviceman, but nothing else is known about him: the relationship did not last long.

8. Matriarch (1945–1956)

In the spring of 1942, the composer Benjamin Britten and his partner, the tenor Peter Pears, had returned from the United States where they had spent the first years of the war. Britten already owned the Old Mill in Snape, and, until 1948, was to spend around half of his time living and composing there.

Music had always been one of Margery's passions, as it had been Stephen's also: in the last few months of the war, raising the initial funding from family and friends and with local authority administrative help, she set up the Suffolk Rural Music School in Stephen's memory.[1] The Rural Music Schools movement had arisen out of the adult education movement of the nineteenth century: the first such school, in Hertfordshire, was founded in the late 1920s by Mary Ibberson and had a close link with the Settlement in Letchworth Garden City.[2] It not only matched up pupils with peripatetic music teachers, but also made instruments available.

In June 1945, in the cause of the Suffolk school, which would be the seventh, Margery wrote to Britten, a staunch advocate of amateur music-making, to ask him to become honorary music advisor to the school. He agreed to do so and, together with Pears, gave a number of benefit concerts in aid of the school. It was not long before Britten and Margery were addressing each other in affectionate terms. Musically, Margery was determined not to settle for second best: after one 'atrocious' concert (artists unrecorded), she wrote to Britten: 'I just don[']t believe that it is

---

1 Mary Ibberson, *For Joy that We are Here: Rural Music Schools 1929–50* (London: Bedford Square Press, 1977). The Suffolk school no longer exists as an independent entity, but much of its work is carried on by Snape Maltings.
2 The Settlement was (and is) an adult education organisation founded in 1920. Ibberson was the sub-warden and ran a music course there before founding the Rural Music School.

    https://doi.org/10.11647/OBP.0215.08

any good gett[i]ng less than the very BEST'. She would have liked to be able to call on Casals, Arrau and Toscanini!

According to the fragmentary memoirs Margery wrote in her old age,[3] it was she who suggested that one of the Britten/Pears concerts should take place in Aldeburgh's Jubilee Hall, an idea that initially caused hilarity from Britten and Pears, who said that Aldeburgh would never provide an audience for a concert of classical music. It went ahead, however, and was a great success. Margery and Britten, and Fidelity Countess of Cranbrook[4] who became president of the Suffolk Rural Music School, shared a conviction that amateur musicians should aim for the highest musical standards of which they were capable. When Britten's cantata *Saint Nicolas* received its first London performance in June 1949, the choir included pupils from the Suffolk school.

The contact between Britten and Margery led to a long friendship, although eventually Margery became, to her distress, one of his many 'corpses', as the friends he dropped came to be known. However, for some years it remained a fruitful and affectionate relationship, and Margery retained her admiration for him and his music until the end of her life. The sentiment she expressed in a letter of 24 January 1947, '[w]hat a tragic muck mankind can make of its civilisation and knowledge and power, and with what thankfulness one thinks of you and Peter [Pears] who are making a constructive and abiding contribution', never changed on her side.[5] On 1 June 1962, the day after hearing the first performance of his *War Requiem*, which spoke to Margery's deepest humanitarian values, she wrote to Britten:

> That is a sublime work, exquisitely performed. It brought back all the heart-aches and yearnings of two wars, — and revivified the dwindling hopes for the future. I haven't been so deeply moved for many many years.

In the autumn of that year, she went to London to hear it again in Westminster Abbey.

---

3 Margery Spring Rice, fragmentary memoirs, recorded 24 November 1968 by Sam Garrett-Jones, transcribed 12 January 2006 by Sam Garrett-Jones.

4 Fidelity's father, Hugh Seebohm, a banker, had been treasurer of the first Rural Music School. Margery introduced her to Britten. The Seebohms were a Quaker family in Hitchin, and Hugh's father Frederic had been involved in adult education.

5 The correspondence between Britten and Margery is owned by Britten Pears Arts and is housed with the archives at the Red House in Aldeburgh, Britten's final residence.

Margery remained as Vice-President of the Suffolk Rural Music School for some years, but in 1947, a new possibility was coming over the horizon, a long-term plan that was to engage much of her energy into the 1960s. Britten and Pears, returning from performing at the Holland Festival, conceived the idea of holding their own festival in Aldeburgh — a project that must have begun to seem possible partly as a result of the success of the Jubilee Hall benefit concert the previous year. On 4 September Britten wrote to Pears:

> I saw Marjorie yesterday afternoon — she isn't well, bad lumbago — but I think the 'Festival Idea' has cheered her — she thinks it the idea of the century, & is full of plans & schemes. We haven't been over the Jubilee Hall, but I'm full of hopes. Do you know she got 390 in for our concert last year?.

At the first meeting of the committee that was formed to take the idea further, which took place in October 1947 with Fidelity Cranbrook in the chair, Margery made a personal gift of £100 to be used to cover minor expenses. This is not only a measure of her gratitude to Britten for his support of the Rural Music School, but also an indication of her enthusiasm for the idea of a local festival.

Her contribution was practical as well as financial: when the first Aldeburgh Festival took place in June 1948, in addition to buying three tickets for every performance, she sorted out a green room for the artists in a local care home, organised refreshments, put up posters in local shops and arranged stewards for the festival club (a single room in one of Aldeburgh's hotels). In her Iken Hall visitors' book, there is a page signed by Britten, Pears, the singer Nancy Evans and others to celebrate the first festival, with a musical quotation in Britten's hand and the words 'Notre amitié est invariable — vide Schubert, passim'. It was sad for Margery that his friendship did not remain 'invariable', though she was by no means his only friend to be dropped: in her case, the later coolness may have been a result not only of Britten's psychological need to keep his composing space absolutely sacrosanct, but also of the fact that Imogen Holst, who became his right-hand person, found Margery tiresome. But while Margery and Britten were still close, he made the big dining room chimney of Iken Hall the setting for one of his first works for children, *Let's Make an Opera*.

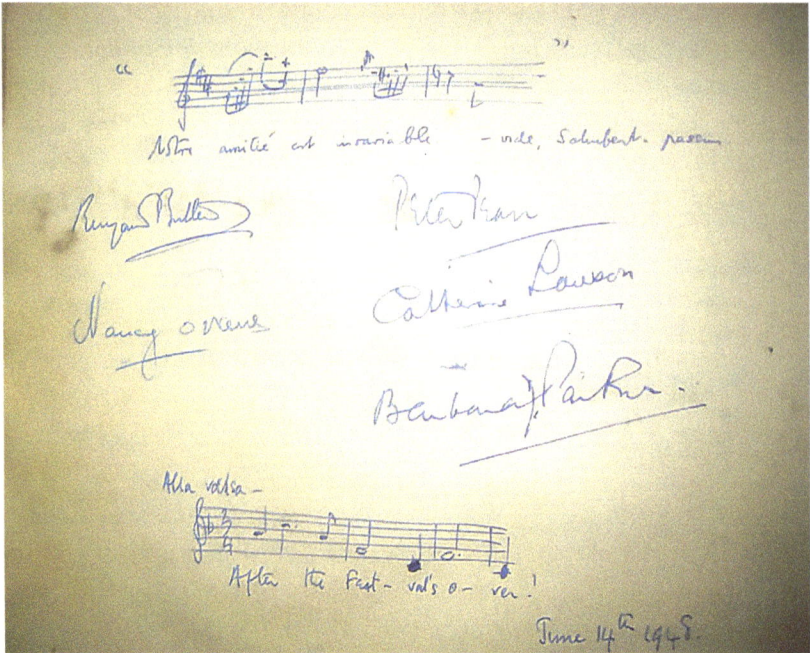

Fig. 20. Page from the Iken visitors' book. Photograph: the author (2016).

Margery remained on the festival committee for sixteen years, through some difficult times: in 1953, for example, there was a question mark over whether there would be a festival at all, because the pressures put on Britten by his commission to compose an opera for the coronation were so great.[6] After the first year, the committee itself was, to some extent, side-lined by the establishment of a separate executive council, which took the more important decisions. In spite of this, Margery continued to worry like a terrier over the festival's financial viability, making various suggestions over the next year or two about how to lure subscribers with the bait of priority booking, and how to find more guarantors, since the festival 'did not exactly make a profit'.[7] It was felt that ticket buyers and potential ticket buyers did not understand that ticket sales did not cover the costs of putting on performances.[8]

---

6   At the time of writing, the Aldeburgh Festival has been going for seventy years without a break, though very sadly, owing to the coronavirus pandemic, it will not take place in 2020. Britten wrote his coronation opera, *Gloriana*.

7   Festival Committee, meeting minutes, 22 October 1949 (Britten Pears Arts Archive, MSC10/1 [Aldeburgh Festival Executive Committee minute book]).

8   The same could also be said of today's audiences.

With her strong sense of her family inheritance, Margery was deeply rooted in Aldeburgh and its hinterland, which soon provided another cause for her activism. In the mid-1940s, the old rectory (at some stage renamed The Anchorage) was bought by Gabriel Clark. There had traditionally been a footpath from Snape along the south bank of the Alde to Iken church but Clark closed the last section of the path so that walkers had to detour via the road to reach the church. Margery, outraged, fought a long but unsuccessful battle to reopen it. The case went to the County Court; Margery's solicitor, her brother Douglas's son Roderick, believed (though there is no independent corroboration of this) that one local inhabitant, the river pilot Jumbo Ward, had been bribed to give false evidence.

Whatever the facts, there were several acrimonious encounters between Clark and Margery or her family and friends. On 30 January 1946, Margery wrote to Brenda Gillingham, wife of Stephen's old school friend Anthony:

> Ben Britten, Ursula Nettleship[9] & I did the 'grind' again last Sunday! Clarke [sic][10] met us at the fallen tree & after the usual sort of ding-dong argument backwards & forwards he became extremely rude to me, saying it was well known that I ought to be in trousers, & that he sympathised with my husband having left me etc. etc. Ben was so angry that there was <u>nearly</u> a fight. Clarke threatened to use violence if we went on, — but I ignored him & we went on, & he merely followed us hurling abuse at us, of the above sort.

She goes on to say that the County Council had appointed a sub-committee to settle the dispute, but 'as Ben said it is extraordinarily depressing to think of Clarke as my only neighbour'. Many years later, Britten's niece remembered —

> that horrible Clarke, and the fight to keep the path along the river to the church open. We were walking along it one day with my mother and Margery, when he came towards us with large and frightening dogs. My mother wasn't as tough as Margery, and she said we should go back, so we did. It was a long battle and I remember the disappointment when 'we' lost. I was only a child but I remember it very clearly.[11]

---

9   Trainer of the Aldeburgh festival choir. Margery had known her since at least 1944. She was the sister of Augustus John's first wife, Ida.

10   Clark's name is consistently misspelt by Margery and her friends.

11   Sally Schweitzer, private correspondence to the author, 24 March 2016.

Margery was not the only person to fall out with Clark. In 1948, he was elected to the Parish Council, on which Margery also sat, but when he arrived for a meeting, according to her account, the chair walked out in protest. Furthermore, when she went out to try to persuade him back in, he said

> 'Do you want to see murder committed, ma'am?' I said I wouldn't mind but I did not think that the Parish Council held in Jumbo Ward's house was a very good place. So he said 'Well let me find my gun, and I'll take the man outside and do it there. He is like a snake in the grass to me, and I won't sit in the same room with him'.[12]

There was evidently a pro-Clark faction as well, since shortly after this, he became chair of the Parish Council and stood for the Rural District Council. Margery thought she should probably resign from the PC but 'can't make up my mind to hand the whole caboodle over to the enemy'.[13] It is not clear how long she stayed.

Footpaths continued to cause local ructions long after Margery had left Iken. In 1961, her son Charles wrote that he had walked through Tunstall Forest and across the Iken estate —

> where we were stopped by the new owner, Gill, down by his new irrigation reservoir [...] in the dip of the land where there used to be an old well. He evidently kept a watch (with field glasses) on that side while his wife watched the cliff side (she stopped Stella[14] at the top of the cliff). Gill came down to stop us [...] After some cool feelers on either side I introduced myself and asked him his name — I had forgotten that Mann had even sold the estate. Then we became friends, he pointing out what footpaths he has purposely left open (not nearly enough, of course) and I telling him the old route of the sailors' path. We found some common ground in slating Clarke's attitude and the action of the previous owner in destroying hedges and woods; Gill has planted some new ones as wind-breaks. He is not a bad sort I think.[15]

A couple of years later, Margery was writing to one of her grandchildren that —

> The whole business is a farce, because there is a tr[i]ennial enquiry into which paths are public and during the three years that the footpath

---

12   Margery Spring Rice, letter to Ronald Garrett Jones, 24 March 1948.
13   Margery Spring Rice, letter to Ronald Garrett Jones, 25 April 1948.
14   Margery's daughter-in-law, Ronald's wife.
15   Charles Garrett Jones, letter to Margery Spring Rice, 17 August 1961.

committee are considering the matter farmers plough up the paths & 'commons' & put barbed wire around them! As the Iken farmer has done.[16]

It is certainly true that from the late 1950s, much of the land around Iken Hall that had been open heath, covered with bracken, was ploughed up and turned over to agricultural land. A big gravel pit across the road opposite the house also disappeared. Perhaps from the agricultural point of view this was justified, although it changed the character of the countryside. As early as 1945, when the battle area was still in place, Charles had written:

> I still feel that the place would be <u>more</u> beautiful if its natural beauty were supplemented by a modern agricultural community. That would give it a richer and more varied character altogether, without in any way marring your bit of heath or the marshes or the river itself.[17]

He hoped that even if the battle area was retained, the boundaries could be redrawn so as to give a clear route to the Slaughden ferry.[18]

Margery engaged more positively with local government when, in the light of her North Kensington experience, she was co-opted to the County Council's health committee,[19] on which she sat for many years. She also remained active on the committee of the North Kensington clinic until 1956, making frequent trips to London to attend meetings.

She had not lost her taste for foreign travel, and in 1948, she made a trip to Italy and Malta where she visited Stephen's friend Tina Price and her parents, whom she had entertained at Iken in 1946. In the winter of 1952–1953, she took advantage of the fact that Charles, now a malariologist, was working for the World Health Organisation and living with his family in Lebanon. It was a good opportunity to escape from Christmas too, which usually meant a large family party at Iken but inevitably reminded her that Stephen was no longer among them. On 6 November 1952, she wrote to Britten describing how she loved visiting —

> Aleppo, Crusader castles, Phoenician ports, & the magnificent memorials of the centuries of the great Roman peace in this land. It is all incredibly

---

16   Margery Spring Rice, letter to Stephen Robertson, 13 June 1963.
17   Charles Garrett Jones, letter to Margery Spring Rice, 20 May 1945.
18   At that time, there was a foot ferry across the Alde from the Iken side to Slaughden, the area at the southern end of the town of Aldeburgh, where the river makes a right-angle turn to run south for several miles to its mouth at Shingle Street.
19   She had stood unsuccessfully for the County Council, probably as an independent.

beautiful. The landscape itself, with high mountains, - the sea & the rich fertility of the plains, - on the very edge of the desert, makes the setting of the buildings quite breath-taking. And through it all this great antiquity & space & depth.

She had been bowled over by the beauty of Syria and its rich history. In contrast, she was having a 'nightmare puzzle' trying to arrange a visit to Israel (via Cyprus), for which she had deliberately acquired a second passport to avoid the problem of showing that she had been in an Arab country.

How absurd it is, — but at the same time how insoluble. I shall probably end up in some Jordanian dungeon for trying to smuggle myself & small suitcase across the border.

She was quite capable of mischievously producing the wrong passport just to see what might happen, but in fact the only hitch seems to have occurred in Egypt at the end of her tour, when she had —

an exciting and rather dangerous encounter with the Egyptian police, [...] who had been opening my letters to the P. and O office in Port Said, and thereby discovered that I had visited an enemy country immediately before coming to Egypt to catch my P. and O boat home. However we finally parted on the best of terms, and the impressive Major Achmed Hassan, chief of the Security police expressed the hope that I would look upon him as my Egyptian son! a quick jump from the role of gaoler which he had been playing for two so[li]d hours beforehand.[20]

One small perk of visiting the Middle East was her discovery that an Arab headband was just the thing for keeping her hair in order: she used the one she acquired on her Lebanon trip for the rest of her life. From her girlhood into her old age, she had beautiful waist-length hair, of which she was justly proud, and which Dick Mitchison had specially loved. Although sometimes an eccentric dresser, she cared very much about her appearance. Rather surprisingly, given her feminism — but perhaps partly because of being very overweight — she never gave up wearing a corset.

One of the most important aspects of Margery's life in the post-war years was being a grandmother, friend and hostess. Having ended the war with three grandchildren, by 1958 she had thirteen. In 1953, she

---

20   Margery Spring Rice, letter to Brenda & Anthony Gillingham, 8 February 1953.

had written that she could 'rest with honour on my oars, and take a little timely grandmotherly birth control', but she was not to be allowed to do so quite yet. Charles had two by his second marriage, Ronald had three, and Cecil eventually had six. If Margery had had a lot of failings as a mother, she was the best of grandmothers, and Iken was an almost perfect setting. In the 1950s, children spent a great deal more time outdoors, and with more freedom, than their counterparts in the early twenty-first century. Iken offered the river for sailing, mudlarking and swimming, trees for climbing, sheds for messing about in and quiet country roads for cycling. There was an area in the corner of the garden where visiting families, for whom there was no room in the house, could pitch their tents and, at some stage, Margery acquired an old gypsy caravan which children could use as a play house or to sleep in on summer nights.

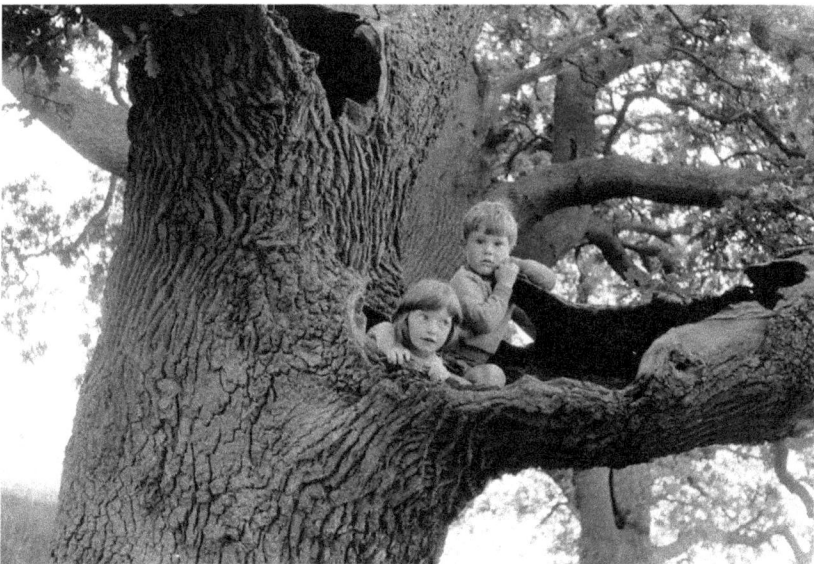

Fig. 21. Iken oak with grandchildren. Photograph: Ronald Garrett-Jones (late 1950s).

Indoors, the big double drawing room was divided by curtains, making a perfect stage for grandchildren to put on plays, music being provided by a magnificent musical box or live on the piano by Margery, and interval drinks consisting of water mixed with drops of red or green colouring for 'wine'. In this room, too, Margery regularly set up a party-piece called 'the Prince of Crim Tartary', which enchanted all the children who saw it. A table was put in front of the closed curtains, covered with a rug, and with a stool on it. The Prince was created by two adults standing one behind the other, behind the table. The front adult made the head, body and legs of the Prince, wearing his boots on his or her hands, while the back one put his or her arms through under the armpits of the front one to make the Prince's arms. He wore a turban and, on his 'feet', a pair of beautiful embroidered children's boots brought back from China and given to Margery by Eileen Power.[21] This small, dumpy but magical personage would answer questions, give out presents, do a stately dance, and demonstrate that he could remain sitting cross-legged in the air if his stool was removed from under him. At the end of his appearance, his audience were told they must close their eyes while he flew away on his magic carpet. His spell was such that one grandchild recorded in adulthood 'I fully believed in him [...] I remember looking out of the window [when he left] [...] there was a moon and scudding clouds, and we definitely caught a glimpse of him as he sped away'.[22]

Fig. 22. Margery with her Land Rover. Photograph: Francis Minns (1953). Courtesy of Julian Minns.

21   The boots are now in the V&A Museum of Childhood in Bethnal Green, London.
22   Matthew Robertson, recollections of Iken, 2014.

Fig. 23. The Prince of Crim Tartary's boots (now in the Victoria & Albert Museum of Childhood, Bethnal Green). Photograph: the author (2011).

Friends, family and acquaintances flocked to Iken and Margery kept up with many of her children's friends as well as her own. Any breach with her Jones in-laws had long been healed, so Gil and Hilda in particular came from time to time, the latter sharing a passion for gardening with Margery. Many German and Austrian names crop up in the Iken visitors' books, as do the names of friends from all periods of her life. She was always willing to offer sanctuary to friends in trouble: an example is her kindness to two other divorced friends, Betty Waddington and Angela Wheeler.[23] Although she had domestic and some gardening help, she did virtually all the cooking herself, which cannot have been easy when food was rationed, as it continued to be until 1954. Everyone was excited one Christmas when a big sack of tinned food arrived from the Rothschilds, who had settled in New York. But even during the war years, the visitors' books sometimes record the names of thirty or forty people a year, excluding her extended family. In 1946, the number topped fifty. There were always musicians among them: Annie Newson (who lived in the village and did domestic work for Margery) later remembered

---

23   Divorce was still less common at that time than it is now, and less socially acceptable. Some divorced women felt they had to leave the country and live abroad, for a time at least, to escape the scandal. Margery and Angela tried sharing Iken for a period, but they were both strong and self-willed women, and the arrangement came to a mutually agreed end.

her delight at hearing Kathleen Ferrier sing, although Ferrier's name does not appear in the visitors' book as she probably came in a day with Britten and Pears and did not stay. Some of the musicians were performers at the Aldeburgh Festival, like the boys from a Danish choir who contrived to go mudlarking in their singing clothes and had to be laundered in a hurry— just the kind of challenge relished by Margery.

In 1942, the year in which he and Margery's daughter Cecil married, Martin Robertson had written an acrostic poem in the Iken visitors' book on the words 'Spring Rice of Iken Hall'. It ends with these lines, to be amply fulfilled in the years to come:

> Here kindness does not fail
> At this or any pass:
> Long live this house into the thaw of peace;
> Long live the name 'Spring Rice of Iken Hall'.

Margery could be an autocratic host as well as a generous one. On one occasion, Ursula Nettleship and her cat Humpy were guests and Margery had cooked halibut for dinner. When handed her plate, Ursula immediately divided her portion of fish in half and made to give one half to Humpy — at which an outraged Margery said she had not cooked an expensive fish like halibut in order for cats to eat it, and if Ursula didn't want all of her helping she could give it back. However, she also loved Ursula for her disregard of convention: once, when Ursula wanted to go for a swim in the river but had not brought a costume, Margery offered to lend her one. Ursula dismissed that idea, saying that her knickers would be quite good enough (though she generally regarded even knickers as unnecessary, since she was happy to swim naked).

If friends were of huge importance to her, there is a gap in the evidence when it comes to her sex life after her return to Suffolk in 1936 in her late forties. Whether this is because it was over and she fulfilled her emotional needs through her friendships, her family relationships and her many activities, or whether it has simply vanished from the record, we will probably never know.

When the east coast of the United Kingdom was struck by terrible floods in early 1953, Margery was anxious to help. However, she learned that all the homeless families had been found accommodation and she recognised that Iken was impracticable for anyone without a car. Like others, she was deeply shocked at the devastation and loss of life. She described the situation in the village:

> Even this village is flooded in its low lying parts, and the whole of the marshes between here and Aldeburgh on both sides of the river and right down to Orford are still deep in water. It is not true that the river made a new mouth for itself. There are 14 large breaches in the mud wall on the Aldeburgh side between Slaughden and the brick kiln dock. The river poured through these, and the sea came over the road between the end of the town and Slaughden quay and with each tide brought of course thousands of tons of shingle, as it always does, so it did not dig a new [mouth] for the river, but merely joined the river over the road and the marshes. Bull dozers and low tides have done their work since last week-end, and at present the sea is not coming over any more. The water [i]n the marshes is lower, because of the lower river tides, but it is still all a [huge] lake coming right up to the wall at the bottom of the old kitchen garden of Gower house![24]

It was not the first bad winter experience. In March 1947, during the worst winter of the century up till then, she recorded terrible blizzards and blocked roads, snow two-feet-deep in her garden and no water supply or coke for the stove (but she had very much enjoyed getting a lift back from London in Britten's Rolls Royce). In February 1949, Cecil was at Iken expecting her third child. The second had been born there without any problems,[25] but this time she haemorrhaged very badly and had to be rushed first to Ipswich Hospital and then to Colchester because Ipswich had no supply of blood for her blood group. The following day there was a dreadful storm, and Margery struggled with awful driving conditions to take her son-in-law to see Cecil. She was an audacious driver, though not a good one. She had driven her nursery children around in an open-topped car, but in about 1950, she acquired a Land Rover, which meant she could (and did) drive on rough farm tracks as well as roads. From the nursery days, she had used her car to tow a trailer: if she had lots of children in the house, she delighted them by ferrying them about in the trailer.

In the early fifties, she was beginning to get tired. She was very overweight and suffered badly from rheumatism and back pain,

---

24 Margery Spring Rice, letter to Brenda & Anthony Gillingham, 8 February 1953.
25 Both were delivered by Dr Robin Acheson, for many years a much-loved Aldeburgh GP.

although it did not stop her cooking or gardening or undertaking any of her other activities. On 8 October 1951, when she was sixty-four, she wrote to Brenda Gillingham that Cecil was expecting her fifth child (as Brenda too would soon be) and 'I am a little daunted at the thought of yet another, when the holiday season comes round again'. The following autumn, again to the Gillinghams, she confessed that Cecil and her children 'have first call on my accommodation and personal energy, which does not increase with the years'.[26] She wondered about letting one end of the house to a young couple to provide help, since 'the time has nearly come when I can't cope with 12–14 people at a time as I have been doing for this summer for about three months'. And yet, she suggested that if some children were willing to camp, she could have Cecil's family and the Gillingham family to stay at the same time — in the summer of 1953, this would have meant ten children in total.

Margery continued to take an active interest in the work of the North Kensington clinic, wholeheartedly encouraging and supporting the liberal attitude prevalent among its staff which is illustrated by the trajectory of the careers of several of them. Margaret Pyke, clinic secretary who succeeded Trudie Denman as chair of the Family Planning Association in 1954, became, in 1966, a director of the Brook Advisory Centres which gave advice to unmarried people. Helena Wright, who in her earlier life had been a medical missionary, did not disapprove of pre-marital or extra-marital relationships (of which she had more than one herself). Joan Malleson campaigned for abortion law reform.

A turning-point in the respectability of contraception, if only for married couples, came in 1955 when the Minister of Health, Ian Macleod,[27] bravely (in the context of the time) visited the clinic. This came about because Lady Monckton, a member of the executive committee of the Family Planning Association (FPA), was a family friend of Macleod's and introduced him to Margaret Pyke. The press turned out in force for the occasion, and the audience included mothers and children, as one of Margery's letters refers to babies crowing during his speech. On the same evening, Pyke appeared in a television programme,[28] and the

---

26 Margery Spring Rice, letter to Brenda & Anthony Gillingham, 25 September 1952.
27 Even in 1950, the BBC had refused to allow a broadcast appeal on behalf of the Family Planning Association: Evans, *Freedom to Choose*, p. 162.
28 Lella S. Florence, *Progress Report on Birth Control* (London: Heinemann, 1956), p. 22–23.

following day, a *Times* leader celebrated the existence of a family planning service 'as a voluntary movement, used by the public health services within defined limits, but remaining free of control or direction by the state'.[29] The leader-writer also recognised that family planning services were concerned with many different factors that contribute to 'wise and happy parenthood' including infertility as well as contraception.

Fig. 24. Ian Macleod, Minister of Health, visits the North Kensington clinic in 1955. Margery is on the right and the mayor of Hammersmith in the centre. Photograph: Wellcome Collection SA/FPA/NK 237 (1955).

A file of North Kensington correspondence dating between 1954 and 1956 shows Margery as chair of the committee interested in every aspect of the clinic's work. The many subjects covered include publicity, a proposed special clinic for the treatment of vaginismus, discussions about women unsuited to using the cap, the annual report, funding, international links, a project on the history of the movement and research into new methods of contraception. Here and there personal issues are mentioned, making it clear how busy she was in other ways too. In June

---

29   *The Times*, 30 November 1955. The clinic visit was on 29 November. There was also an item on the BBC Woman's Hour programme.

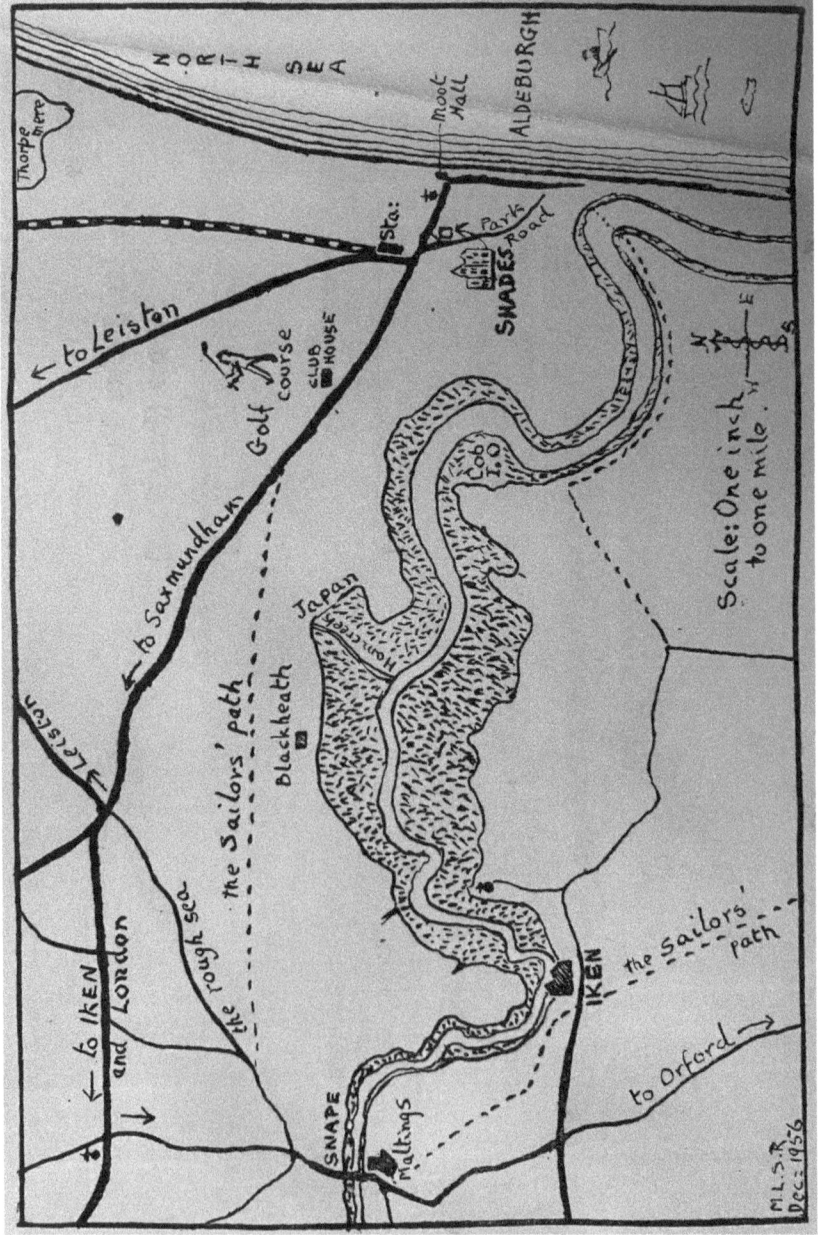

Fig. 25. The map made by Margery when she moved from Iken to Shades in 1956. Photograph: the author (2020).

1954, she reports having four Aldeburgh Festival guests staying, with seven more due to arrive. On 20 June, she mentions that earlier in the week she had nineteen people sleeping in the house. That autumn, she looked after one grandchild who had had scarlatina and another who was recovering from a serious illness; in the following year, she cared for a third grandchild who was in quarantine for measles. At one point in July, there were six small children in the house, in this case, presumably, with one or more parents.

During this time, Margery was also worrying about whether she would be able to stay at Iken: her landlord was anxious to get her out, though he could not legally do so, so 'unless the ideal house, slightly smaller and equally well placed, comes into the market, there I stay I hope till my coffin is [taken] out of it'.[30] Nevertheless, she was beginning to find it difficult to manage house and garden; in 1956, with the help of a loan from her landlord, she bought a house on Park Road in Aldeburgh (in the same road as her parents' old house, Gower House) that had also, very appropriately, been built by her grandfather Newson. On a beautiful October day, when the river looked golden, Cecil and some of her family came from London to help her with a move that — after twenty years — was a sad occasion, though they accepted that it was the right thing to do. In honour of the ghosts of her ancestors, Margery named the new house 'Shades'.

---

30   Margery Spring Rice, letter to Brenda & Anthony Gillingham, 25 September 1952.

9. Running down (1956–1970)

Life at Shades carried on much as it had done at Iken. The house was
not as large, but visitors still found their way there in a constant stream.
The garden was smaller too, but Margery built a big shed, named
'Shambles', for younger relatives and friends to mess about in, or to use
as a bunkroom if the house was full. Of her siblings, her brother Ronald,
who lived near Bury St Edmunds and with whom she had an affectionate
but combative relationship, was now the only one left — Douglas and
Geoffrey both having died in 1949. However, there were members of her
extended family in the area. It was still difficult to get domestic help and
she was not the easiest of employers — those who got along with her
tended to be people who had enough self-confidence to stand up to her.[1]
But it was a happy house, and though she missed Iken, Margery loved
being so close to the sea and living in a place that was so essentially a
part of her family history. For the grandchildren, staying with Margery
still offered wonderful opportunities for adventure, sometimes not a
roaring success. Cecil's son, Stephen, remembered —

> a disastrous camping expedition [with his younger brother], sailing
> up to Snape, and camping in the Maltings grounds, while it was still a
> Maltings, before it was taken over by the festival. The trip was disastrous
> because that night there were fierce thunderstorms and we got flooded
> out. A kind caretaker let us bed down in one of the Maltings buildings.[2]

In 1957, Margery finally stood down from her work at North Kensington,
though she was fully engaged in the work up till the last minute; for
example, she urged the Family Planning Association (FPA) to press
university medical faculties to fill the glaring gap in their curricula by

---

1   A policeman once delighted her, when she leaned out of her car window and said 'I
    want Croydon Airport!', by replying 'You can't have it, madam': she took pleasure
    in repeating this story against herself.
2   Stephen Robertson, recollections of Iken, 2014.

    https://doi.org/10.11647/OBP.0215.09

taking over the FPA's training role.[3] However, in the mid-1950s, there had been changes in the relationship of the clinic to the FPA. In the words of one colleague, Margery had brought the baby into the world,[4] and it was right that she should see that baby safely married to the FPA, but she felt that she had done her work, many other things were going on in her life and she resigned from the chair of the committee. Apart from personal reasons, she was unhappy with the clinic's relationship to the FPA, on the executive committee of which she also sat. Owing to a shortage of space at FPA headquarters in Sloane Street, three departments were moved to the North Kensington premises in Telford Road, entailing a huge reorganisation; but when, quite soon afterwards, more space was acquired near to headquarters, two of those departments were moved back. Margery was frustrated, feeling that the North Kensington staff had not been properly consulted. Papers in the clinic archives also imply that there was a dispute over the boundaries between the roles of paid staff and those of honorary officers. Certainly, as someone determined to get what she wanted, she cannot always have been easy to work with; but the other side of that coin is that she was prepared to fight tooth and nail for what she thought right. The annual report of the clinic for 1957 paid tribute to Margery's imaginative vision and empathy, describing her as realising —

> that it was not only the women overtaxed by excessive child-bearing who needed skilled medical help, but also the couple childless against their will, the husband and wife encountering difficulties in the marriage relationship and the young man and girl engaged but fearful of the future because brought up in sexual ignorance.[5]

After thirty-four years, Margery had seemed a fixture to her colleagues. Their personal tributes to her work were heartfelt. One wrote 'there has <u>always</u> been Mrs Spring Rice to depend on for a progressive attitude'. Another, Isabella Herbert, reported that many of the committee had been 'too near tears to speak' when her resignation was announced:

---

3   After standing down, she kept in touch through her daughter Cecil, who served on the committee for several years, and through other friends who were active in the field, particularly Nancy Raphael, Marjorie Farrer and Letty Gifford.

4   Doreen Agnew, letter to Margery Spring Rice, 24 March 1957.

5   Wellcome Collection, SA/FPA/NK/206/33. North Kensington Marriage Welfare Centre, *Thirty-Third Annual Report 1ˢᵗ January–31ˢᵗ December, 1957* ([n.p.]: [n.p.], 1957).

you have been an inspiration to me all my life — from the early days of the Womens [sic] Liberal Federation. I have always thought of you as one of the most outstanding, right-minded, courageous & above all <u>loveable</u> of women that I have ever known — & I want to tell you this now, instead of writing it to Cecil when you die![6]

For another: 'The F.P.A. Executive Committee seemed all wrong without you. Very tame without your "combative spirit!". I do wish you could have heard all the pleasant things which were said about you'. One of her colleagues had expressed the view that Margery had been 'far in advance of the rest of us & far in advance of [her] time'. The most vivid image came from Helena Wright, with whom Margery had had such a fruitful — if sometimes difficult — relationship for all those years:

> I was stunned to hear that you have decided to leave N. Ken. You are one of the people, whom we, your most appreciative fellow-workers think of as going on for ever! [I want to] give you my vivid regrets at your decision, & my most warm thanks for our many years of happy co-operation. I do hope that your disappearance won't be absolute, but that you will float invisibly in the atmosphere to be appealed to for wisdom whenever events become too stubborn.[7]

The incongruity of the idea of Margery, who though short was very fat, floating in the atmosphere would probably have delighted her sense of humour.

In the spring of 1959, Margery's granddaughter Rachel, Ronald's daughter, was diagnosed with a brain tumour. When they seemed to have run through all the possible treatments available in the UK, Stella, Ronald's wife, managed to discover the names of doctors in the Soviet Union to whom she wrote for help and in whom she placed great faith. She was terribly distressed to receive a letter expressing their sympathy but also their inability to do anything more for her daughter. Rachel died on her seventh birthday, in December of that year. Margery did what she could to support Ronald and Stella and their two other children, both during Rachel's illness and after her death, while coping with her own grief. In January 1960, she took a trip to Kuwait on board an oil tanker with her brother Ronald and his wife which helped to restore her well-being. At some point after her return, however, she had a car

---

6   Isabella Herbert, letter to Margery Spring Rice, 8 December 1957.
7   Helena Wright, letter to Margery Spring Rice, 6 March 1958.

accident which set her back a bit: it is not clear what happened, but she fell out of the car (it was in the days before seat belts, and the car had primitive door catches), which rolled back over her leg and bruised it badly. One family comment was 'We have strong bones in our family': Margery somehow managed to take in her stride something that would have devastated a less resilient person. By the autumn of 1960, she had again recovered some of her energy and was planning a trip for the following summer to Saas Fee in Switzerland, where Charles and his family were now living, taking two of Cecil's younger children with the idea of looking after them and Charles's children while Charles and his wife took a break — hardly a rest-cure for herself! But notes of anxiety began to creep into her letters: on 6 October 1960, she was writing to Charles 'I forget things so quickly', and on 12 July the following year she confessed to being tired and anxious after the strains of hosting guests for the Aldeburgh Festival (Ursula Nettleship and her cat — a fairly demanding pair — had stayed for a fortnight), and to finding the running of Shades too much. She also had problems with the car, which needed extensive and expensive repairs. She was thinking of getting something smaller, but did not want to 'offend the grandchildren too seriously', since they loved her Land Rover.

In spite of increasing deafness, Margery remained a faithful member of the Aldeburgh audience, continuing to support Britten and his musical baby to the end of her life. In 1961, she wrote to Charles about that year's festival providing 'some dazzling highlights, particularly Ben and Rostropovich the fabulous Russian cellist. They played a new "Sonata" by B.B. written for Rostro: and the kissing and tears and hand-shaking etc, that went on afterwards, to say nothing of the shouting of the audience, was terrific. We all liked the new work immensely'. To Britten and Pears she wrote, on 11 July 1961:

> one likes to think that you have forged a link between Russia & ourselves which cannot be broken by these wretched politicians [...] [the Festival] made me feel more than ever that great art has no frontiers [...] Aldeburgh is indeed blessed, & my own old age deeply privileged.

When, in 1967, Snape Maltings (which of course was for Margery, born a Garrett, a place of great emotional significance) reopened in its new incarnation of a much-needed concert hall — seating more than twice as many as the tiny and unsatisfactory Aldeburgh Jubilee Hall, and with far better backstage facilities — she was at first doubtful, but soon become a convert. She wrote to Britten and Pears at the end of that year's festival:[8]

> I had been sceptical and rather disapproving of the adventure of Snape Maltings; but having been at 10 wonderful concerts there, I am a whole-hearted convert to this bold venture; and the great care taken not to disturb the beauty of the range of old buildings has won universal praise.

In 1961, her brother Ronald was widowed, and it appears that the idea of setting up house together crossed both their minds independently, in both cases to be hastily dismissed. Margery expressed the view that she and he could never share a house, not only because his 'material standards' were much higher than hers, but because 'we hardly share one opinion in common'.[9] They were nevertheless glad to see something of each other, if not to live together, and enjoyed each other's occasional company in a slightly combative way. Margery later told a story about having a meal with Ronald somewhere near Aldeburgh, and falling into a furious argument about who should pay the bill: he said she should pay because she was the host, and she said he should pay because he was so much richer than her. The outcome is lost in the mists of history. On another occasion, her nephew Alasdair, Ronald's son, was going to take her for a sail on the river, but —

> Bro: Ronald said he was sure I shouldn't be able to get into the boat from a <u>rubber</u> dinghy, (which was all they had.) I assured him that if <u>he</u> could do so, I could and a 'trial' was arranged; but then it was pelting with rain, so the adventure fell through.[10]

A more attractive solution to where to live was the possibility of a self-contained flat in the house that Cecil and Martin were buying in Oxfordshire, as a result of Martin getting a professorship at Oxford. Margery, however, was reluctant to leave Suffolk and the sea. On 14 November 1961, she had written:

> We had a terrific gale yesterday. I walked down to the beach at about high tide (I thought the L.R [Land Rover] might be blown over if I took her out!) to look at the sea, which was magnificent; breakers at least ½ mile

---

8   Margery Spring Rice, letter to Benjamin Britten & Peter Pears, 29 June 1967.
9   Margery Spring Rice, letter to Ronald Garrett Jones, 22 September 1963.
10   Margery Spring Rice, letter to Stephen Robertson, 13 June 1963.

out, — & the din incredible. This morning I drove down to Slaughden to see the damage. The Y.C [Yacht Club] large boat shed is practically gone, roof ripped off; and the whole road is covered deep in shingle, and the shingle bank (protected on the sea-side by the concrete wall) is badly disintegrated. I couldn't walk further than the Town Quay, & only that by wading through deep pools & muddy shingle.[11]

For the moment, however, she decided to stay put.

In the winter of 1962–1963, Margery and her brother Ronald took off for a holiday in Sicily, which she greatly enjoyed, despite having been desperately anxious beforehand that the heavy snowfalls (in Oxfordshire, where she was staying with Cecil) would not allow her to get away. But her problems had not disappeared: her hearing and her sight were both deteriorating, though she had not lost her zest for a fight. In 1963, a friend in Snape involved her in another footpath campaign. In 1964, to her great delight, she became a great grandmother, when Maurice (unfortunately in Canada) and his wife produced their first child. She created a flat on the top floor of Shades and started to look for a tenant, but in the following year, she finally made the decision to move to Oxfordshire.

Both Cecil and Margery approached the arrangement with the desire to make it work. Margery lived with Cecil and her family for two years, but both of them found it extremely hard. Margery hated feeling dependent, and desperately missed the sea, while Cecil was holding down a demanding teaching job and found it difficult to be patient with Margery's unhappiness. She made visits back to Suffolk, for the 1965 Festival and then to give evidence in the County Court in Ipswich:

about the Iken footpaths [...] I had always understood that our triumph last year, before an officer of the Ministry of [Housing and] Local Government, was final. But it appears it was only final for <u>our</u> side, and that the owner of the land, having lost the case then, could appeal against the Ministry's decision. As my father used to say 'The Law is an Ass'.[12]

She still owned the Land Rover, but reported to her grandson Stephen on 6 March 1966 that it would not go above thirty miles per hour: 'I haven't tried her on a hill, as there are none sufficiently near & sufficiently steep for the purpose'. She was unwell with heart problems

---

11   Margery Spring Rice, letter to Stephen Robertson, 14 November 1961.
12   Margery Spring Rice, letter to Stephen Robertson, 25 May 1965.

and diabetes, and went into hospital for tests, but found it irritating that, in her view, 'the patient is the last person to be told what is the matter with him/her'.[13]

In September 1966, Margery returned to Aldeburgh, buying a flat on the seafront and writing in her visitors' book 'ALDEBURGH again, and until the END'. To her distress, her memory was worsening, and getting sorted in her flat was a struggle: 'I still cant [sic] find any object of my own hiding! Such is life at 79+'. Her anxiety levels were high: she worried constantly, though unnecessarily, about money, and when her grandson Stephen got married at the age of twenty-one in 1966, she thought it could not be a good step for someone so young, perhaps forgetting that she had been only a couple of years older at the time of her own happy first marriage. She never stopped wanting or welcoming visitors, even when she was in a muddle about the date. On 5 February 1967, she wrote to Britten:

> Wont you come down to have a look at the pearly sea, and the oldest of your Aldeburgh friends [...] I dont want to bother you, — but I would love to see you and give you a humble tea, — and a view of a pinky blue sea at sunset.

He almost certainly did not come, but perhaps she was a little consoled when he replied to tell her that he had been at Buckingham Palace at a banquet for the Russian Prime Minister, Kosygin, at which the Duke of Kent had asked to be remembered to her — he had come to Iken in 1950, riding pillion on a motor bike driven by Christopher Ellis, who was his tutor at the time. On 17 March 1967, Margery wrote twice to Stephen, to whose marriage she had quickly become reconciled, to invite him and his wife to visit:

> I have one spare room which is capable of sleeping two people (<u>perhaps</u> one of them on the floor, on a mattress) and I should have to ask a little help from Judith, with the cooking [...] you can dive (or fly) from the bay window [...] straight into the sea.

She went to festival events that year, but found it rather 'bewildering'.[14] Children, grandchildren, other relatives and friends continued to visit: in November 1968, Anthony Gillingham came for a night and recorded

---

13   Margery Spring Rice, letter to Stephen Robertson, 19 March 1966.
14   Margery Spring Rice, letter to Stephen Robertson, 16 June 1967.

that it was the thirty-second anniversary of their first meeting in his Eton days.

Fig. 26. Margery on top of Orford Castle. Photograph: Sam Garrett-Jones (late 1960s).

In June 1969, a disaster overtook the Festival when, on its first evening, the Maltings concert hall caught fire and was damaged to the extent that it would need almost complete rebuilding. Like many others with an attachment to the festival and the hall, Margery was shocked and upset, writing to Stephen on 16 June:

> The Maltings tragedy seems to pervade a large number of visitors and inhabitants of Aldeburgh; and somehow it seems to me that the Festival can never be the same again, in spite of B.B.'s and P.P's[15] optimism about the rebuilding. Almost the saddest part about it is the destruction of Ben's beautiful new piano of which he was extremely proud; and now it is dust and ashes.

Astonishingly, and thanks to heroic efforts by many people, the hall was rebuilt in under a year, so that it could accommodate the performances

---

15   Benjamin Britten and Peter Pears.

of the Festival in 1970 there again. Sadly, Margery did not live to see the phoenix rise from the ashes, though fittingly, one of her grandsons had a Hesse studentship at the Aldeburgh Festival in June that year.

In August 1969, writing to another of her grandchildren,[16] she put at the top of her letter 'Date unknown, but somewhere in August, and on my calendar it says the 29ᵗʰ but I dont [sic] feel very sure of that'. If a visiting family member or friend went out, she worried about where they were and often set off to look for them. Over the next few months, her confusion took over more and more aspects of her life, although she had lucid periods, and with some domestic help was more or less able to look after herself. Her family, while they found it terribly painful to watch her decline, understood that her independence was of fundamental importance to her and that she needed to stay in her own flat. One day in the middle of April, she drank the entire contents of a bottle of morphia that she had probably been saving for about thirty years, just in case. It was so old that it was no longer potent enough to kill her at once and she was found very quickly because her charwoman was in the flat when she took it. Did she really intend to kill herself? Cecil certainly had doubts, writing to her own children on 19 April 'she does not seem to have been altogether whole-hearted about it'. She was taken to Ipswich Hospital in an ambulance, had her stomach pumped, and was sent back to the Cottage Hospital in Aldeburgh. Cecil rushed over to Aldeburgh and spent time sitting with her:

> you will easily imagine that the ordinary difficulties of conversing with her [because of her by now severe deafness], combined with the fact that she is ill, that she is sharing a room with a woman who is <u>not</u> deaf, and that all the doors of the Cottage Hospital, if they exist, are left open, do not make confidences easy.

Several friends and acquaintances dropped in to visit, but did not stay long as her longstanding habits as a hostess seemed to make her feel that she was under an obligation to entertain them. She was cared for with great compassion by Dr Nora Acheson, widow of the doctor ('Doctor Robin') who thirty years earlier had looked after the ailments of her war nursery children with humour and kindness, and who had delivered two of her grandchildren. After a day or two in the hospital,

---

16   Margery Spring Rice, letter to the author, ?29 August 1969.

she contracted pneumonia, and on 21 April 1970, aged almost eighty-three, she died.

***

Margery was a person full of contradictions. She made enemies, but she also made many close, long-term friends, young and old. She could be snobbish (she loved to associate with the great and the good), yet her friends came from all walks of life and her practical sympathy for those less fortunate than herself, particularly women, was boundless. Her parenting can be heavily criticised, but she was the best of grandmothers. She was also a combative peacemaker. She was a doer rather than a thinker: when she saw a need, she set about filling it, being prepared to turn her hand to almost anything. In the late 1940s, Cecil and a group of parents in Hammersmith, unable to find the right nursery provision for their children, had set up a little nursery class in the house in St Peter's Square. One day when Margery happened to be staying there, the teacher was ill, so Margery simply stepped in and got on with the job of teaching the class. Friends learnt to live with her ability to ignore the norms of polite behaviour: on one occasion, she visited a couple who were out when she arrived but returned while she was there. They thought there was something a little odd in her manner, as she stood in their garden with her hands behind her back: it turned out that she had unabashedly picked a bunch of flowers from their garden for herself.

Sometimes her plans did not work out: at some point in the 1950s, she decided that she would like to adopt a Jewish child, and was hurt and disappointed when her family united in opposition, pointing out that it was hardly sensible or practical for a single woman in her sixties to undertake such a task. But above all, she was immensely generous, making her house a haven not only for her nearest and dearest but also for all kinds of people in all sorts of trouble. Her generosity as a host is evidenced by the number of times her friends came to visit: Ursula Nettleship, for example, stayed at Iken at least nineteen times between 1944 and 1949,[17] which is astonishing given the number of ongoing projects Margery was pursuing during that period. In her public life, Margery was a pioneer, whose vision for women's health and family

---

17   She went on visiting until 1964, but less frequently than before.

planning services was always ahead of public opinion. It is fitting that she lived to see the passing of the Health Service (Family Planning) Act of 1967, as well as the liberal reforms piloted into law by Roy Jenkins as Home Secretary on abortion and homosexuality, and the abolition of the death penalty.

Margery was not much given to self-reflection or self-doubt and she generally had such a positive attitude to life that it is all the more striking and poignant to find her writing to Charles on 30 March 1952 that about twenty years before, when Stephen and Cecil would still have been minors, she had thought about killing herself:

> I thought that nothing was any good, least of all myself, and that it would be best for everyone, most of all myself, that I should vacate my seat for another potential occupant.

For Charles, her words struck a note that had thus far been missing in their relationship:

> you did administer the right medicine this time! To reveal your own experiences, instead of hiding them as you can do so successfully under heroic strength of character, is the most helpful thing for anyone who is having similar experiences.[18]

It is to her credit that for once she was able to appear vulnerable. In her turn, on 16 April, she replied that one's forties are —

> the time of the severest self-criticisms, the purging, the discarding of certain youthful ambitions, the always painful adjustments between what one has wanted to do and what time, nurture, nature, and opportunity are going to allow one to fulfil [...] Idealists are the salt of the earth.

The day after her death, Benjamin Britten wrote to Cecil:

> I hadn't quite realised how unhappy Margie was, because whenever we met her she was so lively & cheerful — but one should have known, because for a person of her enormous energy & intelligence it must have been unendurably frustrating to become more and more incapacitated [...] I shall always think of her with the greatest love & admiration, & gratitude that we were priviledged [sic] to know her. She was a brave woman, of highest integrity & intelligence — what a marvellous and important generation of thinker, hers was — & she was one of the best!

---

18   Charles Garrett Jones, letter to Margery Spring Rice, 8 April 1952.

And her warmth & affection was something very special, & we'll never forget her. You will all miss her greatly, & so shall we — she helped us in so many ways.

After her cremation, Cecil collected her ashes and took them to scatter on to the river Alde at Iken. Unfortunately, there was an onshore wind, and Cecil had to wade into the river to do it: all she could think of was how Margery would have laughed at this scene. There is a legend among Arab peoples that places mourn for the people who have loved them, and if this is so, then both Iken and Aldeburgh must mourn for Margery. But Iken cliff and beach are no longer what they were, since the cliff has been defended against erosion by hideous concrete blocks and old car tyres, the ancient oak trees are coming one by one to the ends of their lives, and what was once bracken-covered heath is now farmland, firmly fenced off from public access. Perhaps it is better to remember her in Aldeburgh, where she was so glad to return for the last years of her life. Six months before her death, she spoke of sitting in her flat at dusk on a grey October evening, 'looking out onto the Crag Path, and beyond, to the sea. As always, if one watches carefully the light from the Lightship keeps up its constant flash', a sight that took her back to her childhood Christmas visits to the lightship. I like to think of her sitting there, emulating the ship's figurehead who kept a lookout at her front door in Iken.[19]

Suffolk was in her blood, but she retained her national and international interests until the end of her life. She admired those who got on with life, and got things done. During her time in Oxfordshire, she had had the opportunity to read — with great pleasure — the page proofs of Jo Manton's biography of her aunt and godmother, Elizabeth Garrett Anderson:

I find it enthralling, and am for the 1000th time lost in admiration for Aunt E. and for her mid-Victorian evangelical father, (Newson Garrett my grandfather[)] who supported her struggles, both financially and academically s[o] to speak. He was ready in every emergency, and they were frequent, to rush up to London (from Aldeburgh) or Edinburgh or Paris to support her cause [...] And at the end of her life (she died in 1917) came the Suffrage campaign.[20]

---

19 Margery Spring Rice, fragmentary memoirs, recorded by Sam Garrett-Jones, October/November 1969, transcribed 12 January 2006 by Sam Garrett-Jones.
20 Margery Spring Rice, letter to Stephen Robertson, 14 February 1965.

Margery came by her determination — obstinacy, even — honestly.

There had been a time in her early adulthood when Margery might have been set for the life of a salon hostess, doubtless one with wide cultural and social interests, but probably not someone to leave an important legacy. In the short-lived diary that she kept in 1910–1911, the entry for 18 November describes, among other social events, celebrating her father's birthday, but does not even mention the big suffrage demonstration that took place on that day ('Black Friday'). However, it was partly Margery's own character that prevented such a future: she could never have been satisfied with salon life. In the end, also, she could not — nor did she want to — escape the heritage of a family in which women were expected to take equal responsibility with men for the world into which they were born. She was greatly influenced in this attitude by two of her redoubtable aunts, though in personality she was much more like Elizabeth Garrett Anderson. Millicent Fawcett, while still possessing her share of determination, was both quieter and more tactful than either her sister or her niece. Margery also owed much to her father — Ray Strachey, in her biography of Fawcett, records that Millicent wrote of Sam after his death: '"He was a most dear brother and friend, and such a staunch supporter of all we have ever worked for for women"'.[21] Besides her family, three other factors were crucial in setting Margery on the path — or paths — she eventually followed: first, the way in which her own life and others were drastically changed by World War I; second, the turning upside down, again, of her personal life by the miseries of her second marriage; and finally, the conditions she encountered on the poorer side of the London borough of Kensington. Once she had found a cause to excite and absorb her, and one that demanded the range of skills she could offer, she did not look back but whole-heartedly enjoyed the challenges. She described herself as a 'promoter of lost causes':[22] although she would have been saddened by the huge social gap that still exists today in the London borough of Kensington, the cause of contraception in the UK (which she fought for there so determinedly and for so long) has been triumphantly won.

One of the obituaries of Margery was written by Letty Gifford, her colleague in the family planning movement, but also her close friend

---

21 Ray Strachey, *Millicent Garrett Fawcett* (London: John Murray, 1931), p. 355.
22 Evans, *Freedom to Choose*, p. 133.

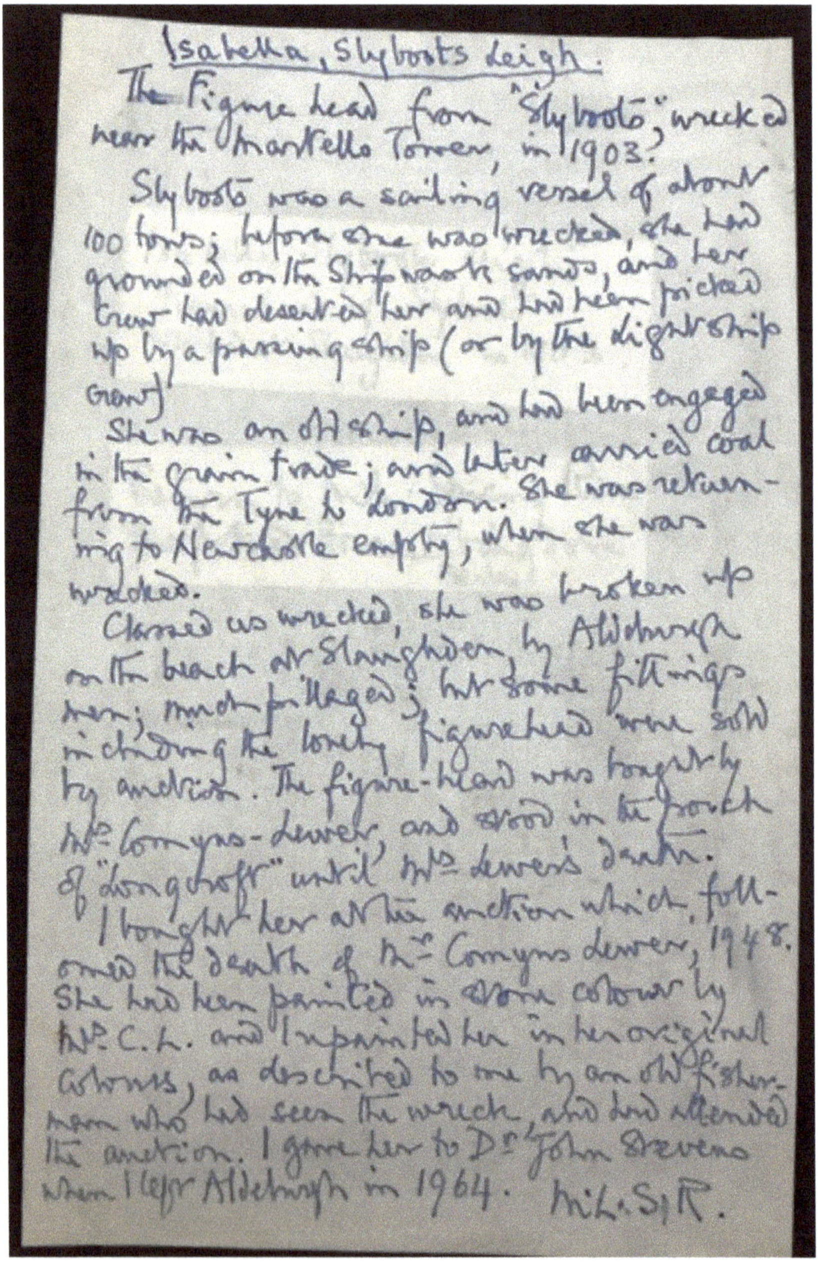

Isabella, Slyboots Leigh.

The Figure head from "Slyboots" wrecked near the Martello Tower, in 1903?

Slyboots was a sailing vessel of about 100 tons; before she was wrecked, she had grounded on the Shipwash sands, and her crew had deserted her and had been picked up by a passing ship (or by the lightship crew)

She was an old ship, and had been engaged in the grain trade; and later carried coal from the Tyne to London. She was returning to Newcastle empty, when she was wrecked.

Classed as wrecked, she was broken up on the beach at Slaughden by Aldeburgh men; much pillaged; but some fittings including the lovely figurehead were sold by auction. The figure-head was bought by Mrs Comyns-Lewen, and stood in the porch of "Longcroft" until Mrs Lewen's death.

I bought her at the auction which followed the death of Mrs Comyns Lewen, 1948. She had been painted in stone colour by Mrs C.L. and I repainted her in her original colours, as described to me by an old fisherman who had seen the wreck, and had attended the auction. I gave her to Dr John Stevens when I left Aldeburgh in 1964. M.L. S.R.

Fig. 27. Margery's handwriting, which retained its characteristic vigour into her old age. 'Isabella' is likely a slip of memory for 'Annabel'. Photograph: the author (2017).

and fellow Aldeburgh resident. Paying tribute to Margery's North Kensington work, Letty recalled how Margery 'bullied and charmed until schemes were started and her nervous Treasurer had somehow complied with her imperious command to "find more money"'. In Suffolk, Margery had always enjoyed pointing out Yarn Hill, which overlooks the river Alde between Iken and Aldeburgh, as the site on which Boudica had supposedly stood ready for action as she watched the Roman legions advancing on the territory of her Iceni tribe, so Gifford's final, more personal image is an apt one:

> Pursuing [Margery] in her Land Rover down a sandy track, with half a dozen ecstatic children bouncing dangerously in the trailer behind[,] was to have an inkling of what Boadicea might have looked like in her chariot.

Bibliography

Archival Sources

Britten Pears Arts Archive, MSC10/1 [Aldeburgh Festival Executive Committee minute book].

Britten Pears Arts Archive, BBA/SPRING RICE [Correspondence between Britten and Spring Rice].

Brotherton Library, University of Leeds, Leeds Russian Archive MS 1372/2 [Francis Lindley's Memoir].

Cambridge, Cambridge University Library, Add. MS 6762–6802 [Diaries of Stella Benson].

Cambridge, Cambridge University Library, Add. MS 8367 [Dominick Spring Rice's letters to Stella Benson].

Church of England Children's Society, War Nursery Papers.

Garrett Family Papers.

Girton College Archive, Cambridge, GCPP E2/1 [Eileen Power Papers].

Jones Family Papers.

London, British Library, Add. MS 60699 [Dominick Spring Rice's letters to James Strachey].

Royal Voluntary Service Archive and Heritage Collection [Iken Hall War Nursery Report].

Suffolk Record Office, HA436 [Elizabeth Garrett Anderson Letters and Papers].

Suffolk Record Office, EC1/2/17/121, A348/5/2/37 [Coroner's Inquest on the Drowning of Mary Garrett Jones, 24 November 1939].

Wellcome Collection, SA/FPA/NK [North Kensington Clinic Papers].

Wellcome Collection, SA/FPA/SR [Spring Rice Papers].

Wellcome Collection, GC/105 [Interview Transcripts].

Women's Library, London School of Economics, 8SUF/B/177 [Nancy Raphael Interview].

Secondary Sources

Allbutt, Henry A., *The Wife's Handbook*, 45th edition (London: George Standring, 1913).

Anderson, Louisa Garrett, *Elizabeth Garrett Anderson* (London: Faber & Faber, 1939).

Benton, Jill, *Naomi Mitchison: A Biography* (London: Pandora, 1990).

Berg, Maxine, *A Woman in History: Eileen Power 1889–1940* (Cambridge, UK: Cambridge University Press, 1996).

Birn, Donald S., *The League of Nations Union 1918–1945* (Oxford: Clarendon Press, 1981).

Bradbrook, Muriel Clara, *That Infidel Place: A Short History of Girton College, 1869–1969* (Cambridge, UK: Girton College, 1984).

Bowden, R. E. M., 'Cullis, Winifred Clara', in *Oxford Dictionary of National Biography* (2004), https://doi.org/10.1093/ref:odnb/32661

Brailsford, Henry Noel, *A League of Nations* (London: Headley, 1917).

Bristow, James Philip, *Aldeburgh Diary* (Aldeburgh: Aldeburgh Museum Trust, 2000).

Brown, Beatrice Curtis, *Isabel Fry 1869–1958: Portrait of a Great Teacher* (London: Arthur Barker, 1960).

Calder, Jenni, *The Nine Lives of Naomi Mitchison* (London: Virago, 1997).

Chamberlain, Geoffrey, *Special Delivery: the Life of the Celebrated British Obstetrician William Nixon* (London: Royal College of Obstetricians and Gynaecologists, 2004), https://doi.org/10.1017/cbo9781107784666

Clarke, Peter, *Hope and Glory: Britain 1900–90* (London: Penguin, 2004).

Clay, Catherine, *British Women Writers 1914–45: Professional Work and Friendship* (Aldershot and Burlington, VT: Ashgate, 2006), https://doi.org/10.4324/9781315261256

Clodd, Harold Parker, *Aldeburgh: The History of an Ancient Borough* (Ipswich: Norman Adlard & Co., 1959).

Cowman, Krista, *Women in British Politics, c.1689–1979* (London: Palgrave Macmillan, 2010), https://doi.org/10.1007/978-1-137-26785-6

Crawford, Elizabeth, *Enterprising Women: The Garretts and Their Circle* (London: Francis Boutle, 2002).

—, 'Suffrage Stories: House Decorating and Suffrage: Annie Atherton, Kate Thornbury, And The Society of Artists', *Woman and Her Sphere* (8 May 2017) https://womanandhersphere.com/2017/05/08/suffrage-stories-house-decorating-and-suffrage-annie-atherton-kate-thornbury-and-the-society-of-artists/

Davies, Amanda, '*A Room Worthy of the Town'*: *A History of Aldeburgh Jubilee Hall* (Leiston: Leiston Press, 2016).

Debenham, Clare, *Birth Control and the Rights of Women: Post-suffrage Feminism in the Early 20ᵗʰ Century* (London: I. B. Tauris, 2014).

Draper, Elizabeth, 'Birth Control in the Modern World', *The Times* (26 February 1964)

—, *Birth Control in the Modern World* (Harmondsworth: Penguin, 1965).

Evans, Barbara, *Freedom to Choose: The Life and Work of Dr Helena Wright, Pioneer of* Contraception (London: Bodley Head, 1984).

Fawcett, Millicent, *What I Remember* (London: Fisher Unwin, 1924).

Fisher, Kate, *Birth Control, Sex and Marriage in Britain 1918–60* (Oxford: Oxford University Press, 2006), https://doi.org/10.1093/acprof:oso/9780199267361.001.0001

Florence, Lella S., *Birth Control on Trial* (London: Allen & Unwin, 1930).

—, *Progress Report on Birth Control* (London: Heinemann, 1956).

Gillingham, Anthony, *Young Rebel: Memoirs 1917–39* ([n.p.], privately printed, 2007).

Glynn, Jennifer, *The Pioneering Garretts: Breaking the Barriers for Women* (London: Hambledon Continuum, 2008).

Gras, Constantine, https://www.grasart.com/blog

Gwynn, Stephen, ed., *Letters and Friendships of Sir Cecil Spring Rice*, 2 vols (London: Constable, 1929).

Harris, Jose, *Private Lives, Public Spirit: A Social History of Britain 1870–1914* (Oxford: Oxford University Press, 1993).

Heaney, Seamus, *The Spirit Level* (London: Faber & Faber, 1996).

Hibbert, Christopher, *The English: A Social History* (London: Paladin, 1988).

History, Gazeteer and Directory of Suffolk, 1891–92 (Sheffield: William White Ltd., 1891–1892).

Holtby, Winifred, *Letters to a Friend* (London: Collins, 1937).

Holst, Imogen, *A Life in Music*, ed. Christopher Grogan (Woodbridge: Boydell, 2010).

Hopkinson, Stephan, *Encounters* ([n.p.]: privately printed, [n.d.]).

Ibberson, Mary, *For Joy that We Are Here: Rural Music Schools 1929–1950* (London: Bedford Square Press, 1977).

Jeger, Lena M., 'The Politics of Family Planning', *Political Quarterly*, 31 (1962), 48–58, https://doi.org/10.1111/j.1467-923x.1962.tb01919.x

Jones, Emily Elizabeth Constance, *As I Remember: An Autobiographical Ramble* (London: A. & C. Black, 1922).

J. S. R.: Sketch of a Background ([n.p.]: privately printed, [n.d.]).

Karsavina, Tamara, *Theatre Street: The Reminiscences of Tamara Karsavina* (London: Dance Books, 1981).

'The Late Mr. Samuel Garrett', *The Law Society's Gazette* (May 1923), 20, p. 108.

The Law Society Gazette, 'Memory Lane', *Obiter* (6 August 2018), https://www.lawgazette.co.uk/obiter/memory-lane-6-august-2018/5067167.article

—, 'Memory Lane', *Obiter* (30 April 2009), https://www.lawgazette.co.uk/obiter/memory-lane/50540.article

A League of Nations: Report of a Meeting held at the Central Hall, Westminster, May 14th, 1917, in *Publications of the League of Nations Society, the League of Nations Union, and the League of Free Nations Association/League of Nations Society* [*and others*] ([n.p.]: [n.p.], 1917).

League of Nations Society, *Second Annual Report, March, 1917–March 1918, as Approved at the Annual Meeting, June 14, 1918* (London: League of Nations Society, 1918).

Leathard, A., *The Fight for Family Planning: The Development of Family Planning Services in Britain 1921–74* (London: Macmillan, 1980).

Lewis, Jane, 'The Ideology and Politics of Birth Control in Inter-War England', *Women's Studies International Quarterly*, 2 (1979), 33–48, https://doi.org/10.1016/s0148-0685(79)93008-2

Liddington, Jill, and Elizabeth Crawford, *Vanishing for the Vote: The Story of the 1911 Census* (Manchester: Manchester University Press, 2014), https://doi.org/10.7228/manchester/9780719087486.001.0001

Macdonald, Kate, 'Women and Their Bodies in the Popular Reading of 1910', *Literature and History*, 22 (2013), 61–79, https://doi.org/10.7227/LH.22.1.5

Mackenzie, John, *The Scots in South Africa* (Manchester: Manchester University Press, 2007), https://doi.org/10.7765/9781847794468

Manson, Janet M., 'Leonard Woolf as an Architect of the League of Nations', *South Carolina Review* 39/2 (2007), 1–13.

Manton, Jo, *Elizabeth Garrett Anderson* (London: Methuen, 1987; repr. London: Taylor & Francis, 2018), https://doi.org/10.4324/9780429401374

Marks, L.V., *Metropolitan Maternity: Maternal and Infant Welfare Services in Early 20th Century London* (Amsterdam: Rodopi, 1996), https://doi.org/10.1163/9789004418455

Martin, D. E., 'Malleson [*née* Billson], Joan Graeme', in *Oxford Dictionary of National Biography* (2004), https://doi.org/10.1093/ref:odnb/54690

McCarthy, Helen, *The British People and the League of Nations: Democracy, Citizenship and Internationalism, c. 1918–45* (Manchester: Manchester University Press, 2011), https://doi.org/10.7765/9781847794284

McWilliams-Tullberg, Rita, *Women at Cambridge — A Men's University, Though of a Mixed Type* (London: Gollancz, 1975).

Megson, Barbara, and Jean Lindsay, *Girton College 1869–1959: An Informal History* (Cambridge: Heffer, 1961).

'Men of Mark: Dominick Spring Rice', *Financial News* (8 April 1931), p. 3.

Mitchison, Naomi, *All Change Here: Girlhood and Marriage* (London: Bodley Head, 1975).

—, *Comments on Birth Control* (London: Faber & Faber, 1930).

—, 'Elizabeth Garrett Anderson', in *Revaluations: Studies in Biography*, Lascelles Abercrombie, Lord David Cecil, G. K. Chesterton, et al. (London: Oxford University Press, 1931), pp. 155–95.

—, *You May Well Ask: A Memoir, 1920–40* (London: Fontana, 1986).

Moore, Katharine, *Cordial Relations: The Maiden Aunt in Fact and Fiction* (London: Heinemann, 1966).

National Secular Society, https://secularism.org.uk

Nicholson, Virginia, *Among the Bohemians* (New York: William Morrow, 2002).

North Kensington Marriage Welfare Centre, *Thirty-Third Annual Report 1st January–31st December, 1957* ([n.p.]: [n.p.], 1957).

O'Cleirigh, Nellie, *Valentia: A Different Irish Island* (Dublin: Portobello Press, 1992).

Raverat, Gwen, *Period Piece: A Cambridge Childhood* (London: Faber & Faber, 1960).

Robinson, Jane, *Hearts and Minds: The Untold Story of the Great Pilgrimage and How Women Won the Vote* (London: Doubleday, 2018).

Royle, Edward, 'Bradlaugh, Charles,' in *Oxford Dictionary of National Biography* (2004), https://doi.org/10.1093/ref:odnb/3183

Rouse, William Henry Denham, *A History of Rugby School* (London: Duckworth, 1898).

Rowbotham, Sheila, *Dreamers of a New Day: Women Who Invented the Twentieth Century* (London: Verso, 2010).

Rudolf, Mildred de M., *Everybody's Children: The Story of the Church of England Children's Society, 1921–48* (London: Oxford University Press, 1950).

Scarfe, Norman, 'Victorian Aldeburgh', in *Programme Book for the Fifteenth Aldeburgh Festival* (1962), pp. 16–20.

Searle, G. R., *A New England: Peace and War, 1886–1918* (Oxford: Oxford University Press, 2004).

Spring Rice, Margery, 'The Case of the Under Fives, 1. Is there a Demand for their Evacuation', *Times Educational Supplement* (5 July 1941), p. 313.

—, 'The Case of the Under Fives, 2. The Government's Policy and the Work of the Panel', *Times Educational Supplement* (12 July 1941), p. 324.

—, 'The Case of the Under Fives, 3. The Question of Accommodation', *Times Educational Supplement* (19 July 1941), p. 336.

—, 'The Health of Working Women', *Eugenics Review*, 32 (1940), 50–54.

—, *Working-Class Wives: Their Health and Conditions* (Harmondsworth: Pelican, 1939; repr. London: Virago, 1981).

Strachey, Ray, *Millicent Garrett Fawcett* (London: John Murray, 1931).

Szreter, Simon, and Kate Fisher, *Sex before the Sexual Revolution: Intimate Life in England 1918–1963* (Cambridge: Cambridge University Press, 2010), https://doi.org/10.1017/cbo9780511778353

Thompson, Dorothy, *Sophia's Son: The Story of a Suffolk Parson* (Lavenham: Terence Dalton, 1969).

Tuke, Margaret J., *A History of Bedford College for Women 1849–1937* (London: Oxford University Press, 1939).

Watt, D. Cameron, and D. C. B. Lieven, eds, 'Report on the Work of the British Mission to North Russia from June 1918 to 31st March 1919', in *British Documents on Foreign Affairs: Reports and Papers from the Foreign Office Confidential Print, Part 2, From the First to the Second World War. Series A, The Soviet Union, 1917–39*, vol. 1 (Frederick, MD: University Publications of America, 1984), p. 158.

Wilson, Romer, *If All These Young Men* (London: Methuen, 1919).

Wingate, John, *The Fighting Tenth: The Tenth Submarine Flotilla and the Siege of Malta* (London: Leo Cooper, 1991).

Winkler, Henry R., *The League of Nations Movement in Great Britain, 1914–19* (Metuchen, NJ: Scarecrow Reprint Co., 1967).

Wood, Clive, and Beryl Suitters, *The Fight for Acceptance: A History of Contraception* (Aylesbury: Medical and Technical Publications, 1970).

Woolf, Leonard, *Letters of Leonard Woolf*, ed. Frederic Spotts (London: Bloomsbury, 1990).

Young, Edward, *One of Our Submarines* (Harmondsworth: Penguin, 1952).

List of Illustrations

Index

About the team

Alessandra Tosi was the managing editor for this book.

Adèle Kreager performed the copy-editing and proofreading.

Anna Gatti designed the cover using InDesign. The cover was produced in InDesign using Fontin (titles) and Calibri (text body) fonts.

Luca Baffa typeset the book in InDesign. The text font is Tex Gyre Pagella; the heading font is Californian FB. Luca created all of the editions — paperback, hardback, EPUB, MOBI, PDF, HTML, and XML — the conversion is performed with open source software freely available on our GitHub page (https://github.com/OpenBookPublishers).

This book need not end here…

Share

All our books — including the one you have just read — are free to access online so that students, researchers and members of the public who can't afford a printed edition will have access to the same ideas. This title will be accessed online by hundreds of readers each month across the globe: why not share the link so that someone you know is one of them?

This book and additional content is available at:

https://doi.org/10.11647/OBP.0215

Customise

Personalise your copy of this book or design new books using OBP and third-party material. Take chapters or whole books from our published list and make a special edition, a new anthology or an illuminating coursepack. Each customised edition will be produced as a paperback and a downloadable PDF.

Find out more at:

https://www.openbookpublishers.com/section/59/1

Like Open Book Publishers

Follow @OpenBookPublish

Read more at the Open Book Publishers BLOG

You may also be interested in:

Non-Communicable Disease Prevention
Best Buys, Wasted Buys and Contestable Buys

by Wanrudee Isaranuwatchai, Rachel A. Archer,
Yot Teerawattananon and Anthony J. Culyer (eds.)

https://doi.org/10.11647/OBP.0195

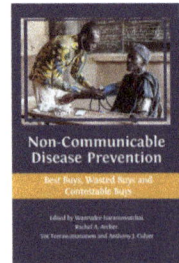

Undocumented Migrants and Healthcare
Eight Stories from Switzerland
Marianne Jossen

https://doi.org/10.11647/OBP.0139

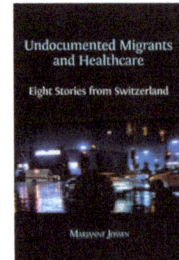

Intellectual Property and Public Health
in the Developing World
Monirul Azam

https://doi.org/10.11647/OBP.0093

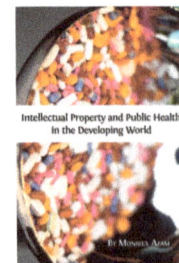

www.ingramcontent.com/pod-product-compliance
Lightning Source LLC
Chambersburg PA
CBHW040256290326
41929CB00052B/3431